FAMILY

FAMILY

A Twenty-Fifth Anniversary
Collection of Essays about the
Family from *Notre Dame Magazine*

Edited by Kerry Temple

University of Notre Dame Press
and Notre Dame Magazine
Notre Dame, Indiana

Manufactured in the United States of America

Library of Congress Cataloging-in-Publication Data

Family : a twenty-fifth anniversary collection of essays about the
    family, from Notre Dame magazine / edited by Kerry Temple.
    p.   cm.
    ISBN 0-268-01178-8 (alk. paper)
    1. Family—United States.   2. Family—Religious aspects—Catholic
Church.   I. Temple, Kerry.   II. Notre Dame magazine.
HQ536.F3382   1997
306.85'0973—dc21   97-1798
                                                                        CIP

∞ The paper used in this publication meets the minimum
requirements of the American National Standard for Information
Sciences, Permanence of Paper for Printed Library Materials,
ANSI Z39.48-1984.

CONTENTS

INTRODUCTION

THE FIRST ISSUE of *Notre Dame Magazine* arrived in my parents' home when I was a student at the University. On the cover was a grainy, gray-green mezzotint photograph of a lustily squalling newborn, still moist with the vernix and blood, being lifted from the womb by a doctor who was blurrily focused and virtually faceless behind a surgical mask. The cover blurb: "Who Shall Live and Who Decides?"

That was 25 years ago.

In that premier issue a half dozen writers took on those perennially volatile issues of abortion, euthanasia, contraception, genetic engineering and the convergence of nature, science, technology, humanity, and God. The magazine has been intelligently and honestly engaging such topics—those affecting family life—ever since. In fact, *Notre Dame Magazine* launched its second year with one of its most controversial covers. It depicted, discreetly shielding certain key elements, a naked couple holding aloft their naked child. The cover blurb: "The American Christian Family—Is It Worth Saving?" The answer was argued inside by Notre Dame faculty members exploring the nuances of sex and parenting, fidelity, divorce, and the meaning and merits of family.

Throughout the magazine's quarter-century history, writers have continued to think out loud about societal forces and cultural trends, politics and current affairs, Catholic truths and earnest truth-seeking, education and social justice, literary and scientific pursuits, the meaning of life, the search for God, questions of souls and love and death and immortality. But no theme, no subject, no enigma has been more persistently dissected on the pages of *Notre Dame Magazine* than the family. This is partly due to the revolution that has taken place in America over the past twenty-five years, altering forever the way we live and relate to one another. But it is also due to how fully family concerns consume our lives.

So it seemed appropriate, as we mark the quarterly's twenty-fifth anniversary, to republish the best of those essays that have dealt personally, thoughtfully, and candidly with those timeless family matters. The essays in this collection are personal family portraits that reveal private truths about having and raising children, caring for elderly parents, managing headstrong adolescents, enduring the deaths of loved ones, making sense of loneliness and family obligations and abuse and comic idiosyncracies. But they also offer universal truths, insights, and wisdom into that most fundamental manifestation of the human condition—what it means to live in family.

This collection is not a comprehensive treatise on family life, but a gathering of what has appeared on our pages. We did not solicit manuscripts to fill what gaps we saw. But the editors are proud that the magazine has, through the years, dealt as widely, thoroughly, and honestly as it has on such issues. We also recognize how very rare it is for a university publication to be able to do this. *Notre Dame Magazine* is not the typical college alumni magazine but has from the outset devoted itself to exploring the broader themes which challenge its readers navigating the menacing white water of twentieth-century America.

This requires the vision and support of those ultimately responsible for the University's place in higher education and its role in the wider society. The magazine has indeed been fortunate to have been guided by the leadership of two extraordinary University presidents, Theodore M. Hesburgh, C.S.C., and Edward A. Malloy, C.S.C., and two exceptional vice presidents of University relations, James W. Frick and William P. Sexton. Without their support the magazine simply would not have been able to be what it is or to publish the kinds of stories contained in this volume.

The marking of any anniversary also brings to mind those who have made major contributions through the years and that must include Ron Parent, the magazine's founding editor who piloted the magazine through its initial formative decade and more, and Walton R. Collins who was at the helm for another dozen years. Every staff member and every reader of the magazine is indebted to these two fine journalists for their vision, talents, and care in directing the magazine for virtually all of its first quarter century. Others, of course, have had a major impact on *Notre Dame Magazine,* most notably Richard W. Conklin, longtime University relations chief and loyal ally of the magazine, and Jim Winters, a former managing editor who was instrumental in shaping the magazine as it exists today. Thanks are also owed to former staff members as well as the current crew, a veteran team dedicated to the magazine's mission and quality—Carol Schaal, Don Nelson, John Monczunski, Ed Cohen, and Julie Ettl—whose good work is evident in this collection and in each issue of *Notre Dame Magazine.* And we are all grateful to Jim Langford and Jeff Gainey and all those at the University of Notre Dame Press who wanted to do this book with us and for us and who have been so patient and helpful in showing magazine people how books are done.

Finally, *Notre Dame Magazine* is most appreciative of two groups of people. On one side are the authors, those who labor with words to create from human emotion and memory and feeling and belief and intellect—from thin air, essentially—a work of art that touches the heart, the soul, the mind of another. And on the other side are our readers, for whom all this is done and who so generously support us in that work. It has been an incredibly pleasurable and gratifying enterprise to bring all these people together for twenty-five years, to share with each other the most elemental spaces of our being, the good and bad of family living, and to make—we hope—the world a warmer, brighter, better place in the process.

Kerry Temple
Editor, *Notre Dame Magazine*

A PERFECT PLACE

Scott Russell Sanders

WHEN OUR FIRST child was born, a rosy wriggle of a girl we named Eva, my wife and I were living in a second-floor apartment on the noisiest avenue in Bloomington, Indiana. Every truck grinding its gears, every belching bus, every howling fire engine and ambulance, every unmufflered pickup and overhorsepowered jalopy in town roared past our windows, morning, noon and night.

To begin with, Eva weighed only six-and-a-half pounds, all of them fidgety. Like any newborn she was pure appetite. With a stomach so small, she hardly seemed to close her eyes between feedings. When they did fitfully close, they would snap open again at the least sound. Ruth nursed her to sleep, or I rocked her to sleep, and we'd lay her in the crib as gingerly as a bomb. Then some loud machine would come blaring down the street and Eva would twitch and wail.

Once an engine had frightened her, mere milk would not soothe this child, nor would a cradle endlessly rocking. Only songs would do, a rivery murmur while she snuggled against a warm chest, and the chest had to be swaying in rhythm to a steady walk. Fall silent or stop moving and you had a ruckus on your hands. Night after night, I worked my way through *The Folk Songs of North America* while carrying Eva in circles over the crickety floorboards. It took hours of singing and miles of walking to lull her to stillness in my arms, and then a siren or diesel would undo the spell in seconds.

After seven sleepless months, Ruth and I exchanged bleary stares over the breakfast table one morning and muttered, as in a single breath, "We've got to move."

* * *

That day we set out looking for a house. Not just any house, but the right one, the inevitable one, the one made in carpenter's heaven to fit our family. How to find this perfect place among the countless ones available? It was a problem as difficult, and nearly as consequential, as finding a mate to marry.

To compound the difficulty, Ruth and I carried in our heads quite different postcards of the ideal house, for she had grown up in a city and I had grown up in the country. She wanted a sturdy old box shaded by sturdy old trees, within a few steps of the place next door, in a neighborhood of sidewalks and flower beds where folks traded recipes and sat on their porches and pushed babies in buggies at dusk. I wanted a log cabin beside a pond in three hundred acres of woods bordering on a wilderness. Failing that, I would settle for a run-down farmhouse on a dirt road unknown to maps.

* * *

We compromised by buying a house in town that was as badly in need of repair as any cabin in the country. Five lines in the "For Sale by Owner" section of the newspaper led us there: "CHARMING 2-story brick, walk to work, Bryan Park & Elm Heights. 3 bedrms., bath, liv. rm. with fireplace. 1113 East Wylie. $25,000."

Now that was cheap, even in 1974—not so cheap that I ever supposed we would live long enough to pay it off; nor so cheap that the loan officers at Workingmen's Federal didn't stare at us hard with their fiduciary gaze—but still, we could cover a monthly note on $25,000 without going naked or hungry.

More alluring than the price was the location. That section of Wylie proved to be a two-block sanctuary of silence, cut off at one end by a cross-street, at the other end by woods. No trucks, no sirens, no hustling jalopies. You could hear birds in the big trees, crickets in the grass, children on screened porches. At night, in the hush of a bedroom, you could hear a baby breathe. The houses were old and sturdy enough to please Ruth; the park just around the corner gave me a taste of country, with its green swells, sunsets and star-spangled skies.

We had already toured more houses than Washington slept in before we set our hearts on 1113 East Wylie. Whether it was charming, as the ad promised, the eye of the beholder would have to decide; but no one could doubt that it needed work. Realtors, in their cheery lingo, would have called it a fixer-upper or a handyman's dream. On our initial visit we made a list of items that would require swift attention, from roof to foundation. Of course we'd patch up that plaster, Ruth and I assured one another. We'd tear out that threadbare carpet and refinish the floors. We'd mend the chimney, ventilate the attic, dry up the basement, enclose the front porch, hang new doors, make over the kitchen, patch and paint and seal.

We moved in 18 years ago, and we are still working on that list. The list, in fact, has grown, season by season, like adult grief or the national debt. For every job completed, two new jobs arise. Reglaze a broken window, and before you've put away your tools a gutter sags or a switch burns out. In an old house, when handyman or handywoman takes on entropy, entropy always wins. Things fall apart, as Yeats memorably warned us, and not only in politics and religion. Pipes rust, nails work loose, shingles crumble, wood warps. The smooth turns rough and the straight grows crooked. A house is a shell caught in a surf that never stops grinding.

* * *

Over those same 18 years, our girl grew up. No longer a light sleeper, Eva went off to college last fall, having lived up to every beautiful promise in those original six-and-a-half pounds. The vague bundle of possibilities that lay in the crib, suckled on milk and swaddled in song, has become a definite person.

More than a little blue about Eva's going away, I work on the house and consider how it holds me. Of course there is no single right place to live, any more than there is a single right man or woman to marry. And yet, having made my choice, I feel wedded to this house, as I do to my wife and my neighborhood and my region. To become attached to a woman, sure, and to neighbors, fair enough, and maybe even to the local terrain—but to a pile of brick and wood? How has this box, this frame of possibilities, come to fit me so exactly? By what alchemy does a house become a home?

* * *

The short answer is that these walls and floors and scruffy flower beds are saturated with our memories and sweat. Everywhere I look I see the imprint of hands, everywhere I turn I hear the babble of voices, I smell sawdust or bread, I recall bruises and laughter. After nearly two decades of labor, the house dwells in us as surely as we dwell in the house.

By American standards it's small, plain, old-fashioned: a cube roughly 25 feet on a side, encased in yellow brick, with a low porch across the front, a wet basement below and on top a roof in the shape of a pyramid. I have touched every one of those bricks, scraping ivy or pointing up the joints with fresh cement. I have banged every joist and rafter, brushed every foundation stone. I know its crooks and crannies, its faults and fillings, as well as my dentist knows my teeth.

I could blame or thank my father or mother for the itch that keeps me tinkering. During my childhood, they fixed up their own series of dilapidated houses, thereby convincing me that a place isn't truly yours until you rebuild it with your own hands. Thoreau, who cobbled together the most famous cabin in our literature, complained that "I never in all my walks came across a man engaged in so simple and natural an occupation as building his house." Had he been a contemporary of my father or me, he could have walked by our doors most weekends and found us hammering.

A month after we moved in, my parents came from Oklahoma to inspect the house and dandle Eva. As soon as my father could bear to put the baby down, he walked to the basement and opened the fuse box, hummed darkly, then came back upstairs and removed the faceplate from a light switch and peered inside. Turning to me with a frown, he said, "Son, you've got to rewire this house. I won't have my granddaughter sleeping in a firetrap."

"I've been meaning to get to that," I told him.

"We'll start this afternoon," he said. "Where's the nearest lumber yard?"

We did start that afternoon, and Ruth and I kept on for months after my parents went back to Oklahoma. Room by room, we re-placed every outlet, every switch, every wire, fishing new three-strand cable down from the attic or up from the basement, driving copper stakes into the soil to drain away any loose amps, until the juice from Public Service Indiana flowed innocuously.

* * *

During their visit the next winter, my father ran his hands over the walls in Eva's room. More dark humming. He lit a match, blew it out, then held the smoking stub near the window beside her crib. I knew what was coming. "Son," he announced, "you've got to insu-late and weatherstrip and caulk or my baby's going to catch pneu-monia."

That job took two years, because Ruth and I decided not just to dribble loose fill into the wall cavities but to rip them open and do it right, with fiberglass batts and polyethylene vapor barrier and new sheetrock. Eva slept in our room while we tore hers apart. When I pried away the lathe and plaster next to where her crib had stood, I found a message scrawled in carpenter's chalk on the pine sheathing: BILLY WALES IS A STINKER! JUNE 12, 1926. I thought about leaving that part of the cavity exposed, with a frame around it, but that would have allowed a draft to blow on my girl, and so I closed it up tight.

Inch by inch, as though the house were a ship in dry dock, we overhauled the place, driven by concerns about Eva and then later, when our second child came along, by concerns about Jesse. Who knew what corrosion lurked in the heart of those old iron pipes? Replumb with copper. The cracked chimney might allow sparks into the frame, so re-lay the bricks, then line it with stainless steel. Sand those oak floors to protect small toes from splinters. And what if there was lead in that peeling paint on the woodwork? Better pry loose the baseboards and trim, the moldings and sills, the mullioned windows; better carry it all outdoors, then scrape and sand and strip everything down to the bare wood, seal it anew with harmless finishes, and put every piece back where it belonged.

In our patching and repairing, our tightening and securing, Ruth and I could have been a pair of hawks tucking sticks into the nest, or beavers smoothing mud inside the walls of our lodge, or prairie dogs hauling dry grass into the burrow. We could have been parents of any species making a haven for our young.

* * *

Unlike the hawks, of course, we fetch our sticks from the lumber yard; unlike the beavers, we get our mud ready baked into bricks; unlike the prairie dogs, we buy fibers that have been woven into blankets, curtains, carpets, mats. But for all that artifice, the house is still entirely derived from the land. The foundation is laid up with chunks of limestone from nearby quarries. The frame is a skeleton of pines. The white walls are gypsum from the bed of a primeval sea. The iron in the nails has been refined from ore, the glass in the windows from sand, even the unavoidable plastic has been distilled from the oil of ancient swamps. When I walk up the stairs and notice the oak treads, I feel their grain curving through me.

Because so few of us build our own homes, we forget that our dwellings, like our bodies, are made from the earth. The first humans who settled in this part of the country fashioned their huts from bark, their tepees from tanned hides held up by saplings. They warmed themselves at fires of buffalo chips and brush. How could they forget that they had wrapped themselves in the land? In his oral autobiography, the Lakota Sioux holy man Black Elk said that "Our tepees were round like the nests of birds, and these were always set in a circle, the nation's hoop, a nest of many nests, where the Great Spirit meant for us to hatch our children."

When white settlers came to this region, they sometimes camped inside a hollow sycamore while they built a log cabin; so when at length they moved into the cabin, they merely exchanged life inside a single tree for life inside a stack of them. The bark on the walls and the clay in the chinks and the fieldstone in the chimney reminded them whence their shelter had come. Our technology has changed, but not our ultimate source. Even the newest ticky-tacky box in the suburbs, even the glitziest high-tech mansion, is only a nest in disguise.

Nature does not halt at the property line but runs right through our yard and walls and bones. Moss grows on the shady side of the roof, mildew in the bathtub, mold in the fridge. Roots from our front-yard elm invade the drains. Mice invade the cupboards. (The best bait, we've found, is peanut butter.) Male woodpeckers, wooing mates, rap on the cedar siding of the front porch. Wrens nest in our kitchen exhaust fan; the racket of their hungry chicks spices up our meals. Water finds its way into the basement year round; for all our efforts to seal the joints, rain and snowmelt still treat the basement like any other hole in the ground.

When we bought the house, it was covered with English ivy. "That's got to come off," Ruth said. "Think of all the spiders breeding outside Eva's window!" Under assault from crowbar, shears and wire brush, the ivy came off. But there has been no perceptible decline in the spider population, indoors or out. Clean a corner, and by the time you've put away the broom new threads are gleaming. The spiders thrive because they have plenty of game to snare. Poison has discouraged the termites, but the carpenter ants still look upon the house as a convenient heap of dead wood. (When Eva first heard us talk about carpenter ants, she imagined they would be dressed as her daddy was on weekends, with sweatband across the forehead, tool belt around the waist and dangling hammer on the hip.) Summer and fall, we play host to crickets, grasshoppers, moths, flies, mosquitoes and frogs, along with no-see-ums too obscure to name.

Piled up foursquare and plumb, the house is itself a part of the landscape. Weather buffets it, wind sifts through. Leaves collect on the roof, hemlock needles gather on the sills, ice and thaw nudge the foundation, seeds lodge in every crack. Like anything born, it is mortal. If you doubt that, drive the back roads of the Midwest and look at the forsaken farms. Abandon a house, even a brick one, and it will soon be reclaimed by forest. Left to itself, the land says bloodroot, chickadee, beech. Our shelter is on loan; it needs perpetual care.

* * *

The word *house* derives from an Indo-European root meaning to cover or conceal. I hear furtive, queasy undertones. Conceal from what? from storms? beasts? enemies? from the eye of God?

Home comes from a different root meaning "the place where one lies." That sounds less fearful to me. A weak, hairless, slow animal, without claws or fangs, can risk lying down and closing its eyes only where it feels utterly secure. Since the universe is going to kill us in the short run or the long, no wonder we crave a place to lie in safety, a place to conceive our young and raise them, a place to shut our eyes without shivering or dread.

Perhaps the most familiar definition of *home* in the American language comes from Robert Frost's "The Death of the Hired Man," in lines spoken by a Yankee farmer: "Home is the place where, when you have to go there, / They have to take you in." Less familiar is the wife's reply: "I should have called it/Something you somehow haven't to deserve." The husband's remark is pure Yankee, grudging and grim. I side with the wife. Home is not where you *have* to go but where you *want* to go; nor is it a place where you are sullenly admitted but rather where you are welcomed—by the people, the walls, the tiles on the floor, the flowers beside the door, the play of light, the very grass.

I am acutely aware that thousands upon thousands of people in my own country have no roofs over their heads. Like anyone who walks the streets of America, I grieve over the bodies wrapped in newspapers or huddled in cardboard boxes, the sleepers curled on steam grates, the futureless faces. This is a cause for shame and remedy, not only because the homeless suffer but because they have no place to lay their heads in safety, no one except dutiful strangers to welcome them. Thank God for dutiful strangers, yet they can never take the place of friends. The more deeply I feel my own connection to home, the more sharply I feel the hurt of those who belong to no place and no one.

The homing pigeon is not merely able to find the roost from astounding distances; it *seeks* its home. I am a homing husband and father. Away on solitary trips, I am never quite whole. I miss family, of course, and neighbors and friends; but I also miss the house, which is planted in the yard, which is embraced by a city, which is cradled in familiar woods and fields. The house has worked on me as steadily as I have worked on the house. I carry slivers of wood under my fingernails, dust from demolition in the corners of my eyes, aches from hammering and heaving in all my joints.

The real estate ads offer houses for sale, not homes. A house is a garment, easily put off or on, casually bought and sold; a home is skin. Merely change houses and you will be inconvenienced; change homes and you bleed. When the shell you live in has taken on the savor of your family, when your dwelling has become a taproot, then your house is a home.

* * *

I heard more than hunger in Eva's infant cry. I heard a plea for shelter from the terror of things. I felt called on to enfold her, in arms and walls and voice. No doubt it is only a musical accident that *home* and *womb* share the holy sound of *om,* which Hindu mystics chant to put themselves in harmony with the ultimate power. But I accept all gifts of language. There is in the word a hum of yearning.

It is hard not to think of our home as a chrysalis from which the butterfly has flown. I miss my daughter. The rug bristles with the absence of her dancing feet. The windows glint with the history of her looking. Water-rings on the sills recall where her teacup should be. The air lacks a sweet buzz.

Unlike a butterfly, a daughter blessedly returns now and again, as Eva came home last December for winter vacation. Ruth and I had been preparing the house to receive her. The storm windows were snug; there was a fire in the stove. Before leaving in August, Eva bet me that I would not have finished remodeling the sunroom by the time of her return between semesters. I stole hours to work on it all the autumn. Just in time I put on the last coat of varnish, so that, when she entered, the place would shine.

WHERE HAS CHILDHOOD GONE?

Patricia O'Brien

I STILL REMEMBER the first time I saw a Barbie doll. It was on a summer evening in the late '50s, in the Los Angeles living room of a friend. A salesman from the Mattel Toy Co. was present, and he regaled us with tales of an unusual new doll that he said was about to revolutionize his industry.

Noting my skeptical face, he handed me a small, miniaturized female form. "Here," he said proudly. "Look at this. I guarantee you, childhood will never be the same."

I couldn't believe what I was holding. This was no doll: This was a tiny plastic woman, complete with breasts and hips, molded with sly sophistication. The facial features were saucily non-virginal, the limbs were pleasingly curved. It was angular and hard, not soft and cuddly. It was different.

"What little girl would ever want this?" I burst out.

I soon learned.

A few years later, my own children were clamoring for Barbie. She wore such pretty clothes, they said; it would be so much fun to dress her up.

Like most parents, I resisted at first, then gave in. Barbie had taken over, and soon it was commonplace to watch a cluster of 10-year-olds busily tucking and snapping tiny creations of silk and lace (often made by doting grandmothers) onto the plastic woman with the somber face.

Children didn't exactly play with Barbie; she was much too sophisticated for that. Instead they took her through the motions of consuming, and in the process, sharpened their own list of wants.

Barbie brought a new and revolutionary message to the world of childhood, and it was this: Hurry up, children! Don't waste time cuddling teddy bears or playing "let's pretend." Here is grown-up glamour, and it's more fun. Make your mommies buy as many new outfits for Barbie as you can. This is what growing up is all about.

Parents resigned themselves to ever-increasing quantities of Barbie paraphernalia. Grandmothers sewed busily.

But Barbie was never satisfied. It was not in her nature to be satisfied, and you could see the reflection of her discontent on the faces of children eyeing the wardrobes of their friends' dolls. Somehow, other Barbies always had it "better." Their Barbies needed "more."

It all seems like a long time ago, and my daughters long ago discarded Barbie and moved on with their lives. But the Barbie phenomenon was a prelude to a significant development that has only recently come into our consciousness.

Childhood is not what it used to be. It is a period of life that is shrinking rapidly.

This disturbing process did not, of course, begin only because of a hard-bodied doll. Television, family breakdowns, the sexual revolution of the 1960s and the rapid increase in working mothers all have contributed to pushing children into premature adulthood.

It was only in recent years, as the evidence came in, that we could see how children are changing. The statistics tell the story:

Close to four million children between the ages of seven and 13 spend at least part of every weekday at home without adult supervision. Half of all girls between the ages of 15 and 19 have had sexual intercourse (and the greatest increase is at the lower end of that age scale). Teenage pregnancies are epidemic. Suicides among children are up and alcoholism among teenagers is common.

Where has childhood gone?

"There's no question that something major is happening," says Dr. Peter B. Neubauer, director of New York's Child Development Center. "There are enormous pressures on children and young adolescents now, and we are running behind in our understanding of what's going on."

We know a few things. We know that once upon a time, children could afford to remain innocent through a slow maturation period. They were left some time to believe in certitude, to remain comfortable in their knowledge of what was "good" and what was "bad."

The rules of life were clear and simple. It was possible for them to believe that all policemen were kindly protectors, that all teachers were dedicated, that all parents stayed married, and that all adults shared a kind of wisdom that came with age.

When children, who were much too smart to stay in the dark about the changes of the 1970s, ceased to believe all those things, they quickly "grew up." They became cynical and disillusioned, and they walked away from childhood.

Waiting in the wings, primed to capitalize on what is happening, are today's commercial advertisers, the direct descendants of the toy salesman who showed me the future in one tiny doll.

They know what to do: Sell sex. Sell excitement.

And so we have Brooke Shields, a 16-year-old model, posing for television commercials with her legs sprawled provocatively, cooing, "If my jeans could talk, I'd be in trouble." And we have Remco, a children's toy manufacturer, launching a trade advertising campaign for a line of children's cosmetics with an ad showing the made-up face of a little girl. "She's your market," trumpets the ad. "She's between the ages of four and nine."

In the movies, Tatum O'Neal and Kristy McNichol have a contest to see which nubile teenybopper can lose her virginity first. On the radio, Rod Stewart sings about sexual desire ("We'd be a fool to stop this time, spread your wings and let me come inside"). Eleven- and 12-year-olds laugh and listen and learn.

I am most concerned by the impact of all those high-pressure messages on ordinary children. Yet a special sadness surrounds those children co-opted by the advertisers to sell the illusions.

I look at them and think of Barbie. But they're not plastic, they're real.

Not long ago, I appeared on a television show with a group of young fashion models to discuss the pros and cons of the growing sophistication of children. One girl I remember well.

She sat bored on a sofa, a child-woman whose smoky, languorous beauty was accentuated by heavy makeup and high style clothes. She tried to explain how detached she felt from her beauty and her job.

"It's packaging, you know," she told me earnestly. "I sell an image. Thank goodness everything for my body is tax-deductible." She giggled, the high-pitched giggle of a 14-year-old, which was natural, because she is 14.

But she had learned to be an illusion.

I am quite sure she is the envy of her friends, but how strange and sad to have one's body be tax-deductible at the age of 14.

Like any parent, I have watched with apprehension as my children made their way through the labyrinth of childhood. The rules have changed so drastically and the stakes are so high.

I look at other parents just beginning the struggle and I see how meager their resources are. Those who try to impart moral values find themselves talking to children deafened by the siren songs of the sexual revolution. Those who try to prepare their children against disaster by providing practical information and prescriptions for the pill worry that they aren't doing enough. Everybody tiptoes over eggshells.

Many parents choose silence. They don't know what to say.

And yet I hear from children conflicting cries for freedom and direction. That's when something important seems lost, or at least left behind, like a mitten or a hat.

A friend once told me about a mother whose 15-year-old daughter asked whether she should have sex with her boyfriend. The mother launched into a modern talk, the kind she felt was required of her, about the "ifs" and the "whens." When she was finished, the girl asked, "Can I tell him you won't let me?"

I am convinced that children would give anything to be allowed to stay children just a while longer. When I watch them curl up in their Calvin Klein jeans, their eyes glazed over from listening to records, I sometimes can detect a crack in their sophisticated armor.

They want something they do not have: They want boundaries.

In a way, the saga of Barbie has come full circle. Children who learned to want too many things, to crave things that were bigger, better and faster, have found themselves unsure and anxious. They hurried too much and only some will learn to slow down.

Sometimes I wonder what happened to that toy salesman I met so long ago. I wonder if he ever had children of his own. If he did, he probably spent some years with a plastic doll who couldn't be cuddled or nurtured. He must have seen the quickening pace of childhood, then the headlong dash towards sophistication.

If he saw all that, I wonder how long he stuck with selling toys.

ONE FINAL HARVEST
Kent Meyers

I DON'T REMEMBER being told that the combines were coming, but I knew that they would, so that when they arrived they went to work as if I had planned them. So much of my life that summer and fall exists to me now as a kind of habit-molded dream. I must have planned things, discussed them with others, made decisions. But I can't distinguish now between making decisions about work and life and being decided by work and life. It wasn't until three years later, when for a composition class in college I wrote an essay about my father's death, that I wept for that death.

It's not that I was holding myself aloof from grief. It was more that life for me, strangely, continued much as it had before. A week after my father's death I participated in a regional high school speaking contest in a town near my own in Minnesota, and I remember the sympathy in my English teacher's face when she met me in the hall. The tears moistening her eyes seemed to me odd and out-of-place. There was work to do.

We rose every morning and put on our work clothes and went out to the expectant cattle and began to fill baskets with ground corn and carry them down the rows of bunks, and the cattle knew nothing and cared nothing. Sweat formed and muscles loosened. This was the way it had been for as long as we could remember, this work in the mornings and afternoons. And there was something natural and right in that unalteration, and the sweat that returned, easy and full of the body's grace, to the surface of the skin.

The work went on, through the sorting and selling of cattle and the preparation of the soil and its planting, all unavoidable and never thought to be avoided. And all that time the combines were coming. The neighbors were wondering whether Wayne Meyers's sons were going to manage all right, eyeing the crops we'd planted with critical, professional eyes and, seeing that the crops were good, maintaining their silence, keeping the important illusion that we were and they were independent farmers doing the work defined by the fences.

Only in their own talk—which I imagine now taking place at the grain elevator and the pool hall, and over those sagging fences buried in long grass where two tractors stop and neighbors converse for a while—does an action begin to form. It is as if the talk, unknown to me then and only imagined now, urges something into existence, or is urged by something, as we go about our daily work that spring and summer, and the crops rise, and pollen floats, and the air swells with the milky smell of ripening corn. The unripe future ripens. Words touch against it tenderly, to test the moment. When the moment comes, corn and community ripe at the same time, there appear in our driveway combines and trucks, coming down the long, gradual slope from the county road, raising dust. I watch them, knowing they would come but not expecting them, and I point them to the fields as if with my own voice I had called them, with my own finger beckoned.

It took two days. Had my father been alive, it would have taken two weeks. The neighbors (how many of them? six? seven? eight? I don't know, and I am pleased at this unspecificity of memory, that I cannot name their faces but only know that they appeared when needed)—the neighbors with their combines glided up and down the fields, dumping the corn from their tanks into trucks that we drove directly to the elevator, selling it instead of storing it, knowing that this was the last year we'd farm, that the old patterns were broken, that the cattle's steamy breath would not fill the barns in the coming winter, that their hooves would not tramp the frozen ground as they waited to be fed.

Now I can see the patterns both fulfilled and broken now, the combines coming as a communal and healing gesture, help arriving only when help was needed, the neighbors letting us do what we could in all the dignity of accomplishment, and never advice offered by any of the men who drove the roads, who slowed to watch our progress that summer and kept to themselves our transgressions, until the time ripened when we might stand within our harvest as adults and men, and they witnesses more than helpers, provers and acknowledgers of who we were and what we'd done—witnesses formed by history and community and stamped by the land, and this harvest a testament to our father's guidance and his sons' abilities and learning, the shelled corn pouring from the combines' spouts and brimming in the trucks, lapping against the sideboards like labor liquid and refined.

Later the talk would come back to us through the crooked meandering of rumor—part of dignity and part of harshness and part of rectitude being that on the plains you speak a compliment to the winds so that it is carried through the community before it finally flows to the person for whom it was meant. It was only much later that we heard from others how the men who ran the combines spoke to each other of how they couldn't believe that we, the sons, had grown corn this productive, had brought from the land—not so much out of knowledge of the land, not so much from our own feel for the seasons and soil, but from our knowledge of our father's knowledge, doing what we knew he would have done—this harvest that, the rumors finally told us, surpassed that of many of the men who combined for us.

For two days the combines roamed up and down the rows, the trucks ran regular circuits between our farm and the elevator in town, and my mother spent all day cooking for men who, many of them, had never set foot in our house and never would again, not because they'd never been welcome but because they were neighbors—not relatives, who are allowed in regardless of affection, and not friends, who enter for the ease of being there, but neighbors, for whom necessity rules. In those two days those neighbors did not become our fast friends. I can't even honor them with memories of their faces, or the ways their laughter echoed in the kitchen, or their requests for the salt. Through the door of necessity they walked into our lives—though of course they had always been there, silent and observant and for the most part ignored, just as we had been in theirs, my father as ready as any of them to spring that latch into their lives.

Then the fields lay bare. The harvest finished, the neighbors dispersed to their own fields while we continued in ours, discing the cornstalks and then plowing, preparing the land for whoever would rent it come spring. Once again the land appeared to be farmed by individual farmers making their own uses of it.

The alluvial soil upon which I grew, which is one of the richest in the world, a Clarion-Webster silt-clay-loam, is formed from old waters and centuries of wetland grasses. The sod, busted by German and Scandinavian settlers, turned black—pitch black, shiny black— when the long grasses fell and decomposed. Corn and soybean crops today grow from a reservoir of time and water and humus, thousands of plants that have fallen: purple coneflower and swamp milkweed and phlox and false indigo and blazing star and black-eyed Susan and lead plant and wild rose and thimble weed and purple loosestrife and bluestem grass and Indian grass and gramagrass—the long-grass prairie, taller than the people who walked through it, who turned it under.

The soil itself of a living, virgin prairie is nearly barren. All the nutrients are drawn into the blaze of flower and stem. The prairie lives above the earth, the minerals and nutrients flowing through the plants, and things so interdependent and entwined, so eager and opportunistic, that nearly every molecule of nutrient is taken in by the root system, which has its own tangled levels, some shallow and others driving deep into the earth. All the richness of the prairie is alive, and the soil itself is merely the substrate of exchange.

Only since the sod was turned, barely 100 years ago, have we been able to speak of the "richness" of the soil, the nutrients even in the middle of summer, when the land is so green it stuns the eye, lying mostly within the soil, mono-culture farming unable to draw them all up, to use them, so that farmers spread fertilizer to encourage single crops while nutrients that might grow hundreds of other plants go to waste, and the plants that do attempt to use them, the weeds—and a weed is just a plant that has lost its relationship to other plants—are doused with chemicals and killed.

Still, the virgin prairie is a metaphor for the communities that exist upon this land, as if nothing is ever escaped but only changes form, as if walking on the prairie were enough to draw from it its consciousness and power, until its way of being emerges in the communities that shape themselves upon the land, and the tangled words that form these communities are dumb to know what they form, like the roots of plants that cannot know the blossom.

Communities on the northern plains are made manifest by disaster. Thus it is that an individual or family can be graced by loss, as the land, never stopping or waiting, absorbs the seasons, and the people who have chosen to live upon it must make the ritual responses. When these responses cannot be made, the community, which appears to the casual observer to be non-existent, to be nothing more than a collection of individual landowners working at their own pace, defines itself by its reaction, shapes itself by its talk, and is made manifest in the clumsy, lumbering grace of combines silhouetted against the far sky, and the small dust they raise on the road, blown instantly away, and by the unnameable faces of neighbors. And the community is expressed, too, by the embarrassment they would each feel were they ever remembered, or thanked beyond the restrained and ordinary thanks that comes when a job is finished, and that is offered as water is offered, with the knowledge that we all thirst.

In the moment of disaster to one of their members, these plains communities draw into themselves, out of the rich substrate of tradition, all the unused nutrients, all the quiet charities, all the powerful stories that have told them how to live—stories that have never, in ordinary times, prevented them from bickering, from denigrating their neighbors' crops or coveting their neighbors' Harvestore or machine shed, or from engaging in vicious gossip or praising their own children at the expense of someone else's. It can sometimes appear that the injunction to love thy neighbor passes unheeded through the ears of these people.

But when the worst that can happen happens, when the resources of the individual or family are exhausted, when neither insurance nor capital can compensate the loss, talk, like the tendrils of roots, draws from the old stories their essential meaning and power, old divisions are put aside, land and stories and people and belief for a time become unified and real, and though no one ever expects help, everyone knows it will come.

This may be a good definition of a living culture, one in which the old stories are made real in daily life, in simple relationships and actions, when the telling and the acting-out reinforce each other and become part of the same pattern. As I look at the desperation with which people in our age are seeking community, I am struck by the thought that few people any more know what a community is, both how awful and how comforting a true community can be. Having forgotten the complexity of community, people form mono-culture communities, seeking any similarity around which to group, accidents of biology and fundamentals of all sorts. These mono-culture communities are frail and in need of tending, as unable to draw from the substrate of their cultures all of the nutrients as the great mono-culture farms of the Midwest are unable to draw from their rich soils all the nutrients deposited by the past.

The full richness of a culture can only be drawn up and made day-by-day alive by people as different as lead plant from coneflower, but who know their interdependence and who live as neighbors. I suspect, though I don't know for sure, that some of the men who drove down our driveway and into our fields with their combines were men with whom my father had disagreements. Perhaps some of them, even, were men fundamentally different from him in their outlooks, their senses of humor, their beliefs. But when he died, these men appeared to witness his sons, to fulfill the patterns, to complete the ritual.

I will take them. I will take their silence that summer, and their distance. I will take the respect they showed us by letting us do the work we could do, by letting us succeed on our own. I will take them in all their restraint and all their imperfections and prejudices. They were neighbors. They knew what was necessary. And when necessity called, they drew up into their individual differences the strengths of their traditions, and formed from those strengths a community, and made us part of the whole.

I will take their witness. I will take a man who will not take thanks, a man whose face I can't even remember and who has no need to be remembered, hidden behind the sunglance off of plexi-glass or the dust raised by the immense machine he has driven slow miles over gravel roads, to help me, to help my family—because the corn is ripe, the time is ripe, the talk is ripe. I will take men whom, could I remember them, I might not even like, and I will take their compliments directed not to me, and their faith that nevertheless I would come to hear them.

I will take their witness to my passage into the community of men and women, and the community of the land itself, the ancient plants and waters whispering in it, the cycles that repeat, that end but are never ended, the stories that go so far back and are so rich that they begin with the beginning, the stories of our communion with all things and with each other, the stories of our needs, of our living and dying and being.

"MOM, PLEASE!"

Barbara Turpin

MY NAME IS Andrea Turpin and I'm 14 years old.

I'm 5 feet, 10 inches tall and I weigh 125 pounds. I'm fat and ugly.

Jeesh, does my mom get upset when she hears me say that! But that's what I see when I look in the mirror. She says I don't see straight, but *she's* the one who wears glasses.

That's why *I'm* writing this. I have 20/20 vision and I want to tell what it's really like to be 14 years old.

No adult knows what kind of hell it is. Oh, my mom thinks she does. *She* thinks *she* knows *everything.*

"I know what you're going through," she tells me. I hate it when she says that. What does she know? That's why I couldn't let her write this. She'd get it all wrong. She was never 14, never had parents bugging her all the time, never had to worry about school and friends. She just sort of hatched one day, fully formed. She was put on this earth for one purpose: to make my life miserable.

Take last fall, for example.

She knows that I go to all the rallies on Friday nights before home football games and that I count on her to pick me and my friends up afterwards. She never has anything better to do; she never goes out. So what did she tell me on the way to school on Wednesday? That an old student of hers was coming into town for the game and she was going out to dinner with him on Friday night. I'd have to find a ride home from the rally.

22

I was so angry, I couldn't even look at her. But I wanted to let her know I had her number.

"Well," I said to her, staring out the window, "I guess we have our priorities."

Whoa! Were *we* upset! Can you believe it?

Things like that happen all the time. She gets mad at me for no reason.

She hardly ever gets phone calls, and anytime the phone rings it's almost always for me, so she knows the phone is really mine. One day last winter, I was on the phone with a friend when I heard the call-waiting "beep, beep." I put my friend on hold and took the call. It was Michael from Boston, one of mom's best friends from her flower-child period. I looked out my bedroom window and saw her shoveling snow in the driveway. I knew if she took the call she'd be on the phone forever. So I told Michael that she was out of town for two days.

Okay, so maybe that wasn't very smart. But how was I to know that he'd call back two days later wanting to know how her trip was? She yelled at me while she was still on the phone with him! *Then* she stayed on the phone for an hour!

I was so mad. I kept going into her room every five minutes or so to give her dirty looks, but she didn't get the hint. So then I stayed in the room and just stared at her. She *still* didn't get off the phone, though she knew I was there because she returned the dirty looks. She left me no choice. I *had* to scream at her to get off because she was cutting into my phone time.

Her face went white. Her mouth dropped open. It was like she was in shock or something.

For what? It's *my* phone! I keep telling her to get a separate line for herself, but she just rolls her eyes at me and mumbles stuff like "over my dead body" or "when hell freezes over."

Then there was the day she left work at 5:30 and found her car had a flat tire in the parking lot. She called me and my sister at home to tell us that she'd have to wait for the man from the garage to come change the tire, and it could be a couple of hours before she was home.

How could she do that to me?

"I have to be at Tim's party by 7!" I reminded her. "And I have to eat, and we have to pick up Clare, and we have to stop at the store because I have to bring something!"

She exploded at me—for no reason. All she could think about was herself.

"Do you think I *enjoy* standing out here alone in the cold and the dark?" she asked me. Jeez. Like it was *my* fault or something.

I heard her messing around in the kitchen when she came home from work one night a few weeks ago. She'd promised to make my favorite dinner—marinated chicken. All of a sudden I heard a crash. I ran down the steps and saw her standing in the middle of the kitchen, the pan of chicken smashed to smithereens on the floor, glass and marinade everywhere. She was trying to wrap a towel around one finger that was dripping blood all over the chicken. It was disgusting.

"So," I asked her, "what'll we have for supper now?"

"Hot dogs!" she barked at me, squeezing her finger in the towel and making a face like she was in real pain.

Like I'm really gonna eat hot dogs when I could've had marinated chicken. "Forget it," I said. "I'm not eating."

She gave me this look like I was some creature from another planet. What did I say to deserve that?

Besides flying off the handle for no reason, she isn't consistent. What she says and what she does are two different things.

She *says* she's willing to help me with my homework, but when I ask her for help with geometry as soon as she comes home from work at night, she tells me that she wants to get changed and get supper out of the way first; then she can help me without interruptions. But if she really wanted to help, she'd do it on *my* schedule.

And when she does try to help, she's worthless. I asked her to help me study for a biology test by explaining 20 pages of class notes I'd taken. She looked them over and said, "They don't make any sense!"

I knew that! If they made sense, would I have asked her to explain them? And this woman has a Ph.D.!

I know she's trying to do the best she can, raising my sister and me on her own since dad died, but I wish she'd lighten up and get a life. She worries about the stupidest things.

Like the laundry. She complains that I ball up towels and jeans and sweaters and shove them down the laundry chute. What's the big deal? So what if she has to stand on a chair and shove the handle of the broom up the chute to prod them loose?

And then she gets mad at me for putting in a wash with just my shirt in it. "It wouldn't be so bad if you didn't have to step over a mountain of dirty clothes to do it!" she yells at me. "Why can't you throw other stuff in, too?"

But hey! I need my shirt washed. And what does anybody ever do for me around here that I should wash *their* clothes?

Then there's my room.

Well, maybe she's right about that.

"Words haven't been invented to describe it," she says.

"But it's *my* room," I tell her, "not yours."

"When you pay the mortgage, it'll be your room," she says. She always has a comeback like that. It's so annoying.

And *cheap!* God! How's a 14-year-old supposed to survive on 10 bucks a month?

"You don't even deserve that," she tells me. "You don't do anything to earn it."

Can you believe it? I wash my shirt, don't I?

So she wouldn't give me any money to eat supper at the Huddle the last time I went to a rally, just because I'd turned down a baby-sitting job earlier in the week because I wanted to watch my favorite TV show.

"You can't need money all that much," she said, "if you turn down opportunities to earn it." She's so unreasonable.

To save money, she actually voted for uniforms at my old school. Can you believe it? Uniforms? So everybody can look like everybody else? I want to express my individuality and wear sweaters like the ones Gina has and slacks like Leah's. And I want the same running shoes that everyone's got now. Uniforms—the ultimate expression of conformity. Spare me.

Now, to top it off, she's humiliated me, too. She's hobbling around on crutches because she broke her ankle last weekend. She always crosses her legs Indian-style when she writes, and when she got up off her chair last Saturday, her foot was asleep. As soon as she put it down on the floor, it twisted under her. We heard a "crack!" and down she went. Worse yet, she hyperventilated and passed out.

Only *my* mom would break her ankle in her own kitchen. My friends will see her, and I can't possibly tell them the truth. What'll they think of me? I'll have to lie and tell them she broke it while skiing in the Alps.

I really hate to see her incapacitated like this. How will she take me into Chicago next weekend, like she promised?

She's so selfish.

That's why I don't understand why she let me write this when I asked her. She let me say whatever I wanted; she said she's tired of getting mad at me. But I don't get it. If it's me talking here, how can this be "getting even"?

THE LIFE I CHOSE
Kerry Temple

JIMMY AND I were boyhood friends and together we cast our adolescent fantasies. Jimmy grew up to live our dreams and I grew up to ponder the road not taken.

Raised in Louisiana, we spent our barefoot years chasing through scruffy pine woods and splashing naked into drowsy bayous. As restless teenagers, we were New World explorers, racing down country roads, finding fresh swimming holes and investigating all the rural stores and cemeteries. We canoed Arkansas rivers, backpacked in the desert mountains of southwest Texas, and vowed never to live near the confines of Shreveport, Louisiana.

We were restless products of middle-class security; what mattered most to us was freedom. We would be drifters. We dreamed of train-hopping hobo lives spun from John Steinbeck stories.

But while I worked summers in such exotic locales as Cedar Grove, Louisiana, and Gulfport, Mississippi, Jimmy went off to the wilds of Montana and California. While I attended graduate school, Jimmy went off to the Yucatan, then spent a year bumming around Europe. The last I heard of him he was running a country store in west Texas in the winter and working a fishing boat out of Kodiak, Alaska, in the summer.

I was reminded of all this the other day when I stood at a railroad crossing and watched a freight train accelerate as it headed out of town. The thought of jumping it still strummed in me some romantic chord, the way sailing ships allured others in generations past.

On this day, however, I had in one hand the leash of the family dog and in the other the handle of a wagon containing our boys, aged 2 and 3. As the boxcars thundered past and the rails bent beneath their weight, I stooped to explain the dangers of playing near train tracks.

The moment brought back one particularly heated debate I once had with my parents. Jimmy and I were trying to talk our way out of school. We said we would live in a mountain cabin and write a book. What I remember best was my parents' argument that what I wanted from life then would not be the same as what I would want five years later; so "Don't botch up your life tilting at windmills." I countered by paraphrasing Albert Schweitzer who once said something to the effect that people become great by holding firm throughout their lives to those ideals that burned in their youth.

Standing at that train crossing during this summer that I turned 30, I realized we all were right.

When I was 19, I never thought I would prefer zoos to bars, *Sesame Street* to *60 Minutes* or someone else's birthday to my own. I never thought "camping out" in the backyard with kids would be as much fun as hiking alone. I never imagined I would work in an office from 8 to 5, then be happy to come home to play ringmaster to a circus of unidentified flying children.

We have rented the same box house in the same tightly fenced neighborhood for four years and have no prospect of owning our own home. We have too little money and too many debts. When the car needs repair, we pray it doesn't break down on the highway before we can afford to make the bumps and grinds go away.

The last time my wife and I disagreed over the seriousness of the car's ailment, she declared, "This is what I hate about marriage. I like to be independent, to do what I want, to be in control."

"Me too," I said, before I stormed from the house and clobbered the lawn with our dull-bladed push mower. These concessions to domesticity do not enhance the images I concocted as a sophomore in the Age of Aquarius.

I am certain that part of my unease with reality has its roots in the love and peace times of my teenage years. I became aware of the wide, wild world during a period of extreme idealism and freedom. We actually believed the gospel according to the songs and posters which filled our rooms. "We can change the world," we sang. All we needed was "love, sweet love."

But the choruses said little about responsibility, obligation and commitment to entangling relationships. Today my wife and I talk more about life insurance, medical plans and sibling rivalry than we do about living off the earth, thumbing to Big Sur or moving to Australia. This is normal for many people; but for those of us who made heroes out of renegades, it raises questions of identity and compromise.

Dreams say a lot about our values and ideals and about the lives we want to lead. They give direction and hope to those navigating life's murky currents. But how far can a person bend an ideal before the bending becomes a cop-out? When do the responsibilities of "reality" entrap an individual and prevent him from living his own life? At what point does the dreamer become the dream's victim, defeated by overinflated expectations or unable to deal effectively with real life situations?

At the time, I didn't think turning 30 affected me much, but in the months since that birthday I have caught myself evaluating my lot. The other night at dinner, for example, I was daydreaming about my younger days, when I was again startled by the revelation that the two little guys on each side of me, with whom I had played all afternoon, were not going home after dinner, but were, no fooling, my very own kids. After three years of fatherhood, this thought still jolts me sometimes.

It was especially hard to accept on this occasion when the younger brother opened a bean barrage on his giggling older brother, who retaliated by slinging applesauce. I looked across the table for disciplinary help, but my battle-weary wife had entered the fray, and was escalating it. My calls for a cease-fire were first ignored, then answered with a bean to the forehead.

"What am I doing here?" I asked aloud. "This is not how I planned it. Will someone bring a real parent in here to break up this mess, while I take a hike?"

I left the table but returned, toting a water pistol with which I mercilessly zapped each of the combatants until they joined forces to chase me into the backyard. There the war ended in a pileup of tickling hands and squirming bodies. I fell back on the grass, breathless, happy and full, but hoping my example and leniency would not someday result in Grampa being blasted by a bean or the Washington Monument by a homemade bomb.

Later that night, while the others slept, I stretched out on the living room floor and listened to some old records. Eric Andersen and Jerry Jeff Walker sang highway songs. Then, with a soft breeze drifting through the windows and a train whistling in the distance, Tom Rush sang: "Seems the songs I'm singing now are all about the sea and sky. Seems the scenes I see are city streets; I can't say why. Seems the life I chose is different from my dreams. I'm going home to younger days when things were as they seemed."

I heard the soft click of a latch and standing in the doorway was my 3-year-old, Casey. He rubbed his eyes and walked stiffly to me.

"What do you want, Casey?" I asked. "Some water? The bathroom?"

"I want to do something with you, Daddy," he said softly.

"Do what?"

"Just something."

So with his bear and blanket he curled up on the couch to hear the music with me. He fell asleep, one hand clutching mine, the other arm wrapped like a snake around my arm, while I told him the story of brave Casey Jones, the train engineer who drove to his death because he wouldn't slow down.

TOO BIG FOR HIS BRIDGES

Tom Werge

DRIVING TOWARD THE Jersey shore in the August heat, I am acutely conscious that the road to the sea also leads to my life's half-century mark. Since boyhood I've made the journey from my North Bergen hometown hundreds of times: Jersey Turnpike, shore exit, Parkway, old Route 36, then the shining Shrewsbury River. On one shore, the highlands of childhood summers; on the other, a wall of great boulders restraining the sea. Spanning the river, a concrete bridge made mythic by memory.

Jumping from the bridge through the salt air into the river below—a drop of 30 feet, more at low tide—once braced our souls. As teenagers free of television's dull glare and linked to the sun by our senses and bright days, we shined. In his youth, my uncle jumped from this bridge and landed, inadvertently, in a boat. In so doing he broke a cardinal rule (always have a lookout on shore to sanction the jump) and his leg. And, I guess, the tranquility of the boat's crew.

But ours were leaps of faith. We were innocents abroad in spray and sunlight. Ours was not a bridge too far or too high.

Three decades later, in the accelerating August of my middle age, I have to admit the bridge is higher than I recalled. My son observes, "It's a pretty good drop, Dad," but his implied caution only intensifies the desire at the heart of this trip back home: to make one more leap. Not one "last" leap—that would be ambiguous; just one more for the road of restoration and of memory for a moment made flesh.

Speaking of which, my own flesh turns dizzyingly weak as I climb

31

over the bridge railing and look down. My spirit is willing, but, hey, we're now talking Jimmy Stewart in *Vertigo*. Cars whiz by. It's high noon. My son can't believe I'm going to do this. Neither can I. I decide to climb back over the railing to assess my options.

Only to confront a gathering crowd: young, old, curious, lovers of potential sudden death and the macabre. They appear straight out of Dante. I give them a cavalier smile and pretend I'm just loosening up the leg that had started back over the railing. I stay where I am.

My lookout on the shore below gives the all-clear signal. The demonic crowd edges closer for a better look. Some words of J. Robert Oppenheimer loom before me: "Sometimes the answer to fear does not lie in trying to explain away the causes. Sometimes the answer lies in courage." I jump.

Hurtling downward I think, *Right, Oppy, easy for you to say. That was a simple A-Bomb; this is serious stuff.* Just before I hit the water, I extend my left arm, hand flat, to brace myself.

Bad move. Screaming pain surges through my suddenly immobile left shoulder, and the current takes me seaward. I vaguely hear my son's voice asking if I'm all right. I try to shout "no problem," but what emerges is a cross between a defective foghorn and a flu-ridden sea lion. I try to paddle to safety but the docks, perversely, retreat.

Finally, dog-tired and dazed, I make it to a dock ladder. Barnacles slice my hands and feet, my arms, chest and legs as I climb. Laboring mightily, I heave myself onto the dock, a beached whale, a cast-off jellyfish. I stagger upright, bleeding. My son greets me: "You all right, Dad?"

The searing shoulder and vague nausea give way to horror: We are not alone. We're on the edge of a dock-restaurant—an upscale place whose patrons gape at me rudely, forks frozen midway to mouths. The Creature from the Black Lagoon meets the Nautical Yuppies. They're mesmerized. Only later do I think of the words I should have uttered: "So what did you expect, Esther Williams?" But my potential Mel Brooks moment passes and I exit silently in tragicomic pain.

At the hospital the staff takes sides: To some I am heroic, to most

I am crazy. "*That* bridge?" one asks; "that's *high!*" He edges away from me.

The X-rays show a hairline fracture of the left arm. The edger returns warily. "Tell me," he asks, "why'd you go and do something like that?" I give the only answer I can: "That's a good question. I don't know. I really don't."

I really did, though. I had tried to reclaim the past, my past. In my imagination, my friends and I were—are—unscarred and fresh. My parents are alive, appalled at our jumping but forever loving. My kid brother's blond hair shimmers in the sun. Faith and hope shine too, visible and radiant. We can still go home again.

THE SNOWS OF APRIL
Sonia Gernes

I HAD MEANT to make an end to grief that April. I had come to Ragdale, a refuge for artists and poets in Lake Forest, Illinois, not because I have no private space at home, but because a long relationship had ended some weeks before, and I needed a less haunted space, one not ringing at every turn with little bells of memory that chimed: darkness, pain, loss . . . I had meant to put sorrow behind me and immerse myself in the healing oblivion of work.

It is not easy to fall in love in midlife. Or perhaps the falling is easy and the love is hard. At any rate, I had not succeeded. I had tried for longer than I cared to admit to make a life of a troubled relationship. I had "wept and fasted, wept and prayed" as Eliot says, and more than that: I had reasoned, argued and sought counsel, made resolutions that never seemed to work. The time came when it was right to cease the trying, to walk away and accept the grace one needs to acknowledge defeat.

But to walk away when one is past 40—to be the one who does the breaking—is not to turn to the next romance as a younger woman might, but to step back into the realm of the empty room, the ticking clock, the nights when you open the refrigerator and dinner is whatever's there. It's those odd moments when grief catches you just below the ribs and you cannot breathe without a scalding pain. And in the weeks after that, when the silent phone no longer sears you, it's those moments of doubt when all the spinsters of childhood crowd in and hiss: You threw it away! Last chance . . . Last chance . . .

I had meant to be done with that. Two months have gone by

since I walked alone into a February sky so tightly blue there were no openings, no cushions of cloud to hold me. It was April now. New life, I told myself; new shoots so tender they are not yet green, so tenacious that no quantity of last year's leaves can hold them down. New work, new projects, a resurrection of the novel that in those years of turmoil had finally drowned: I would be a writer again, if I couldn't be a lover.

Tiny blue-petaled bells were all around the gateposts of the old estate where I spent the Easter weekend. The brick courtyard of the old barnhouse was shining with hyacinth leaves, new myrtle shoots. I settled in, unpacked my books and half a ream of paper, went down to dinner to see who else was there.

Good Friday was rainy, but that was all right. I could stand at my window and watch the rain slick the blue slate roof of the studio wing, climb to the cupola where, legend has it, a thousand butterflies once made their way in and, trapped by a falling window, perished in the sun. By 8:30 in the morning, I had found a plug for my electric typewriter, gotten out my notes and started to work.

In the early evening, about an hour before dinner was due, I discovered that I needed to check a reference and decided to walk over to the "big house" to see if, by chance, the book I wanted might be there. The old mansion on the estate is still used on occasion by family members, but visiting artists have rooms there as well, and the library is open to all residents.

It is always something of a fantasy for me to walk through that front door, as though I were chatelaine of such copious living arrangements. The family treasures are still there: framed bookplates designed for the children, a sculpture of a long-dead dog, an antique music box that tinkles in the dining room when you lift the lid. There is a mellowness, a patina, in that house. The light that filters over the now slightly shabby chairs and sofas comes from an expanse of prairie land and woods. It is a beneficent house, a place of people who put their wealth to the test of truth and beauty and a greater good. It is a place where one can curl into a chair and heal, and feel the springtime coming.

The book I wanted did not seem to be there, so I browsed, selected *Late Night Thoughts on Mahler's Sixth Symphony*, measured the increasing sliver of twilight and turned on a lamp. The book was one my old love had in his collection, and perhaps that was the association, but there, in the safest of houses, the most tender time of the day, I read a meditation on how noises are alike but every smell is unique. Suddenly, all my griefs came back to me. Every gesture he had made seemed precious. Every quarrel, every insoluble dispute, every weekend of raging anger slid away like cellophane and vanished from my life.

Will it be ever thus? I thought. Having made my bed, shall I be conscious every waking moment that I must sleep in it alone? I closed my eyes against the sting of tears, then opened them to cast about for anything—another book, a painting, a tinkling music box—that would distract me from the pain that was creeping up my throat. That was when I noticed it—the April snow falling through the depth of twilight. I went to the window and watched it come: an unrelenting whiteness onto a land my mind had colored green.

It was everything of shroud and tomb and winter. It was Good Friday descending with the silent ache they must have felt in Jerusalem when the thunderbolts ceased. But it was salvation too: health and hope and healing, for April snow is brief. It was the knowledge that each season contains the rest, and none can be taken purely— that grief cannot be hurried, as love cannot be held in too tight a grasp.

There would be other snows that April, brief showers of opaque air hurtling toward the grass. There would be other moments of grief. In time there would be hyacinths and a fierce burst of tiger lilies. It was too early to tell if there would be other loves, but there would be days when work and words became a splendid house, and days when sudden gladness darted.

I did not know then that snow in April would come to hold a kind of secret joy for me, but I did know this: Before the final whiteness comes, there would be other Easter mornings.

DANCING IN THE TWILIGHT
Walton R. Collins

THE LAST TIME I saw my father, he danced for me.

In his pajamas and slippers and robe, he got stiffly out of a chair in the tiny nursing-home room that is now his universe and began doing a cross between a jig and the Charleston.

He always liked doing the Charleston for his children, especially the part where he put his hands on his knees and crossed them back and forth. A good salesman, he was blessed with a sunny disposition and has kept it into old age.

He was 91 last October, but if you ask him how old he is he'll reply, "100." That's because he plans to make it to his personal turn-of-the-century, which comes due three years before the turn of the millenium. Mainly he spends his days saying the rosary in his 15-by-15 foot room with two chairs, a bed, two small chests, and a 30-year-old record player whose volume he keeps high so the rest of the nursing-home floor can enjoy the music of Harry James and Glenn Miller. No one ever complains.

On the wall is a photo of his bride—her dark hair cut in the cloche-cap look of 1929; she died three years ago after 56 years of marriage. "Notice how her eyes follow you?" he asks a visitor.

In another photo on the wall, he is one of six young men standing behind a seated couple in their 50s. If the photo had a caption it would say, "Maurice and Florence Collins and six of their seven sons." There also were five daughters.

Nobody in any of the pictures on my father's wall is still alive. Hardly anyone he knows is, except for his three children, none of whom lives in the town where he prefers to dwell. All of us have tried to lure him to our towns, but he's not interested.

A manufacturer's representative who peddled railroad equipment from New York to Chicago, he spent a lifetime on the road. He didn't quit his career until he was well into his 80s, less than a decade ago. By then, his wife was too ill to care for at home. After she died, he lived alone for a while in the apartment they once shared. He liked it hot, and he kept the temperature cranked up into the high 80s no matter the season. One summer night his apartment grew so hot he had a heat stroke; fortunately, the noise of his convulsive fall attracted the attention of someone in the next apartment.

For my sister and my brother and me, it was the moment we had tried to keep at arm's length: We could no longer ignore the fact that the child-parent role reversal was complete, that the children were now the decision-makers in the family unit, not the parent. That role reversal happens more often in our time than ever before, given the achievements of medicine at prolonging life. I had already helped my wife through a similar role reversal with her own father, so I had an understanding of what had to be done now.

The trouble comes in knowing what's best. It's easier to know— or think you know—in the genuine child-parent relationship. In the false one, there are too many emotional overlays for comfort. And that brings guilt, sometimes assisted by outsiders who don't have to make the choices and so find it easy to pass judgment. My sister, for example, found herself being chewed out one day during a telephone call from a cousin who said it was dreadful that we had put our father in a nursing home.

My father doesn't think it dreadful. The home is in his hometown; the alternatives are not. We decided he would be happier there than trying to live with any of his three children, options he himself declined to take seriously.

We visit him as often as we can, but it is never often enough—for him or for us. He is a gregarious man who comes alive in the presence of other people. When he puts on his horn-rimmed glasses, he looks a little like George Burns, minus the cigar. Like any successful salesman he knows how to win the good will of clients: When we send him candy he spreads it around to the nurses and orderlies, and we've had to reduce his pocket money because he distributes it as quickly as he gets it—or else he leaves it out where it's promptly stolen. He has always enjoyed being liked.

I hate visiting the home. The corridor leading to his room seems a mile long, and I sometimes have the Twilight-Zone feeling that the patient I see rounding the corner at the far end is myself in 20 years. A woman in a room near my father's yells "help me" all day long, and other patients sit outside their rooms and watch me blankly as I walk past. Do they envy my relative youth and vigor? Are they sizing me up as a future inmate of a home like this? The trouble with this place, I decide one day, is that there are no dreams here, only resignation.

My father's eyes light up when any of his three children walk into the room, and he pulls together his energies and manners. "I was just thinking about you," he invariably remarks. I find it painful to see the translucent quality of his skin that the very old often acquire, and the shock of white hair turned as fine as angel hair. He is harder to converse with each time, more confused about people and places and events.

He, on the other hand, genuinely likes being where he is. It's the best nursing home in the city, he tells me, as if he were convincing a railroad purchasing agent of the quality of an electrical bond. His room is the best one in the building, with the nicest view out the window. But he refuses to get dressed and go to the common dining room to eat, and the world beyond his four walls grows misty and unreal to him.

The orderlies tell me he is always cheerful. And every now and then, they say, he turns up his record player to top volume and goes to his door and dances a little.

THE HONORABLE THING TO DO
Mark Phillips

M Y SISTER AND I riding the old yellow school bus home over bumpy curvy country roads. Kids bouncing into each other and sometimes onto the aisle floor. A screaming cursing laughing shouting kissing spit-wad throwing canned jungle of yahoos. Brakes screeching, jerking stops. Kids sprinting across muddy lawns to farmhouses, bus doors swishing closed, the odors of manure and diesel fuel, gears grinding and engine growling, kids leaning out windows waving madly and popping the finger and laughing muted into the wind.

I recall one such spring afternoon when I was 14 and Kim 12. I am sharing a seat with Donnie, my best friend, who, because of his physical resemblance to the comic strip character, is nicknamed "Dondie." But now, turned around in the seat in front of us, Kim is calling him other names. What began as teasing is now a contest of adolescent meanness. Donnie's voice stretches high as he calls her fat. After a hurt laugh, she calls him bony and weird looking and adds that it's no wonder he and his mother have to live with his grandparents—his father away because the poor man is ashamed of having a son who's in a comic strip.

Donnie, who lives across the street from Kim and me, climbs down from the bus when we do. He plants his feet and stings one of her shoulders with a bony fist. She drops to the grass, wailing. Before I know it, I'm atop Donnie, pummeling him. When his cry is louder than Kim's, I free him to run home. Kim looks up and thanks me. I don't reply, I don't help her up, just stand there rather surprised at myself. Donnie and I are best friends, and brothers and sisters are supposed to be enemies. Aren't they?

That evening, when our father comes home from his job as a welder in a power plant, he learns what has happened and praises me for protecting my little sister. Then he turns to Kim, pulls off his belt and gives her a strapping.

Honor thy father and thy American courage. Your dad is a brawler, the toughest and best father in the whole wide world, and you proudly try to follow his example. When your best friend hits your sister, in a world where boys never play with dolls, you instinctively fight him. Years later, when your sister suffers kidney failure, in a world where men go to war for the Motherland, you give her one of yours. Having misread a little Hemingway, you think your code is one of American manliness. To hell with *le courage*. To hell with heart. To hell with the French. In American, courage means "to possess guts." Your sister needs some of your guts, so you give her some. You give less out of love than because your code mandates it.

I did read poetry, belonged to Amnesty International, drove a 4-cylinder car, liked to cook, fed winter birds and occasionally wore pink. I never owned a pickup truck with NRA stickers plastered on the bumpers and guns hung on a rack behind the cab seat; never owned a mint '56 Chevy with lacy garter belts dangling from the rearview mirror like fish on a stringer. No muscle shirts, no refrigerator packed with Grizzly-brand beer, or splayed-legged *Penthouse* centerfolds tacked above my workbench. No den bedecked with mounted heads of lions and tigers and bears, or portable gymnasium in my living room, Doberman pinschers in my front yard, Qaddafi target in the back. Never have been one of those men who chew up their sensitivity and digest it into intestinal fortitude. Nevertheless, I sometimes have thought I was.

Of course such thinking is crap. Still, it clings to many of us men until a personal cataclysm shakes it off. Until someone's alienated daughter overdoses, or until his lonely wife leaves him, or until his son returns from war without legs. Or in my case, until I gave one of my kidneys to my sister and my sister died. Until in tragedy she gave me, as she put it in a letter intended to be read posthumously, something "intangible." Kim, who never fought bulls, hunted big game in Africa, boxed or went to war, taught me about *le courage*.

When Kim became ill, she was working as a waitress and maid at a country tavern. My mother wanted her to attend college, but Kim was far happier and better at her job than most people are at theirs; and what more should one want in a job? A working class girl, she was the perfect barmaid for the tavern's working class patrons. She had a full, rolling and musical laugh the men loved. On the other hand, she knew when to look a man in the eye and tell him where to get off. Elbows propped up on the bar, she listened to her share of woeful tales, did her share of social work. She forced herself to work throughout a year of sickness, right up to a day when she almost died.

Kim kept faith in her doctor though he persisted for a year in treating her for recurring flu. Then one day—Kim's temperature alternately soaring and plummeting, dry heaves, pain everywhere and her body covered with bruises of uremia—our mother drove Kim to the office of the doctor, who was on vacation. His associate saw that Kim had something far worse than influenza. Tests at the local hospital confirmed total kidney failure, and she was transferred to a hospital for hemodialysis.

Three days a week for five years, each session lasting hours, Kim was one with a machine. Patients in reclining chairs were lined up around the large room, the dialysis machines humming like a mass-production line. Rollers squeezed thick bright blood through clear plastic tubing, and visitors worried about leaks. Technician-nurses checked gauges and monitors, adjusted dials, took blood samples. Kim focused on the tiny black and white television suspended above her chair, trying to concentrate on soap operas and game shows. She weathered the sessions better than many patients but always was nauseated all the days she received dialysis and sleepless during the nights. Regardless, she considered the machines to be gifts from God.

Transplantation had been postponed because of Kim's intermittent bone and tissue infections. However, the dialysis began enlarging her heart. She and I were perfect matches; "as good as perfect twins," said the nephrologist, who told me that if Kim were to receive the kidney of a cadaver, the odds of rejection would be about 50 percent, a parent's 30 percent, and mine only 10 percent.

A donor's remaining kidney tends to enlarge, its function increasing, and as far as researchers know, the donor's life-style and life span are not affected. Still, many potential donors do deny kidneys to relatives, and the doctors lie for them, telling the desperate patient that the match was inadequate. Common sense says you should keep all the organs God gave you, and fear cries, "Amen." Indeed, some of my friends and relatives tried to dissuade me. What if the researchers are wrong? What if the kidney rejects? What if something happens to your remaining kidney?

Coolly, I stated that I simply must make the donation. Code of honor and American courage. "I can't just let her die." I was uncomfortable when, in the cool sterile hallway outside the nephrologist's office, following our meeting with him to set a surgery date, Kim hugged me and told me she loved me. I halfheartedly returned her hug and had to force out the truth, that I loved her too.

The morning of the surgery, as I was wheeled out of my hospital room, I sat up on the cart, gave my family the thumbs up sign and said, "See you on the other side."

My mother hurried into the hallway to kiss me and said, "Mark, you're so brave."

Damn right.

After the surgery, I woke in the haziness of the post-op recovery room to one of the surgeons, who sounded far away. "Mark . . . Mark . . . It's all over, Mark." Struggling to focus on his face, I recalled where I was and mumbled something about Kim. He said, "The kidney began functioning before we had finished sewing it completely in . . . Kim's fine."

The next day I was refusing pain medication and accomplishing short walks, bent over my pillow and dragging along my IV unit. On the third day, I visited Kim in her room. I teased her about still being sick in bed and about taking a sleeping pill the night before surgery. When she'd heard enough, she bounced a plastic cup full of ice chips off my forehead. I shuffled back to my room, but we made up that evening. On the fifth day, because one of the surgeons had told me the soonest any of his donors had been released from the hospital was six days, I insisted on my discharge. To make my point I performed a toe touch, eliciting a strong warning but gaining my walking papers. And that was the last enduring good news I received.

Kim's new kidney was functioning, but her blood pressure was elevated. For three weeks and despite strong medications, it mysteriously continued to rise. Then one evening a nurse found Kim unconscious, the result of a hypertensive convulsion. In the ICU, a doctor informed my mother that the convulsion may have damaged Kim's brain or new kidney. For two days, Kim gradually regained consciousness but frequently hallucinated. When the hallucinations ceased, a neurologist declared her fully and miraculously recovered. She was returned to her old room in the nephrology unit. But late that night she spiked a temperature. The doctors decided she, somewhere, had an infection.

Returned to the ICU, Kim received massive doses of antibiotics but weakened daily. Finally the nephrologist told me that he believed the elusive source of infection to be in Kim's new kidney. That the kidney might eventually be removed. That even then, because antirejection drugs had suppressed her immunological system, her ability to fight the infection, now in her blood stream, would be minimal.

When it roars in our ears—when the River that has nurtured and gently carried us startles us with the news that it will suck us under—courage all alone, flexing its sinking biceps, is a pathetic sight. In a letter we would discover after her death, Kim wrote, in part, "Some things in life are intangible. I'll remain with you in love." She had earned no college degrees, but she was far from stupid. When the waters swirled around, her courage inhaled love, became buoyant, kept her afloat until she released it to drift intangibly away.

In the ICU Kim is on a refrigerated mattress, her face bloated. She stares at the ceiling. A tube runs to a catheter bag. Three tubes run to three bottles of the IV unit. Wires run to a vital signs monitor. Although she is shivering, she is perspiring. After saying hello, I can utter no words. Minutes pass and then she slowly turns her head on the pillow and asks about my wife: "How's Margaret?"

The infection has worsened for weeks. Her arms and legs are grotesquely black and blue from the hundreds of needles. As a nurse approaches with yet two more resting on a tray like a meal of cacti, Kim whimpers, turns away her face and stiffens. After the nurse is done, Kim turns back to her visitors and apologizes for "being a baby in front of you."

Although it has not rejected, under the stress of the infection the kidney has ceased to function. Kim has resumed receiving dialysis. I visit and find her unusually talkative, asking about my friends and wife and pets. Finally I ask how she is doing and she replies that the doctors have assured her the kidney is functioning well and the infection subsiding. Later I find one of the doctors and suggest that the reality is too much for Kim and that she needs the help of a psychologist. The doctor appears surprised and informs me he has noticed no such problem. That night at home, Margaret asks, "Do you think maybe she was trying to protect you?"

They cut out the kidney, place it on an operating room table, slice it up and find nothing abnormal. Pieces are sent to a lab, but no infection is located. They decide the source of infection is a heart valve. They hope Kim can strengthen enough for another operation. They hope to replace the infected valve with one taken from the heart of a pig.

I cannot sleep and am desperate to feel something other than anger. One night after 2 a.m., I decide to reread the Book of Job; but when God gives back to Job all of Job's blessings I throw the Bible against my wall. I feel only anger until I drink so much whiskey that I feel nothing at all.

I visit for the first time in several days, since before the kidney was removed. Kim awakes coughing, pushing aside her oxygen mask so our youngest sister can dab the blood from her mouth. When Kim sees me she opens her arms; I bend over the bed and we embrace. She says she is sorry I gave my kidney for nothing. I say I needed to lose a pound anyhow. Weeping, she tells me she loves me. Now there is nothing left to do but feel the truth. I tell her I love her too, and we embrace and weep until a nurse, fearful for Kim's heart, like a gentle current tugs me away.

NOBODY'S PERFECT

Carol Schaal

SITTING IN A comfortable chair in my living room, the hour somewhat past midnight, my mother finally revealed her closely held secret to my sister and me. "All I really wanted," she said, "was perfect children."

Her perfect daughters laughed. "We noticed," my sister said. "Yeah," I chimed in; "we've already figured out who we got it from."

The perfectionist's life, the three of us can attest, is one way to drive yourself crazy. Long hours, constant vigilance and low pay: Whatever you do, it's never good enough. This trait is terrific in a brain surgeon or car mechanic; for lesser mortals, it can be a compulsive road to ruin.

My writing career, for instance, was only saved by the advent of word processors. B.C.—before computers—I'd spend hours retyping assignments on a Smith-Corona. One typo meant redoing the entire page. No little bottles of white correction fluid for me, thank you, because the smudge drew attention to the fact that I'd made a mistake in the first place.

Fortunately, my mother, sister and I have managed to overcome somewhat the female perfectionist's big three: house, hair and homework. My mother only dusts every other day; my sister can go to the grocery store without first resorting to the curling iron; I cry for only an hour if I get an A-minus on a research paper. As for my laid-back father, he treats us all as if we're slightly off plumb.

The real kicker of perfectionism, however, is not what it drives you to do but what it keeps you from doing: Taking risks. Any perfectionist worth her salt knows it's better not to try something than to do it badly. The ploy of preference is called procrastination: If you wait until the last minute, the logic goes, then it can't be perfect because you didn't have enough time. Bosses especially hate this one. One of mine did, and she kindly pointed it out to me. "Stop driving yourself crazy," she said.

I can take a hint. So, like a good perfectionist, I attempted to treat myself. My therapy was simple: I vowed always to be awful at one thing.

For years, the thing I did badly was softball. In what's designed to be a hitter's game, I struck out. Fly balls slipped through my mitt, grounders smacked my shins and rolled out of reach. My one-person Three Stooges act wasn't pretty, but it satisfied my soul.

Then terrible things began to happen. I caught some fly balls. I stopped hitting into double plays. Other players started slapping me on the back, saying things like "good job." Then came the day of reckoning, the day the team voted me "most improved player." No longer was I the worst on the team; third-or fourth-worst, maybe, but not the worst. There was no joy in Mudville; I had to find something else to be awful at.

I tried leaving dirty dishes in the sink, dust on the furniture and (forgive me, Mom) crud in the carpets. But this didn't make me a better, less-than-perfect person; it simply made me a perfectionist with a dirty house.

A date of mine offered the perfect alternative: golf. "I once taught a blind man to play," he boasted, "so I probably can teach you." The insult never dented my resolve; I'd do my best and hope for the worst. Then one day we went to a miniature golf course so I could practice my putting. I got a hole in one. I won the game. I lost the golf instructor.

All of which left me metaphysically floundering, still searching for the perfect imperfection.

In desperation, I took more risks. I bought a drill and tackled some home-improvement projects. My upstairs closet, with its do-it-yourself modular shoe racks and sweater shelves and clothing rods, now looks worthy of a spot on *This Old House*. Even my mother was impressed, although I specifically showed her where the shelf dips.

My first Christmas cross-stitch project also showed promise: The design was off-center and its reindeer looked like mutant cows. But it only got easier. Now my sister, the traitor, wants me to make one for her.

Practice makes competent, or at least mediocre, and that's a dangerous place for a perfectionist. For competence leads directly to the idea that, since you've already gotten better, you'll eventually be able to get . . . perfect.

So here I sit, stuck in the middle again—neither perfectly perfect nor perfectly imperfect. Still, all was not wasted. I've got a softball trophy, some handy-dandy closet shelves and a beautiful cross-stitch sampler.

And my mother—the one who instilled this drive in her daughters, the one who remade the already-made beds, who sent us back time and again to re-do, re-fix, re-straighten; the mother who now chides my sister and me when she thinks we're trying too hard to make everything turn out perfectly—this mother ended that late-night talk with the lowest blow of all. "You two aren't perfect," she said, "but you turned out okay."

Repeat after me: That's good enough.

SOMETHING SO NATURAL
Brian Doyle

SOME MONTHS AGO I woke up, took a shower, made a cup of coffee, and masturbated into a plastic cup. I then got dressed and drove an hour through the woods to the hospital. There, cup held closely against my chest in a shirt pocket, I walked up the stairs to the Gynecology Department and handed the cup to an understanding nurse who didn't smile. Then I drove to work.

Why this odd toilette? Children. My wife and I don't have any. We would like some. The number isn't important. Once it was important, and deciding whether to have three or four children was a matter of much discussion. Three? Five? Maybe even six, my wife said, warily. We could get lucky and have a set of twins in there someplace, I said, secretly dreading the stereo screaming and the drooling.

That was five years ago. We haven't been lucky. We've tried to conceive a child in any number of ways: rhythm methods and conception according to the moon; boxer shorts and intricate positions; prayers and tears. No luck. Finally we went to the doctor, who tested our reproductive chemistry (thus my interesting morning a while ago) and prescribed a hormone supplement for my wife. She diligently gobbled pills, charted her daily temperature like Holy Writ, and hoped. But her periods arrived like clockwork, as did her tears and my hidden disappointment.

Then the doctor examined the intricate plumbing of her reproductive gear and discovered blocked Fallopian tubes. These tubes are the highways to the uterus, the path by which sperm cells make their odyssey to the egg cell. For some reason—probably scar tissue

49

from an old infection, the doctor speculated—the tubes are closed, which means that no sperm cell can make its way to the Valhalla of the uterus, where the egg cell waits with open arms.

Repairing the blockages meant opening the pathway. That meant surgery. One summer morning we drive to the hospital, park, register, wait in the humming bustle of the clinic. Before lunch my wife is suddenly wheeled away. I read, pace, read. After dinner I am admitted to her room. Her face is white. We make our way gingerly to the car. She leans on me and gasps when she missteps. I am crying at her pain. At home I put her to bed and sit on the porch, watching nighthawks slice through the dark.

I always assumed I could father a child. It was beyond question, as much a part of me as my nose. Even as a boy, not yet familiar with love and sex and heartbreak, I did not doubt that I too, like my father and his father and all the fathers down into the dawn of the Gaels, would come home, kiss my wife, and listen carefully to the triumphs and despairs of my children's lives. There would be several, of indeterminate size and shape. They would consider me funny but old-fashioned until they grew up enough to realize I was wonderful.

As I grew older I learned how to worry: about what college I'd attend, what profession I'd seek, and what sort of man I'd become, whether a woman would ever marry me. But not once did I wonder if I could make children. Reproduction seemed like a train stop I'd get to eventually, when my life arrived there. Everyone had kids in the end.

But they don't. The easy presumption that you will have children is a lie, like the assumption that you will fall in love and live happily ever after, or that pain and death happen to old people, or that sadness is for others. Sometimes it seems that maturity means accepting the essential inaccuracy of all you hold accurate and beyond question.

My mind accepts our childlessness. It happens, it's not the worst thing in the world. There are evils far worse, more savage, more heart-rending. In the larger scheme of things it is simply a closed door, and other rooms nearby are open. It may be that this door will suddenly swing open one of these days.

But my heart hates it. I am patient and enraged, driven to tears, philosophical. We'll adopt children. Several. All different colors. Think of the lives we'll add humor and meaning to, think of the children who will live differently—one hopes better—than they would have. We'll give them a home, humor, a moral foundation, square meals, decent clothes, a family to call their own. They'll have Dad's T-shirts and Mom's old paintboxes. They'll have the wonderful intricate web of cousins and aunts and grandparents that surrounds a lucky child like a safety net. We'll name them Nicholas, Joseph, Emily and Eulalia, nicknamed Lily.

But I feel a hole in my heart. I pick at it occasionally to test the pain, the way you explore a sore tooth with your tongue. I know it will hurt to think about it, dwell on it, but I can't help it. I reach for the place where my own son would be, with his mammoth Dad nose and his spectacularly curly Mom hair, and I feel as if I've lost the child I never had.

My parents lost their first son, my invisible brother. They don't talk about it. My wife's nephew drowned at age 3. The family doesn't talk about it. All we know of these lost boys is that their photographs suddenly silence the room when the page of the photo album turns and there they are, peering delightedly at the camera, swimming, eating, grinning, vanished.

There are other operations, the doctor says. We can implant the seed. We can do many things. Miracles happen. I watch my wife's face, that gentle face with the soft lines I know so well. She is sad, hopeful, horrified, hopeless. More operations, each further from simplicity, are not what we want. Long ago we agreed that it wasn't right, at some inexplicable level of right and wrong, to chase after a baby forever.

Another moral fog to wade through: Which operation is the one by which you defy God's decision for you? At what point are we arrogant and obsessed? When does the urge for your own child become selfish? When do you decide that you will be the parents of someone else's unwanted child?

Outside the doctor's office hangs a large chart of the female reproductive system, with lines and arrows pointing out the important organs, the key players. We stand before it for a moment, holding hands. The structural intricacy is astonishing, unbelievable. The design alone deserves applause. With a silent finger my wife points to the tubes. She traces them slowly like a blind person reading. She is crying.

We walk down the corridor, out the door, past troops of children, squadrons of babies, harried mothers, haggard fathers, busy doctors, solicitous nurses. I am crying too.

WHAT CHILD IS THIS?

Sheryl Miller Overlan

FIVE YEARS AGO, when a gynecologist attributed my "flu symptoms" to pregnancy, I couldn't believe it. My husband and I had practiced natural birth control for seven years—since the birth of our last child—with no pregnancies.

At 43, I was thinking not of more children but of more money to pay for the three children we already had. I had been a stay-at-home mother for 12 years, and with all of our children finally in school for a full day, I was looking for an employer. I was not looking for another baby.

I suppose the doctor had seen enough women of my age and in my position to know to send me across the street for a confirming ultrasound. He was right of course. Little Margaret, all 6 weeks of her, was firmly implanted, her heart beating rapidly inside me. A new life had begun already without me even suspecting it. But as soon as I saw her in the ultrasound, I took her as my child. Accepting the consequences of another child, however, was quite a different matter.

My initial reaction was to fall apart emotionally. I made it through the revolving doors of the medical building, across the busy Boston street and into our parked station wagon, where I collapsed into sobs. I didn't care that the trolley continued its regular runs in front of my car or that pedestrians passed by me. I sat there for at least a half of an hour, a lump, trying to figure out what my husband and I were going to do. This new life was not only not planned, it interfered with all the things *we* had planned. And it wasn't fair, I kept saying. I'd turned my body and life over to raising children for 12 years—completely, giving up interest after interest, as well as an opportunity to work and provide us with a better standard of living. Now that I was finally going to take charge of my destiny, like so many other women today, I learn that my plan to direct my life has been foiled—by God. I knew enough not to argue with him, just as I knew that once again I was going to have to hand over my being to another. At that point I couldn't think of much else to do but cry.

Margaret is 5 years old now, and anything I write about her only scratches at the surface of the repercussions of her life. But I make the attempt, because today we live in a society where the trend for one human to decide when another should live or die grows stronger, where abortions continue, and where a small family and working mother are the norm.

There are some hard things to swallow when you are in my situation—middle-age, without a lot of money but with another baby on the way. One of the biggest is the maybe delayed, but probably lost, bigger house and easier life. Without my contribution to the family income, our bills were not going to go away as quickly and the savings weren't going to accumulate any time soon. Instead, Margaret's birth meant we would continue to operate from an overstuffed house, continue to play hide and seek with my too many pots and pans crammed in too-small cupboards and continue to operate my husband's business, store our Christmas and other holiday boxes, and wash our clothes from the same small 10-by-10 "room" downstairs.

We said good-bye to fancy vacations we had hoped for as well as to material extras we perhaps foolishly had told the kids we probably would have in a few years. Instead, we stayed our course of "making ends meet," finding bargains, taking odd jobs for me or the children and accepting "gracefully" last year's clothes. The sacrifices reached down to the dog, who probably forfeited any chance of a professional grooming.

While the "dire consequences" are almost all of the tangible variety, the benefits of adding another being to our family are almost all of the intangible sort. They are translucent enough that on many days they seem to evaporate, if anyone even has the time or inclination to look for them. When they do appear though, they shine with a brilliance that can burn a hole in your heart.

There is the time I opened the door of the bedroom shared by Margaret and our middle daughter, Elizabeth. They had snuggled up together in Elizabeth's bed, similar in appearance and similarly engrossed in reading their books. Together they looked up at me and smiled. I am hard pressed to find words to describe their contentment, their comfort with one another, their bonds. Don't we all look for this kind of moment when we share peace with another?

There is the time Margaret and I were in her older sister Mary's bedroom putting away some clothes, and I told Margaret how Mary would soon go away to college. I wanted Margaret to know she would one day have a room of her own. Instead of being happy as I anticipated, Margaret looked up at me with big eyes full of fear and filling with tears. In a trembling voice, she said, "Mary is going away? I don't want Mary to ever go away." How could I ever have assumed that this little child would prefer a room of her own if it meant that one of her sisters would leave her world?

There is the morning I found my 12-year-old son Alex brushing Margaret's hair. His big boy hands slowly and carefully brushed the strands without causing a whimper. "Alex makes my hair so soft, Mom," Margaret said, smiling. "You should learn to brush hair like him," she advised me.

There is the moment one still, winter's afternoon when time seemed to stop and my husband and I simultaneously looked over at Margaret, who was standing on a kitchen chair to wash her doll in the sink. "What would we do without our Margaret?" my husband asked as much to himself as to me. I'd asked myself the same question only a few days earlier, as if the idea were incomprehensible. What would our house be like with only teenagers and no young child? We both shuddered. Margaret just smiled and continued washing her doll, suggesting the contentment that comes from being cherished.

There is the time each Christmas that the older children plan their outing to shop for Margaret. On their own, they decided to always buy Margaret the most, because "Margaret should always have the biggest Christmas." Their enjoyment in this conspiracy to give to Margaret brings me a warmth and hope for their continued goodness as adults.

But just as significant as these special "times" all of us have had with Margaret are the things we've learned as a consequence of letting God have his way and bring another life into our own lives at this late stage.

Without Margaret, our children wouldn't yet know the sweet joys and hardy laughs only a young child can bring. They wouldn't already know which age of childhood is their favorite (an indication of their budding and realistic appreciation of the responsibilities of raising children). They wouldn't have learned how to perform so many chores and organize their time so well, because I wouldn't have had the additional responsibilities that come with caring for a young child. They might not understand how important their "job" of student is if they want to earn financial aid for college. They wouldn't have witnessed their parents struggling to remain strong as they live out of step with the status quo, nor, I doubt, would they see their parents' growing reliance on God. God has become our rock.

I was raised in a two-child family where, to my parents' sorrow, the age difference between my brother and me was seven years. In their case, the small number of children wasn't planned, but was what God gave them. By most standards, the living was much easier. I never heard anyone yell, my mother's furniture stayed beautiful for years, and each of us children had our own room, our special clothes at holiday time and our ordered, neat and clean life. I don't ever remember a chaotic moment in all the years I lived with my parents.

I watch my contemporaries repeat such a lifestyle, not because it is the one handed to them by God but because they made the decision to order it that way. One of their goals appears to be total self-reliance and direction. As I look at the vast orderings of the many particulars of my contemporaries' daily lives, however, I can't help but wonder if they have left room for God to be himself, or has he too been relegated to a spot they have chosen for him? They don't seem to put much reliance on the Being greater than them.

They don't look like the humble or meek sheep of the great Shepherd. My parents did. I hope I do.

An uncle admonished me once a long time ago for trying to second-guess why God did certain things. Only God knows the reasons for his creation of Margaret as a gift, to force us to face up to choosing either his way or the world's way. Margaret has made all of us confront and test our values and beliefs. Life isn't easy and doesn't measure up materially to the majority of those around us. What are we going to do with this situation? How are we going to handle our status? Will we continue to turn to God for guidance or will the temptations of the world overcome us? Will my children, as adults, make similar choices as mine? Will they let God direct them? Or will they choose a lifestyle more like their peers'?

For me, the decision to have Margaret was never really a decision, even though the gynecologist suggested it was by handing me a brochure on abortion. Margaret's life only necessitated an adjustment to my preconceived ideas about where I was going in my life. While I stumble often on this path, I'm confident that, with God's grace, I will never leave it. I can only hope and pray that in the end, when my children have similar choices in their own lives, they too will let God lead them and not rely solely on their own finite intelligence. The rewards of doing so are of his world and infinite. In this world, reliance on him brings rare, but brilliant hints of unimaginable perfection of peace and love.

PARADISE LOST

Kerry Temple

L IFE HAS ITS seasons. Summer was turning to fall; he would start first grade in a week. The time had come. He followed me to the garage, then waited outside as I pulled out his shiny blue bike with the sleek silver handlebars. He watched solemnly as I wrenched off the training wheels and tossed them into the garbage. There was no going back.

Out on the sidewalk I pushed him along, holding the seat. He wobbled and teetered and veered off the road. Again and again. I caught him each time. "Pedal," I yelled, losing patience. "Keep pedaling. Faster."

"Don't let go," he screamed. "Don't let go."

"I have to." I was mad. "You've got to learn."

He fell again, and I said, "You stopped pedaling." He said, "But you let go." And I blurted sarcastically, "I suppose when you're 15 and riding off with all your friends, you'll want me running along behind you, holding you up." Then I pictured him older, riding off with friends, turning the corner without me. He wasn't even looking back.

But on this Saturday morning he was hurt and mad and tearful, and I said, "You know, this is as hard on me as it is on you." And right away I wished I hadn't said it; I heard that so much as a kid. He ran into the house, and I felt like a heel, having botched this rite of passage.

I remembered when my father taught me, and how mad I got at him. And how big and scary the bicycle felt. And how far it was to fall. Then I recalled the floating sensation, the triumph, when the

58

bike began to glide along. And I remembered riding off into sunsets (hardly glancing over my shoulder) while *my* father waved goodbye . . . and when bike wheels turned to car wheels that carried me out of town.

My father is a thousand miles away; his grandsons are growing up six states away from him. Maybe it isn't so bad, I thought, having them cruise the sidewalk in front of our house—at least for a little while—before they're out on the streets on their own.

I lay on my back and stared at the clouds drifting by. One looked like a sailing ship, another like a swan. The late-August air smelled the way it did 30 years ago. When I was little, I pretended my red Huffy was a black Harley-Davidson. I clothespinned cards to the spokes to make the proper noise. We rode in gangs to look ornery and ramped off boards to look fast. When I was little, I was in a hurry to be bigger. Now that I'm big, I daydream of going back.

It didn't seem that long ago when I lay on the grass like this and watched my father fly a kite. It went so high I could hardly see it—a tiny yellow diamond against the azure sky. I was afraid it would catch on a cloud and be carried away. Some of the clouds looked nice and some looked mean. I remembered hoping—if my kite had to be captured—that the pirate cloud would be puffy and white.

It didn't seem that long ago when Casey was a baby pushing my orange basketball across the floor. Wanting to test his little legs, he pulled himself up onto it (I could see it coming) just before it rolled away and plopped him to the floor. I was new at this too. Do I pull him away? Hold him? Get ready to catch his fall? Or watch as he learns about life's hard knocks?

He fell and cried, and I comforted him. "All of life's bumps should be so good to you," I told him. I shuddered to think of the real-life Humpty-Dumpties who can't be put together again. But I had learned to hold my tongue when the boys later walked too close to the river or climbed a tree too high. I have since learned to look the other way when they hang like chimps from the monkey bars or leap from high-flying swings.

Sometimes I think life is a minefield, whose traps explode, arbitrarily, indiscriminately, on those who either dance or crawl along the way. A softshoe is better than any kind of fearful groping, but it is a tenuous fencewalk between timidity and trust. Where do you draw the line between cautious and afraid? I do not want them playing in lightning, but I like to sit on the porch with them while it is flashing all around.

It isn't easy bringing children from innocence to independence in a world so ugly and cruel. There is too much to hurt these little boys with their sweet blue eyes, vulnerable, sensitive and serene. I do not like warning them about strangers and child molesters, the real-life witches and goblins who lurk behind the trees on the road to Oz. In time the circles will turn, and they will know the raunchy sides of life. Already they are asking about war and dirty words and why grownups kidnap kids.

Sometimes I feel like Holden Caulfield, who wanted to wipe the obscenities from the walls of New York City so the children wouldn't see. I know how he felt when he said, "I keep picturing all these little kids playing some game in this big field of rye and all. Thousands of little kids, and nobody's around—nobody big, I mean—except me. And I'm standing on the edge of some crazy cliff. What I have to do, I have to catch everybody if they start to go over the cliff—I mean if they're running and they don't look where they're going I have to come out from somewhere and catch them. That's all I'd do all day. I'd just be the catcher in the rye and all. I know it's crazy, but that's the only thing I'd really like to be."

I remembered taking Ross to his first day of kindergarten. He was the one standing so straight, with the new blue shirt buttoned at the collar. His purple backpack had three white teddy bears across the back. When I stooped to say goodbye, I saw the tears in his eyes. I asked him if he'd be OK, and he nodded bravely. His lips quivered; he could not talk from fear of crying. I could almost feel the lump in his throat. I was sorry I'd told him to be a big boy now.

Then I wanted to stay and see him through it, to do it for him, to intercede on his behalf, to introduce him around, tell the kids what a great guy he is. But I didn't; it would have hurt him in the long run. The world does not take kindly to those who do not know its ways.

Even Holden Caulfield learned to let go. There is that scene at the end of *Catcher in the Rye* when Holden takes his little sister,

Phoebe, to the zoo in Central Park. She rides the carousel and he watches from a bench. He says, "All the kids kept trying to grab for the gold ring, and so was old Phoebe, and I was sort of afraid she'd fall off the goddam horse, but I didn't say anything or do anything. The thing with kids is, if they want to grab for the gold ring you have to let them do it, and not say anything. If they fall off, they fall off, but it's bad if you say anything to them."

I turned my back on Ross in the school yard, walked a few steps, then looked around once more. He was a lone figure, a fixed point in a sea of schoolchildren swirling about him. He seemed to be falling, floating away from me, as if on a ship slowly heading out of the harbor. Our eyes met and he raised a hand in a mournful wave goodbye: a puppy left on the doorstep of life.

The boys are now at such a tender age: ready to run from the house where they've spent their first five years; eager to join in the bruising chaos of the big-kid world; caught somewhere between the Smurfs and the streetwise kids they emulate when they march down the street with sticks. They tag along, looking up to the older boys the way they once looked up to me. I hope the big kids treat them as well as their father did, but I know they will not. I would give them Magicland if I could. I would keep them this age forever, so we both could believe Santa Claus is more than a myth. But there is no house at Pooh Corner; Jackie Paper never came home to Puff.

It is a big and little comfort, when you see your sons being tackled too hard, to know the neighborhood boys are making men out of them. It is hard keeping your distance when one son dives headfirst into the pile and the other is in a fistfight. But they still come home to curl in my lap with teddy bears and blankets, and they get up early on Saturday mornings to watch *The Muppet Babies* on TV. Now at bedtime when I read them *Dumbo,* they tell me they are certain that elephants do not talk (even though they will then look out the window to wish upon a star). On those nights I want to hug them forever, knowing the hugs will not always be there.

Already they wish they were older. One night last week Casey informed me, "I'm through with silliness now, Daddy. I'm 6 now and ready for 'portantness. We need more 'portantness around here."

"God made the world for children," I wanted to tell him, "although grownups have made it theirs. Be of no mind—though you will know this too late—to hurry down that road. It is not what it appears to be. But you will remember always the firefly summer nights and the autumn scents of childhood in the leaves."

Why is it, I thought as I lay in the grass and watched the clouds drift overhead, that parents spend half their time teaching children to go away, then spend the other half happy when they have stayed? Why are all the joys of raising children punctuated with the pain of a parent's broken heart? Why did I not miss my own childhood until I watched my children losing theirs?

Soon after that Saturday, on a day when I wasn't looking, Casey taught himself how to ride his bike. Now the backyard gate is always open, and he and Ross are always gone. There was a time our yard was big enough. That time, too, has gone away.

They still look like angels when they sleep. I still think of them as emissaries from God. They came as miracles of creation, incarnations of purity and goodness. I remember when they prayed for the animals in winter. They showed me again what Jesus meant when he said, "Unless you become like little children, you will not enter the kingdom of heaven." They taught me to believe in innocence again, and in the possibility of happy endings.

A high school teacher once told me that every baby born was another attempt at human perfection. As a rebellious teenager, I felt like a far-fallen angel. In his classic, *Let Us Now Praise Famous Men,* James Agee wrote: "In every child who is born, under no matter what circumstances, and of no matter what parents, the potentiality of the human race is born again: and in him, too, once more, and of each of us, our terrific responsibility toward human life; toward the utmost idea of goodness, of the horror of error, and of God."

I suppose most parents have felt the weight of this belief, whether consciously or not. At least you are braced in the event Milton was right when he wrote, "Childhood shows the man, as morning shows the day." And later, when you see the little one sinking his teeth into the calf of his big brother or the big brother chasing the little one through the yard with a bat, you remember another poet's admonition: "In the lost boyhood of Judas, Christ was betrayed."

After all, the little person in your arms began with a virgin soul, and you feel compelled to keep it fresh and clean. It is easier in the early years to feel as if you're succeeding. For a little while, you can protect him and shield him. You can surround him with Care Bears and cuddles, nursery rhymes and fairy tales. You can polish out the nicks and scratches, and steer him away from the collisions that can cause major damage.

In the early years you give full flight to your children's imagination. You nurture their naivete, their idealism, their sense of wonder. For now it's all right for them to think that unicorns are real. You let them believe in Bambi, Thumper and Flower; the time will come soon enough to teach them about hunters and fire. And if you are like me, you may secretly wish the world really were as the children see it.

"Know what it is to be a child?" wrote the poet Francis Thompson. "It is to be something very different from the man of today. It is to have a spirit yet streaming from the waters of baptism. It is to believe in love, to believe in loveliness, to believe in belief; it is to be so little that the elves can reach to whisper in your ear; it is to turn pumpkins into coaches and mice into horses, lowness into loftiness, and nothing into everything, for each child has his fairy godmother in his soul."

I think of this when I see parents hurry to turn their children into little adults. With nursery school, preschool and real school, I wonder where childhood has gone. But sometimes I think something is wrong with *me* because I see it as the kids' world versus mine, and that it hurts me to see them leave that world behind. Parents, after all, are not shelters from life but are, as Kahlil Gibran said, "the bows from which your children as living arrows are sent forth." That's not always easy to accept, especially when you don't know when or where the arrows may fall.

But now, all appears peaceful when they sleep. Casey is sideways and uncovered, the Snoopy bedspread wound tight around one leg. Ross is curled into a little ball, clutching his bear, Fuzzy Wuzzy. Ross keeps a stickhorse by his bed to fight off any bad guys who come in the night. He keeps toys under the bed in case he chooses to hide there. Then he will have something to do to bide the time while the bad guys ransack the house. Some nights Casey asks me if he will have a nightmare. I say no; he asks, "Do you promise?" He is disappointed that I can't. I heard once about a boy who was afraid of monsters under his bed; his father sawed off the legs. If only it were all that simple.

There is a night light and a bulletin board with pictures they have done. There are posters of the evil Darth Vader dueling with their hero, Luke Skywalker, the Jedi knight who conquered the Dark Side of the Force. The floor is littered with cars and robots, and the Masters of the Universe—the armies of He-Man and Skeletor who have spent the day engaged in epic battle between good and bad. If only it were all that simple.

Graham Greene once wrote that he lost his childhood when he learned to read and discovered that the world did not come in black and white. It comes, he said, in black and gray. One thing that hurts a parent is watching that happen in a child once innocent and pure . . . and knowing the loss is irretrievable.

I hadn't jumped from a swing since I was a kid. Or built a snow fort. Or climbed a tree. I had not really tried to catch a butterfly or wondered why the sky is blue. It isn't easy explaining thunder and rainbows, but it resurrects the mystery in a grownup brain gone stale. Children see more in a sand castle than grownups see in the sky. Sometimes I think their vision packs a poet's wisdom that is beyond adults, who have grown tired, hard and dull, literal and skeptical. When Ross told me trees make the wind by waving to God, I thought of the Little Prince, who said, "Grownups never understand anything by themselves; and it is tiresome for children to be always and forever explaining things to them."

The best part of having children is going with them on their explorations. They take you to the fields where they play. You, too, can be a mountain lion or a pirate or a knight slaying dragons. You can play hide-and-seek, or just lie in the grass and blow the fuzz off dandelion globes. The magic draws very close when you're there; the bad things go very far away.

Children, like real-life Peter Pans, take you to a world no longer yours to track down alone. They take you to enchanted kingdoms where evil villains can be expelled with the swipe of a sword or the wave of a wand. Sometimes, when the boys spread out their "real life action figures," I will set up the little soldiers, the cowboys and Indians I played with as a kid. They still have the crayon marks for blood and teeth marks from my old dog, Scamp. And when I turn them in my hand, they look and feel like they did then. And when I build forts with my plastic red bricks, the boys build theirs with Legos. And when the players come to life and the battles reach fever pitch, you believe in magic.

Then it happens. You become a kid again and the world goes far away. You laugh like you did and you run like you did. You feel free for the first time in years. And when you play freeze-tag with the neighborhood kids or argue a close play at second or feel the wonderful exhilaration of kicking the can and setting the others free, you become (just in the wink of a moment) yourself again—the person you thought you'd left behind long ago.

In *A Death in the Family* James Agee wrote: "How far we all come. How far we all come away from ourselves. So far, so much between, you can never go home again. You can go home, it's good to go home, but you never really get all the way home again in your life. And what's it all for? All I tried to be, all I ever wanted and went away for, what's it all for?

"Just one way you do get back home. You have a boy or a girl of your own and now and then you remember, and you know how they feel, and it's almost the same as if you were your own self again, as young as you could remember."

Then they grow up. And they leave you alone and empty-handed in a world that's lost its magic, where trees never wave to God. You have only the bittersweet memories, the babybooks and paintings, the notches on the closet door where you measured their growth. There are photographs and feelings, but so much more is left behind. All the things held so possessively in tightly curled little fists, all the animals with whom they shared their bed, all the mystical playgrounds have been discarded for bigger games and broader horizons that they must explore alone.

And you learn again that none of us is Peter Pan; but we all, in a way, belong to the company of the Lost Boys, wanting to partake in the whimsical heroics of Never Never Land. We are all caught somewhere between childhood and maturity, yearning for the days of sweet remembrances—the mornings of boundless horizons; the evenings of carefree calm; the nights when our mothers and fathers pulled the quilts to our chins and kissed us gently goodnight. Childhood is like that. It is a memory that fades too quickly, images wrapped in a longing to feel that way again.

I did not expect to want to stop the clock so soon. But D. H. Lawrence was 31—about my age—when he wrote, "The glamor/Of childish days is upon me. My manhood is cast/Down in the flood of remembrance, I weep like a child for the past." Elizabeth Akers Allen was 28 when she wrote, "Backward, turn backward, O Time, in your flight. Make me a child again just for tonight."

I think of this when I am home from work, changing clothes and watching the gang from my upstairs bedroom window. I'd give anything to join them in play; my heart feels that young. I open my closet to hang up my tie and I remember when I was little and my father came home from work. I remember the way his closet smelled and the suits and ties hanging there. I remember how he'd ride me on his shoulders: my head would scrape along the ceiling; I'd wear his tie around my neck. Sometimes, when the world has been mean to me, I wish I could go back. I'd sit in the kitchen while Mom made dinner, or "rough house" on the floor with Dad.

I suppose part of this ache to return comes from seeing your parents' arms grow frail and watching your children outgrow yours. But part of it is reaching the backstretch of your own life. You come out of the first turn of your youth and look down the straightaway where you can see old age, really see it, for the very first time. The impulse is to go back to simpler, more carefree days when you weren't so tired and you were bound for glory.

But life has its way of turning summer to winter, leaving you to long for the sun-filled afternoons of swimming holes and games of Marco Polo. And even on those rare occasions when life favors you by letting a dream come true, it is never as good as when you had it all.

"And God knows he was lucky, so many ways, and God knows he was thankful," wrote Agee in *A Death in the Family*. "Everything was good and better than he could have hoped for, better than he ever deserved; only, whatever it was and however good it was, it wasn't what you once had been, and had lost, and could never have again, and once in awhile, once in a long time, you remembered, and knew how far you were away, and it hit you hard enough, that little while it lasted, to break your heart."

Your heart is twice broken. Not only must you bid farewell to your children's innocence, but you must say goodbye to *your* childhood and youth as well.

When I was younger, having children was only a passing thought. Fatherhood was a part of life I just assumed would eventually come. What I looked forward to most was playing ball with my kids or taking them camping. I never dreamed they would mean so much so soon. I knew they would need me in the early years; I didn't know I would come to need them. My sons have given new meaning to Wordsworth's observation, "The child is the father of the man."

They have helped me grow up; they have kept me young. They have made me feel so purposeful and needed; I have come to depend on that. They make me feel wise (because I know where the sun goes when it sets) and strong (because my arms can still lift them high into trees). Children are like that. They think you're terrific because you can build paper airplanes and make circuses out of cardboard, crayons and string. And on days when the world has been rotten to me, when the plaster is cracked and there are too many bills to be paid, they make it all right with a kiss and a hug.

They have returned to me a child's vision of the world and made me promise to remember what Wordsworth vowed when he was my age: "My heart leaps up when I behold a rainbow in the sky. So was it when my life began; so is it now I am a man; so be it when I shall grow old. Or let me die."

They have taught me that Homer was wrong when he said, "You ought not practice childish ways, since you are no longer that age." And that the Confucian teacher, Mencius, was right when he said, "The great man is he who does not lose his child's heart."

And when I am caught in adult "matters of consequence" and think I have too little time for them and their handlebars that need to be straightened, I remember the time will come too soon that they will have nothing to do with me. And that the Little Prince was right when he said, "Only the children know what they are looking for."

And them? For now, I wish their childhood would be something to carry with them always, and not something left behind. I wish them days like yesterday, when the only monsters were the ones on *Sesame Street*, when their biggest problem was learning to read and write, and when the worst thing that happened was having to go to bed. I wish our yard would always be wherever their imagination said it was, that they would always dance in my arms across the floor and hold my hand when I walk them to school. But I know none of that will happen.

Just yesterday when I asked them to play, they said, "Aw, Dad. Can we go down to T.J.'s instead?" And this morning, when I was about to ride my bike to work, Casey was out teaching Ross how to ride his.

But then (while Ross was scooting down the sidewalk, one foot on the ground) Casey came and hugged me around the neck and said, "Kiss me, Daddy, on top of the head." So I did and he said, "I will wave to you as you ride away. I will wave until you cannot see me anymore." So there he stood as I pedaled away, waving his little hand in the air, getting smaller and smaller as I rode down the street waving back over my shoulder at the little boy whose dreams are now more important than my own. Waving and smiling, front teeth missing, till we couldn't see each other anymore.

I know the time will come when they will ride through life without me. They will grow strong and my arms will grow frail. Their childhood and I will fade into memory, like the distant, green shoreline of a land left behind. But before I go I need to remember to tell them what an aging poet once wrote to his godchild, "Please remember to look for me in the nurseries of heaven."

AND ONE OF THEM
WAS MY BROTHER
Robert F. Griffin, C.S.C.

WHEN GEORGE DIED seven years ago, I chose Robert Louis Stevenson's *Requiem* as his epitaph, as if my brother had been the happy wanderer, worn and weather-beaten from being blown by the wind: "Here he lies where he longed to be; / Home is the sailor, home from the sea, / And the hunter home from the hill." But his life was no child's garden of verses, and my excuse for glossing over his sufferings (for which he deserved a gold medal in the Special Olympics) was that his pain was my pain, too, and I wasn't willing to face the memories that left me heartbroken.

The neatest thing I ever did for him was to unite him in death with Dad in a burial place by the sea, the sailor's snug harbor of a family in which all the men were fishermen. I thought, "Now he's out of harm's way, immune at last from humiliations." Maybe the only decent break he ever got was to be brought there for the long sleep, for he would have been restless buried with strangers, cruelly separated from his loved ones in death as he was in life.

To tell the truth, I don't know which direction to turn for cheerfulness when I remember my brother. I could paper over grief with the customary Christian consolations were it not for the Jimmy Swaggarts warning us of the hellfire that awaits sinners who die without accepting Christ as their personal savior. The Catholic version of doomsday is brought to us by the crepehangers in the church who spend their lives praying for a happy death—to die in the state of sanctifying grace, freshly fortified by the last sacraments.

Once you've buried a brother who's regarded by outsiders as the black sheep of the family, you start looking for schemes of salvation that come, like health insurance, as a package deal for all the family, though it has never troubled me excessively that George, in his life-time, wasn't conventionally religious. I can't really believe that my brother's life, or any life, should mean so little in the sight of heaven that I should have to defend him from God's trashing him in flames for all eternity.

The restoration of peace in the family begins with the recognition that grace works overtime in an incredible way to bring the mavericks home, though sometimes it's over the road of hard knocks. It's not sentimental to say that nothing is impossible with God—that Christ doesn't give up on anyone.

Our Lord was very fond of telling stories about the father who had two sons, both of them in need of paternal love and wisdom. This is why, if I could write my life as a gospel parable, I would begin it, "A man in Maine had two sons, and one of them was my brother." Is it possible that brothers can lead each other into God's presence, that one can appear as a character witness for the other? In the parable of the prodigal, don't you suppose that later the younger lad would willingly go to court to testify to the worthiness of his elder brother who stayed at the father's side, working hard all his life, even when the old man gave half of his savings to be wasted by the playboy of the family?

In bible stories the brother who obeys his father's instructions and the brother who flouts them often strike me as being the same son in different moods. In those stories one son can see in his brother his own better, or darker, half. One brother can see the other as his twin in mediocrity or his counterpart in virtue or vice. This homemade insight may be shallow or unimportant, like pop psychology, but in my house I think it was true. How can I sort out what Christ means in my life except to say that, in my family, I got the vocation to be *alter Christus* and my brother George got the vocation to be Simon of Cyrene, helping Christ carry the cross in a way I never did. It must have been Christ's cross that George was struggling under, considering its size and weight. So I became the priest who got spoiled by attention, and he was the ne'er-do-well brother, expected to keep out of sight. Still, he must have gotten the lion's share of grace or he couldn't have been so patient. I never did as much for him by the influence of my good example as he did for me.

George was my handsome and gentle elder (there were nine years between us), whose name must have been on the short list of the Beautiful and the Damned. Even as one of the boys of summer in their ruin, he still had a head like Lord Byron's. I'm not willing to tell you, even now, how often and how cruelly he was wounded. I could say, as many have said to me, that he was his own worst enemy, but it wasn't true. Life was the enemy that kept defeating him, though only by a TKO. He was a plucky lad with style and class, and he never ran out of that courage called grace under pressure. Unfortunately, that's a secular grace that doesn't sanctify you, but perhaps God accepted it in lieu of the sanctifying grace which is the credential you need for entering heaven.

He never married, though he was in love with an Irish girl named Eileen, sister to his teenage chum, Carl. She may have loved George, though it worried her that he wasn't a Catholic. Then Carl got killed riding piggy-back on a boxcar, his head knocked off by a low-lying bridge, and Eileen gave up dating the young and restless. Soon George had his own injuries to deal with: He fell off the back of a truck and was dragged through the streets until the toes of his shoes were burned off before the driver knew he had a hitchhiker in tow. He was left with a scar on his brain from which he suffered ill effects the rest of his life.

When he was in his late 40s, he started to have anxiety attacks that left him so manic he would have to be hospitalized. Once, when he felt an attack coming on, he tried to take his own life by slicing his throat. After that my mother kept the razor blades out of sight. When he finally died in a nursing home, crippled by a stroke and confined to a wheelchair, this helpless man was a prisoner in a locked room—though he was as peaceable as a nun breathless with adoration—to keep him out of harm's way in case he had a mood swing.

The saddest scene of his life must have taken place on the day he went in a wheelchair from his nursing home to see my old, blind mother in her nursing home where she was confined to a room on the second floor. The home didn't have an elevator—only stairs he couldn't climb up and she couldn't walk down. George, stunningly disappointed, never got to visit the mother he adored and hadn't seen in several years. Because of their illnesses, he never saw her again.

He shouldn't have died at 66 from a stomach aneurism that started to hemorrhage. When the bleeding began, the doctors couldn't figure out where the blood was coming from; no mention had been made on his medical record of the aneurism he had had repaired 10 years before. By this time in his life, he may have felt that his soul was being stretched over a wheel of fire, but I have no way of telling whether he felt ready and willing to die. All you can say, in the words of Thomas Hardy, is that the President of the Immortals had finished using George for his sport.

Years before I opened Darby's as "a clean, well-lighted place" for the night people of Notre Dame, George was trying to open a social club for people who needed a light for the night. It would cater especially to dried-out drinkers who sought something happier or more swinging than an AA meeting as a barrier against feeling empty inside.

George started to drink when he was very young. As a boy, he got into the sneaky habit of sampling the home brew that my uncle made in my grandfather's cellar. My first awareness of what the repeal of Prohibition could mean was when George, at 17, was brought home pissed to the gills and passed out in the back seat of a police car. That's the only time I ever saw him under the influence, for he never drank at home and I never was with him when he took a drink.

After the age of 45 or so, he never touched a drop. Another hail-fellow-well-met had smashed George's leg to pieces by breaking a two-by-four across it, and from then on George was afraid to drink for fear of getting hurt again. The pain from his shattered limb must have bled into the pain circulating through his head. Even if he'd wanted to find the amnesia that lies at the bottom of a cup, the sobriety forced on him when he was hospitalized for months deprived him of the chance to use liquor as a crutch. You'd have to be a shrink to understand the damage so much trauma can cause.

All I can tell you is that after that, his mental health gave him a run for the money.

The first time we noticed that our boy was in deep trouble was when he told us about the "Blackbird Club" he was trying to find premises for. The name came to him from a song: "Make my bed, and light the light / I'll be home, late tonight. Blackbird, bye-bye." From then on, whenever he mentioned the Blackbird Club we knew his mood was switching from depressive to manic, and neither hell nor high water could have kept him from trying to go into business as Toots Shor.

When he was a practicing alcoholic, George didn't like to lush unseen, wasting his sweetness on the desert air. When he started to practice sobriety as a lifestyle, he would stand outside bars—as he once told me—looking through the window, watching the folks inside who were laughing and having a good time. That's when he started to want his version of Hemingway's clean, well-lighted place, where wallflowers committed to total abstinence could meet to dance.

The older I got, the harder I tried to let him see how fond I was of him, partly as a penance, I suspect, for trying to play him as a fool when I was still a college student. Once I wore, without his knowing it, the good-looking new suit he had shopped for to wear at my father's funeral. It was blue, double-breasted and Brooks Brothers—the most expensive set of threads either of the Griffin boys had ever had on his back. I wanted it and was jealous of George's having it, though on me the pants were too short, the sleeves not long enough.

Unfortunately, I fell down while I had it on and ripped a hole in one knee. I hung the suit back in the closet without saying a word. When George discovered the damage, I tried to convince him that he, while drunk, must have torn the pants without knowing it. The look he gave me would have wrung tears out of the eye of a turnip, as he realized I was treating him like a dummy. And he probably wondered why I would want to humiliate him, since he wasn't about to get in a fight with me over a suit I could have had for the asking. God love him, he wouldn't have seemed half so tragic in his lifetime if he hadn't been so transparently sensitive. When he was 60 years old, wobbling like a wino with a wet brain because of his injuries, he still looked elegant in the peajacket and corduroys of a longshoreman.

He was always kind to me and infinitely courteous, full of love and charm for the baby brother. If he was ever unhappy with self-pity or bitterness, he never let me see it. He would have enjoyed my needing him as a big brother, taking care of me as my role model, defender, social coach, guardian angel—and, after my father's death, as the family breadwinner anxious to see that my mother didn't spoil me. He never held it against me that I became a priest, though he could have made it tougher, as the man of the house, for me to continue in the seminary. He could have pointed out, as my sister did, that it was I, not he, who worried my father the most by my decision to sign up as a Catholic.

He was not, in any outward way, remotely religious. As far as I know, he wasn't even baptized. He asked me once why I had taken up with a church that so many scholars, scientists and other bright people regarded as nonsensical. I gave him one of the smug answers that preconciliar Catholics were famous for, then asked him if he believed in God. "I would have to be a fool not to," he said. In the time we spent together that was as close as we ever came to a discussion of religion. I have no way of telling if he was close to God, or if he said prayers, but I may find out in heaven that his prayers were the ones that kept me going all the way to ordination.

The only concern he showed for me as a priest was his worry about my getting too heavy. He asked my mother once if I had to kneel down in performing my duties in church; he was concerned that kneeling could be hard for me, since I was so greatly overweight.

He was intelligent and a keen observer, and the wilder he was on his antic days, the quicker he was to figure things out. Besides, he read a lot. I'm sure that in his own way he must have researched the question of God's concern for his world, especially after he met proselytizing preachers who offered him bibles and born-again nurses who wanted to bring him to Jesus. How could he not have tried to put God to the test, or tested the efficacy of prayer, in all the time he spent alone as he fought to survive the disaster of his life, or to help my mother and my sister carry the burdens that weighed on them like the everlasting hills. It isn't necessarily your consciousness, or the nearness or sweetness of God, that makes you a saint or a believing Christian. The mystics warn us of the long, dark night of the soul: That's when the cries go up from the heart, "Where is God? Where is he when we need him, and what is he doing to help?"

There is a secular version of this divine abandonment that could be described the Gospel According to Hemingway. Everyone has his omega-point of pain, when everything seems lost except the struggle itself. Christ's was not in Gethsemane, when he was still able to make an act of blind faith in his father's will, but on the cross, when he cried, "My God, my God, why hast Thou forsaken me?"—when, as Chesterton noted, it seemed the Son of God had become an atheist.

The saints of Hemingway's gospel are heroes who keep a stiff upper lip and are tender in love, manly in courage and primitive in their instincts, which bond them like brothers-in-survival to the wild things on earth. They are heirs to the kingdom in which God is our *nada*, because when the chips are down they show much grace under pressure and have obvious class as straight-shooters.

Hemingway wrote, "If people bring much courage to this world, the world has to kill them to break them, so of course it kills them. The world breaks everyone and afterward many are strong at the broken places. But those that will not break it kills. It kills the very good and the very gentle and the very brave impartially. If you are none of these you can be sure it will kill you too but there will be no special hurry."

The omega-point of Christ's passion is a mystery to me and everyone else. Though God is Christ's own *Abba,* our Lord as he was dying felt so rejected and abandoned that he had difficulty conjuring up his father's face. How can I build a bridge between this and my brother's mood as he waited for death in a nursing home?

My brother's was the passion of the unwashed have-nots. He was not an uncrowned saint, passionately wounded by splinters from Christ's cross. If he'd found himself in Gethsemane, he'd have left by the nearest exit to drink through the night with Hemingway's sleepless old man. George wouldn't have known what I was talking about if I told him he was a victim drawn into the circle of God's pain. He would have said, "Given the choice, I'd rather be with the sunshine boys."

The heavenly father couldn't have allowed him such a large portion of pain only to allow it to lie fallow and unredemptive. Where love is, there is God, says scripture. Where pain is, there is God's son on the cross. You can get there on the *via dolorosa* which leads to Calvary from a hundred million directions. Getting there, you bow your head and beat your breast as though you were visiting the Wailing Wall. I can believe all this as an act of faith, but it's nebulous compared to Hemingway's gospel of guts. If mercy came into my brother's life, it had no discernible shape. But I didn't see doubts there, either. Though he may have had hopes, I don't think George expected anything. He didn't die beaten or mute with fear.

I've seen my brother's face when the ghosts of old tears behind his smile were struggling to keep fresh tears from emerging. What do you do with the rememberance of things past that dates all the way back to the lost childhood, when innocence is first lost and the child is no longer conscious of himself as nature's high priest, trailing clouds of glory? Of course neither of us brothers was so Wordsworthian, nor would we have wanted to be if it meant perceiving that the shades of the prison house were beginning to close upon the growing boy.

It's only as an adult that you reach for the nearest available metaphor to describe how it felt as a child to discover that you could no longer rely on having a good time every day, that the adults who kept reminding you that you were no longer a baby usually had an axe to grind, and they could get in your way like darkness. But where were any of us when we first became aware of tears and the death of things, and understood the sadness of that time as a warning for the future—realized that the blues we were getting were an affliction that could follow us around like cold germs?

For years and years I saw the sadness in my brother's eyes as I left him behind in hospital rooms, nursing homes and, once or twice, in a jail. Usually, I'd be heading off to have dinner at a fancy restaurant with friends who were picking up the tab. I've been to so many places where he couldn't follow me, for the shy, explorative and easily embarrassed love that existed between us didn't mean that either of us could go trespassing into the other's world.

Carrying an empty suitcase, he once checked into a hotel where I had stayed, just to prove that the place wasn't off limits to him. After checking in, he found he was lonely and had nothing to do, so he went home without paying, leaving the empty suitcase behind. He suspected that I was embarrassed by him, ashamed of him, and he was probably right, though I was ashamed of myself for being embarrassed.

It would be selfish and unfair of me to save up graces for myself with which to grease God's palm if I felt that George would once again be left outside to cool his heels, gawking up at the marquee. I would be sick with guilt if I could even faintly foresee it would happen that way. How could I love God without bitterness if I couldn't trust him not to give my brother the back of his hand? I love him, and am ashamed of him no longer, and am almost tempted to praise him elegically as "the sweetest, wisest soul of all my days and lands." But why make him greater in death than he was in life, except as an act of homage which would bring peace not to his soul but to mine?

When you say *kaddish* for my brother, please don't pull strings to get him into a pie-in-the-sky kind of heaven; don't arrange for haloed Veronicas to meet him or virgin-martyrs to fall over him. He'd take no pleasure from a Catholic heaven, lit with candles and reeking of incense, cluttered with statues from the catacombs. The crowd he runs with in heaven should be composed of simple folk: street people, eccentrics living hand-to-mouth, the invisible drifters who became visible to him after they helped him survive with their gutter-wisdom.

While I was watching him crawl toward the grave, maybe I should have encouraged the Salvation Army to approach him with fife, trumpet and drum, offering to furnish him with midwives capable of delivering him into born-again innocence. My brother would have had a great deal of respect for a religion which makes a duty out of serving coffee and doughnuts to winos who would starve without the charity they receive from a skid-row mission. But he wouldn't have cared to live there as a captive audience. Why would I expect him to be comfortable as the everlasting houseguest of any denomination holding leases to the mansions of glory in a city with jewelled walls and gates of pearl?

Reason, in the Catholic tradition, is regarded as the handservant of faith; and faith, in St. Paul's definition, is "the substance of things hoped for, the evidence of things unseen." What substantial thing can we reasonably hope for in heaven? Oh, says St. Paul, reason doesn't come near it. Out of love for us, God created this incredibly beautiful world—which can't hold a candle, Paul says, to the one to come. God's heart has reasons that our reason cannot know. Heaven is his masterpiece, and we will dance for him there as though we were honored guests at the Stardust Ballroom at the end of the world.

I can imagine God dancing but, of course, God is more supernatural than that. I can imagine an Emerald City but, of course, heaven's more ineffable than that. I can imagine iridescent angels and archangels with aquamarine eyes the color of Yeats' unicorns but, of course, the heavenly choirs are more ethereal than that. What I can't imagine is a hereafter where the lame and crippled aren't allowed to enter first.

Rather than believe those pre-Vatican II diehards complacently assigning the soul of my unbaptized brother to a place in limbo (or worse), I'd trash theology and start over. My brother can slip through the narrow gate as an "anonymous Christian," as Karl Rahner describes those "who are justified by grace even while they remain outside the Christian community—even if they're not church members, have not been baptized, do not confess Christ, and do not believe explicity in God." This hopeful view is a spinoff from the teaching of Vatican II in *Lumen Gentium.*

I don't want to claim my brother was a saint—even an "anonymous saint"—whom the church would be justified in "anonymously canonizing." But I'd like to think the poor, dear chap had as much chance to grab the brass ring as the rest of us. Insisting that "outside the church there is no salvation" seems to leave him doomed.

My brother's funeral service was as simple as could be. The casket couldn't have been cheaper or more modest, but it had dignity and it was better than plain boards and he wasn't buried by the welfare department in a potter's field. I had to borrow the money for the funeral, and dignity was all I could afford.

The casket wasn't opened. The body, zipped in a body bag, wasn't made up for viewing. I was sorry I made that arrangement: Not seeing him made saying good-bye more impersonal than it needed to be. Despite his tough life, my brother never lost his good looks, but I hadn't liked the idea of the cosmeticians practicing their arts on him, applying rouge and powder that would leave his fine face looking waxy, or fussing with that magnificent head of hair until it looked like a wig. Still, I wish I could have seen him laid out, and I realized my sister would have preferred an open casket. My mother wasn't there and couldn't have been even if I had told her of George's death, which I didn't. God love her, she was getting ready to die herself. I should have bought him a new suit for his burial. I felt I owed him one, remembering the suit of his I tried to rip off.

The Congregational minister in charge of the service kept offering to play hymns and asking if I wanted to share the prayers and readings with him, but my prayers were said privately. George didn't have any great taste for hymns, especially those on tape like Muzak. I did ask for Lord Tennyson's "Crossing the Bar," which has always been read at our family funerals.

But religion, too, can be a form of cosmetics used to change the complexion of things. I didn't want to give my "anonymously Christian" brother a sendoff as though he were a doctor of the church. I did for him in death what I knew he wanted: I saw him laid to rest in the snug harbor by the sea next to my father. It was done with love, devotion and sorrow, but without frills.

I owe it to my brother not to turn his life into a lie, and I've had to struggle against the unctuousness that can be a part of the clergyman's style. I've been tempted to say, "He wasn't heavy—he was my brother," but it isn't true. He was a heavy cross to bear, mostly because he was a cross to himself and a cross to my family. I've wept for him again and again, and have died inside when I've seen him forced to live in some of the saddest places in all the world. I could have been a cross to him as a priestly phony, judged by his cronies to be a pompous bastard who wouldn't give them the time of day. If so, he never let me know that his pals had a poor opinion of me.

I would love to claim him for Christ, though he may have lived and died an agnostic. I want his life to have counted for something, but I have no right to try to appropriate him posthumously for the church, as though I had evidence for believing that, in his heart, he was a Catholic lad like me.

I can't rob George of the right and dignity to be who he was, even if he was only a loser who never got the breaks. If he was a victim more sinned against than sinning, maybe his life could count as a protest against man's inhumanity to man. But when you say *kaddish* for my brother, you shouldn't completely disregard the possibility that he may have been one of the unsung heroes who ran secret errands for the powers that be.

THE IMPORTANCE OF FATHERS

John Garvey

MY DAUGHTER MARIA, the first of our two children, was born at seven months. The first month of her life was a struggle to live. I remember seeing her for the first time through two panes of glass. She was fighting for air and looked frightfully small and vulnerable. And I knew in an unexpected rush that, if I could, I would die to keep her alive. It was the fiercest feeling I had ever known. It was my first experience of fatherhood.

That was in the late '60s, when people were saying things like, "How can you love somebody if you can't *communicate?*" The only communication between Maria and me wasn't communication at all, but an agony that she be alive; and she couldn't possibly have known that I felt that way. It took the bottom out of whatever love had meant to me until then.

Until I was a parent I thought I knew what love was like: you willed to do the right thing, even when you didn't feel like it, and of course you knew what the right thing was.

Sweet reason, self-sacrifice, and paying attention to a relationship would all come together to make love work.

Equipped with those reasonable-sounding ideas, I got married. A few months of marriage to someone who was suddenly a stranger taught me, painfully, that growth in a marriage is frequently growth in the dark. Years later a friend complained that her brother and his lover were always observing and talking about their relationship. "That's like watching a radish grow," she said. I recognized the problem; it was an old friend.

I thought that having a child would be a natural development, and of course it was. But I expected it to feel the way I thought natural things should feel. I wanted being a father to dovetail smoothly with being a husband. That, of course, was as mistaken as my earlier belief that marriage would be a smooth transition from the relationship Regina and I had before marriage. Instead, marriage and fatherhood went off like depth charges and rearranged everything.

It takes a long time to learn that not needing to be at the center of your life is a relief, not a deprivation. The consoling thing about marriage is that this learning, if you've been lucky (or, better, blessed), is done in concert with someone you like very much.

One strained metaphor has marriage as a kind of dance, in which both partners make a pattern larger than they could by themselves, a pattern that depends on both of them and has a center all its own, where both husband and wife can grow. The metaphor has its truth: marriage is about the creation of a (God forgive me this California word) space, but the strain comes from the fact that this dance involves such funny elements as inconvenient lust, loud chewing noises, and patience while someone finishes reading a novel in a bathroom you need to use. (I've noticed that the most poetic generalizations about marriage come from celibates and people whose mates are long dead.) Forgiveness, acceptance and humor need to be there. In its best moments—they do happen once in a while—marriage is a conspiracy between people who know and love one another.

No matter who you are, you get a terrible preparation for marriage and parenthood. If you come from a family in which there was deep and generous love, as most of us believe we do, the forms of that love were probably so specific and complicated that their importation into marriage is difficult at best. In addition, you are likely to marry someone whose background is different enough to make your meeting and mating a funny, painful process of understanding.

Each of us comes to adulthood through a process that has as much to do with myth as with rationality. Children are little reverse Freudians, mixing up their images of father and mother with their images of God, and even the children of atheists know for a while that their parents are divinely right. Some of the anger of adolescence is the realization that parents too often are wrong and need forgiving. That means that you must make your own way; you really are stuck in a world you never made. (Later you meet this merciful knowledge: given the way your most disastrous personal choices have been mercifully corrected by the real world, you understand that a world you could make would be hell, compared to the world you did not, thank God, make.)

All of this gives you some fellowship with your parents. In the long run you are blessed and wounded by the same things: love, with all its complications, and helplessness, which is part of love. Yeats begins his "Poem For My Daughter" by telling of "the murderous innocence of the sea." Part of our love is a fear for our children which comes from the realization that this "murderous innocence" is shining at the depth of a universe which is indifferent to us; it would kill our children as easily as it would a sparrow or a clam. The love of God sustains it, but that is a love which somehow can encompass Hiroshima, Shirley Temple, hornets, me, Bach, leukemia and Christ. It isn't something you can be on easy terms with. In this kind of universe we are asked, when we marry or have children, to take a step into the dark.

The risk husbands and wives take is as risky as any radical choice, but at least husbands and wives know one another well enough to have some sense, however limited, of what to expect of the other. Parenthood presents something more mysterious: you do not know who this new one is, or will be. Husbands and wives grow and change, of course, and like parents learning who their children are, they must learn to continue discovering each other. But they began by knowing something of the other. It seems less risky.

Having children is stranger than taking a vow. As scary as it is to be so hopeful or so blind, something in us says that it is profoundly right. You do not know what to expect; you know even less than you did about marriage. There is less possibility for an end to the relationship than in marriage: because you have fathered or mothered this other one you are responsible for life. Husbands and wives find it possible to cut loose from one another; various degrees of pain may attend the process, but it can be done. It is harder to deny your relationship to your children.

The yearning of parents for their offspring can be holy or demonic or a terrible combination of the two. I remember a man, drunk and angry, screaming and hammering on the door of a neighboring apartment. His terrified wife, inside with their daughter, called the police. They were divorced a few months before; he wanted to see his daughter. His wife's fear was real; so was his agony. His wild mixing of emotional self-interest and desire to see his daughter was frightening to everyone who could hear his shouting.

Family ties are as strong as anything human, and nobody can be objective about them. Ulysses on his adventures is a domestic man whose whole urge is towards wife and child; Antigone's loyalty to her dead brother puts her in peril; Abraham's hope is placed in a son he is asked to kill. If Jesus were not the beloved son of God the Father—if something less personal were involved—his suffering, and ours, would mean less.

Whatever the love of God for humanity might be, it must be mirrored in the ferocity and pity of fatherhood. By pity I mean the compassion referred to by the psalmist, who says that God regards us lovingly, "as a father pitieth his children."

It may be that the idea of God's fatherhood is essential precisely because of the ambiguity of fatherhood. We do not carry children to term. We are not the physical center, as mothers are, when our children are very young. We do not seem to be central to our children's lives as mothers must be. But children could not exist without us. We love them, but our love is not necessary in any obvious way.

The weakness and vulnerability of fatherhood are great secrets. Images of power and strength have to give way to the life-giving breath, the still small voice which remains when the storm and fire have passed away. That is where creation begins.

We are met by magic here, especially in early childhood, which is full of real magic and raw poetry. Here you get to see myth in the molten stage. I remember a night at dinner when Maria and Hugh, aged 5 and 3, ignored me and Regina and, with chicken bones in their hands, took up a chant. Maria began, "Before they had sticks, they used bones." Hugh took it up: "I wave over the water with my magic bones, I fly over the water with my magic wings." They chanted that way for a while, little sorcerers.

Poets, too: Hugh, watching the fluid motion of a neighbor's cat, asked me if cats had bones. Another time, trying to imagine a time when he didn't exist—the idea offended him—he asked where he was when Regina and I were married. I told him he wasn't anywhere then; he didn't exist. And he said, "Yes I did. I climbed up inside God's head, I looked out of his eye, and saw you." As they grow, our place in their lives changes. Maria is approaching adolescence now, asking the hardest questions, the kind that has no answers.

Our culture deprives too many men of fatherhood. I know men who leave home for work before their children are out of bed and see them again for a few minutes before bedtime. This busy-ness is culturally sanctioned and for some it may be economically necessary, but it is not good.

One of the most heartening trends today is the willingness of couples to work less and spend more time with their families. For too long motherhood was considered a special vocation, while fatherhood was a part-time job. Mothers held the family together and raised children. Fathers gave advice and earned money, but their real work was to serve as stockbrokers or linemen or journalists or electricians or lawyers. Feminism has helped to show the limitations of that approach to having families, and more men are realizing that fatherhood is as much of a vocation as motherhood.

I grew up with seven younger brothers and sisters, but as an older brother I never saw children the way I see them as a father, perhaps because my solidarity was with other children. Parents were alien and baffling. We knew they loved us and we could depend on them, but we also spent a lot of time trying to outwit them.

The idea that my father, with his hairy hands and bristly face, had ever been a child never occurred to me as a serious possibility. He told me stories about his childhood, but he also told me stories about imaginary kingdoms, and his childhood was as fascinating and unreal to me as the magic ships and castles he told me about.

Now I tell my children stories, and I think of my father.

A friend of mine says that the ultimate ethical questions are: What will you teach your children? What will you hand on? I realize that what I want to hand on to my children may not be what they get from me. The most I can do is to try to understand them, to let them know what matters to me and why it matters, to love them, and while they are young enough to need leading, to lead them the right way.

Trying to be clear about those things, I look at my children and have a sudden sharp memory of a moment when I was very small. I was holding my father's hand as we crossed a street. His hand felt large in mine; the veins that stood out on the back of his hand were soft. As we crossed the street I pressed down on those veins and found their softness reassuring. I hoped he didn't notice, because it seemed like a silly thing to do. But I hoped someday I would have hands like his.

A HAPPY ENDING

Georgie Anne Geyer

IT WAS THE day I had feared above all others, a day I had hoped at times to precede my mother to. It was the day of my mother's wake. And yet, in a strange and unexpected and incongruous way, it was a day wondrous and transcendent.

I recall, in the oddness of the mood, standing in the funeral parlor on Chicago's Near North Side, as people ebbed and flowed about me like tides from the times of her life, and thinking, "My God, this is a happening!" I remember thinking, too, how Mother, who loved parties and gaiety and people (so long as they were "well-behaved") would have loved to see the "happening" her passing had engineered. And I'm sure she did.

What so impressed me about the response to my mother's death, at 80, on June 11, 1979, was the myriad types and sizes and ages and creeds—and the sheer numbers—of the people who came to the wake. At any one time during that long day and evening, more than 200 people were there. In all more than a thousand came. For 10 hours, I never once sat down, there were so many people to greet. They poured in, like the rushing river that had been her life.

There were her old friends, women now facing the grave themselves, with tear-stained cheeks and ashen expectations. There were my friends, journalist types and crazy people in general in several languages. There were my dear brother Glen's friends from the clothing business, where he is a leading designer. There were hairdressers, suburban matrons, old boyfriends of mine come to see how I'd held up through the years, and a friend who came because his mother had just died and we-mourners-seek-out-other-people-hurt-like-ourselves. As a final cap-off, there was the endearing flock of little elderly nuns from the convent next door to my mother's apartment on Barry Avenue. The Helpers of the Holy Souls swept in like a flock of gray and white birds, filled with love and chattering with sympathy.

The next morning in his sermon, Roy Larson, the fine Methodist minister who is also the religion editor of the *Chicago Sun-Times,* summed up the sense of this life that all these people by their presence attested to. I had not heard the types of eulogy which celebrate a life rather than mourn the dead and I was strangely calmed and comforted by it, at least for the moment.

"Like Martin Buber, she seemed to know that the secret of a good life involves a refusal to withhold oneself," he said. "She did not sow her love sparingly, and she did not, therefore, reap sparingly. In her love, she displayed one of love's greatest gifts—a respect for the 'otherness of the other.' She was willing for her children to live their own lives, lives very different from her own. And there was humor in her love, expressed so exquisitely that Christmas when, to a daughter afflicted with an incurable case of wanderlust, she gave three gifts—an evening gown, a bush jacket and a Swiss Army knife.

"We thank God, too, for the way she loved her neighbors. A mutual friend told me this morning that Mrs. Geyer 'created neighborhoods'—in Auburn Park, at [her] summer home in Wisconsin, and in the North Side area where she spent her last years. Her home was a neighborhood center where she acted as a party-giver, a parent to her own children and a second parent to the children of others, and a friend to those who rejoiced in the open-door policy that reflected the spirit of her open heart."

When we took her to the cemetery that sunny spring afternoon, I had a jumble of thoughts, some of them strange. I felt that her life had been victorious. But I had lived and worked as a journalist in the fearful and dark worlds of international revolution and terrorism, and it had affected me deeply. In a sudden rush of feeling, I felt grateful that she was at peace—and that she had been spared the violent and barbaric deaths I had seen all too much of.

That was that, you may say. You just have to bear the agony somehow and eventually you will find some peace. You just have to "get

on with life," "pull yourself out of it," or "remember that this happens to everyone eventually"—or any one of the inane things that
thoughtless people say to you.

As a matter of fact, that was not that: not at all. A mother's death
is quite unlike the death of anyone else in one's life, and my mother's
death set me off on a journey—three journeys, really—that I am
only now beginning to understand. And I, who had known so many
journeys, now undertook new ones, because I had no choice.

My first journey was into the world immediately around me, a
world I had bypassed in my passion for knowing the peripheries of
the outer world. My entree was by way of the manner people responded to Mother's death and behaved toward those of us left behind. For now, I was alone in history. My ties to the past were rent.
And being alone—for the first time in my life, really—made me also,
for the first time, vulnerable.

The first few months were like a deep and ongoing psychoana-
lytical or spiritual experience or purging. I became suspicious of
people, particularly of young people, who were, after all, still alive—
and who still had parents. I found myself pulling back and watching
people for signs of any potential to hurt me. Whereas before I had
been so open and giving, now I waited. I let people reveal themselves; I asked myself, "What are their motives?" I tried to figure
out, with a kind of savage need, "Who will leave me alone the next
time?" I had always been so free and had always needed so little
from other people, but suddenly I became as fearful and as depend-
ent as a troubled child.

The world just around me unfolded like a new play opening in
the neighborhood. The people I had expected the most of never
even came to see me. The woman I had considered my closest friend
called once, sent flowers . . . and never called again. Other people,
from whom I had expected little, showed a nobility and a gallantry
that showered my soul.

But, remember, I had been a foreign correspondent for 11 years,
traveling everywhere in the world. I had been a columnist for four
years, analyzing everything for everybody with thorough ease. I had
looked at Egypt in 1973 and predicted the Yom Kippur War. I had
predicted, without hesitation, the Islamic revolution four years be-

fore it happened. I had laid out the El Salvador tragedy six years before the horror broke. And now I was discovering that I had not known the world—and many of the people—right around me.

That was almost as disturbing as the loss of my mother, whose luminous love had given me the security to bypass the needs that make most people attend to their inner anxieties about people. And so I began the painful process of pulling off layer and layer of skin on the human society right around me. And I came to a painful conclusion: it was my fault that I had not correctly analyzed those around me, my fault that I had not looked deeper into the characters and into the souls of my fellow travelers in this private journey.

Then, months after her death, I found myself embarked upon a second journey. This one started with casual—and, finally, searching—conversations with Mother's friends and relatives. I found myself asking: What was my mother really like? What did she do when she was 25? Or during that summer of '41, when Glen went to the Battle of the Bulge? *What kind of woman was my mother?*

You must understand that, while Mother and I were tremendously close and while I always considered her my best friend, I had always thought that we were different women, and she had never quite forgiven me for taking a path so different from hers. For Mother had been the consummate homemaker, and she always asked me, as I returned from my forays against the world and for the world, "Well, *now* you will settle down?"

Indeed, in the last years, I had become convinced that I had been a failure in her eyes. Even those last weeks at the hospital, she had said once of a roommate, "Imagine, her children even knew your name!" I had been published in Chicago for 20 years, yet she could not acknowledge that I was a success. It was bittersweet.

In my journey, I remembered first my classical picture of Mother: tall, slim, beautiful, with lovely eyes, a warm smile, a lilting sense of humor, and unending graciousness. But then, through my conversations, another picture began to emerge, at first haltingly and tentatively. It was a picture of a woman other than the one I had thought I had known.

I began to see my mother as a transitional woman, a woman who had led me to the path I had taken. She had her feet in two worlds.

She "gave up tennis" when she married, even though she was a champion, because, "When you get married, you give up things." She urged me to read and to know things and to explore the world. She was a woman who was in between, who lived one life and who wanted another, who pushed me on and fearfully tried to hold me back when she realized what she had done, who gave distinctly mixed signals.

Now I began to see a woman herself frustrated, wanting more, wanting more love and more independence but born in an age that forbade it.

I remembered her own mother, a stern, upright Dutch New Yorker, who had lectured my father when Mother was pregnant with me at 36 about how bad it was to have a child at her age. I thought of my father's mother, Martha Geyer, who ran our dairy business on the South Side and who threw the cans of milk around with the best of the men—and who, on Sundays, would dress up in her beaded chiffon dresses and jewelry and be transformed into one of the most elegant ladies anywhere.

I began to see myself in those women and those women in me. So often I had thought of myself as breaking the line. Now I felt the strength of a great river, carrying me along and ahead.

Sometimes that awareness—the sense of the flow, the solidarity of the blood and of the mind—became funny. Two weeks before Mother's Day in 1981, for instance, something hit me with the force of a thunderstorm.

Mother, you see, was a woman who liked happy endings. In earlier years, she had liked Doris Day movies. I, of course, had enjoyed mocking Doris Day, preferring movies that ended in some love tragedy or with someone walking off into the sunset, alone.

When I was home, Mother insisted that I watch Lawrence Welk, and I tried to comply, but it was as if I were all tied up in ropes. "Why don't you like it?" she would ask beseechingly, as though all her life's efforts for me were cancelled by this debit of character I displayed. "It's soupy," I'd reply.

Then, last spring, there I was, sitting—alone now—before the tube, the same person sitting on the same sofa watching the same Lawrence Welk. Suddenly I found myself swaying to that circumspect time and thinking, as he was just a-oneing and a-twoing into gear, "You know, he really does have a talented group!"

"Of all the things that my late beloved mother might be proud of in me today," I wrote that Mother's Day, "one now stands out like a lighthouse during a great storm at sea. Knowing this new fact about me, she would have seen all her efforts and struggles well worth the sacrifice. Her life would now seem justified, all her fears for my sanity and safety (not to speak of my chastity) worth the never-ending cost . . . I have come to like Lawrence Welk."

Now that I was in my mid-40s I discovered that I had come to a point where I liked happy endings and happy music, too. No, scratch that—I didn't just "like them," I needed them.

The age at which you change to needing happy endings marks a generational moment of truth. Tragedy appeals to young people because it is something they think they can change and challenge and confront. In their lifetimes, they are certain everything will change for the better. Happy endings appeal to older people because they have already seen enough tragedy in life.

I finished the column this way: "I suppose other mothers and daughters have similar struggles, although I frankly doubt that they could be at the inspired level of ours over Lawrence Welk. But always inside those struggles is a confrontation of generations, worked out over and over with each new generation of older women and younger women who love and create each other.

"And always, yes, there is a winner. For I realized something else that night. I realized, suddenly, why it is that all you mothers out there put up with all of us idiot children all your lives. It's because you know something we don't know. You know full well that you'll get us in the end."

Lawrence Welk even answered in a letter. "I am heartily in accord with your late mother's feelings about happy endings," he wrote. "Goodness knows, there's enough tragedy and depression in the world without inflicting them on the public in the guise of 'entertainment.' I know that your mother would have been happy and proud to know that your early TV training was not completely wasted and that we did finally 'get you in the end.' "

Yes, she did get me in the end. What's more, she continues to help me, which is the essence of the third and final journey.

It has been almost two and a half years now since I stood by her grave that sunny day. The constant agony, the lying on planes at night and sobbing my heart out, the waves of panic and alienation: all have been replaced by intermittent insight. Whole periods of time I try not to think of her at all. Then the presence and the loss comes back to me and over me as if it were a palpable presence.

I know things now. I know that people should talk about these things beforehand. I know that we should listen to our loved ones as they lay dying, for when Mother tried to talk to me about her death, I would not—could not—listen. I will always wonder what she wanted to tell me.

I think that the generations of women should tell their own real truth to the next generation—and not so many fictitious lies about what "being a woman" really means. I think that people like me, who analyze the world to death, should start paying attention to those immediately around us.

I guess that, if I have learned anything from these last years, it is that you suddenly discover you cannot will everything any more. You can only march resolutely and courageously into the mysteries. You go with the leaps of faith. The demands of "Why?" with their futile adamancy, become tentative. The moment comes when you can no longer explain everything but can rest only by losing oneself in the mysteries—and confirming oneself by them.

The third journey, thus, has been inside myself. My writing is changing. It is becoming deeper, it has new dimensions, it is more complex. For the first time, I can write good fiction because for the first time I understand the vagaries and complexities and convolutions of character. My mother gave me this, too. Even in death, she is giving to me.

One final thing I also know. Having survived my mother's death, I know for the first time that I can survive my own.

LONG BURIED TREASURE

Joe McKenna

THE MOUNDS OF sods along Rockne Drive reminded me of piles of potatoes in the garden at home and in a moment's foolishness I looked around, almost expecting to see my Da standing at his spade, stealing a well-earned rest. If he were here, I knew, he'd be proud of me now. For the day's work was over and the biggest machine in the South Bend city fleet, the articulated John Deere 240, had arrived to collect my bounty of rocks, sods and bushes and load them onto waiting trucks. The teeth on the gaping scoop shaved off the little mounds I had piled along the curb on Rockne Drive. In a few moments the whole thing had been scooped up and loaded into waiting trucks.

It seemed effortless for both machine and operator.

Things had not been so effortless for the 20 of us who had gathered on the city's east side for the "Christmas in April" project. From the untypical 7:30 a.m. Saturday start, 1,500 Notre Dame students had volunteered their muscle power to do a spring cleaning in the Northeast Neighborhood. Our team had blistered through 50 bags of litter and trimmed back bushes and sod to reveal a 100-yard sidewalk buried under 10 years of neglect. These mounds represented a day's toil for the group now reduced to the role of spectator, leaning on our spades and shovels.

As the noise of the trucks moved up the street toward another site, we agreed the day's work had been worth more than a week in the classroom.

For me, the rediscovery of the spade was a high point.

I was just three weeks short of returning home to my parents' farm in Derry, Ireland, having spent four years in the United States, three of them at Notre Dame. The day I spent digging sod in a city that I didn't care about carried me back to the things that were permanent in my upbringing, and to the reasons why I needed to go home.

The blisters on the knobs of my fingers throbbed against the smooth shaft of the spade, and I thought of my father's thick welted skin that knew no such pain. I could picture him at work, his sleeves rolled up beyond the big muscles above his elbows, his peaked cap pushed to the back of the head holding the gray hair in place, the weather-beaten skin and tight, brawny, good looks that never seemed to sweat, and jeans patched with holes and stains tied down over the hobnail boots buried in the brown earth. Over on the cherry tree in the hedge hung his dark sports jacket, the remainder of the spade-man's uniform.

The spade Da used was shorter in shaft than the tool in my hands. It had a T-bar handle the width of a fist at the end, and the blade was small with a horizontal edge shiny and sharp. The instrument I now held was a poor substitute, but it was enough to remind me of the man who had inherited 50 acres of hill country in County Derry and got to know it well at the end of his spade. This day in South Bend served as a refresher course in the value of a hard day's work and the goodness that comes with every turn of a sod.

A man's worth was measured by the way he handled the spade.

Now was the first time that I realized that my Da spoke to me through the spade and in the process turned over little mysteries that soiled my hands with memories I could not easily shake off.

As we walked home toward the University after our spring good turn to some of South Bend's less privileged residents, the students chatted loudly about the work they had done and its value for University-community relations. We resented the ease with which the backhoe belittled our day's work and we talked hard, as if to convince ourselves that we had indeed done a lot.

I needed less convincing about my father's efforts with 50 cows, 20 sheep, a scattering of pigs and hens, and my Ma and nine youngsters squatting on our little belt of green along the face of the hill near Maghera. It was the spade in my father's hands that showed

that soil well tilled, weeds rooted out and hedges trimmed back
meant more food for all of us. Affection was dealt out in grand
doses in the annual rituals of the potato-digging and the turf-cutting that brought our family together. These were the staple supplies
for six boys and three girls who valued a hard-working man who
showed his love in a way expected of a breadwinner.

A man's place was with his spade. Wife, family, church and God
were a lot more important, but it all came together in well-handled
sod and root on drizzly Saturday evenings at the bottom of the
garden.

I remembered how the lessons began when the books were put
away after I had walked home from my three-teacher primary school.
I'd be commandeered to join my father "in the garden." The term
was used affectionately for an area of land where you'd expect to
find a man at work. And in the brisk fall evenings I'd gather my
share of the family's potato crop and toss them into the tin bucket
by my side. By the time I'd arrive, Da would have an afternoon's
work spread out and the shiny skins drying in the early evening
breeze. Sometimes we'd work together so that I could catch up to
the spade. He'd catch four or five spuds in each hand and still be
able to rub the clay off. I'd launch one from each hand from three
yards and they'd bonk against the side of the tin bucket. Now and
again, when my back got sore, I'd crawl on my knees and rise to a
scowl that said, men don't do that.

We worked quietly. We'd stand to break the silence and I'd tell
of Master Stone and how he smoked in class. Da looked down the
valley from our little farm on the edge of the hill, Catholic settle-
ments all around hewn into the little arable lots in the heavy clay
soil of the Sperrin mountains. Down the valley were the Protestant
holdings that had been there for 300 years and stretched for 30 miles
to the south and west. At the 10-mile range around Moneymorc,
my Da could pick out the owner of a field as it changed its color in
the harvest reaping, and he talked of the "quer land" that it was. I
had no idea if the land was rightfully ours, but it seemed that we'd
just been evicted yesterday.

On our side of the hill, known as the "Brae Face," we referred
in whispers to our Protestant neighbors as those who "dig with the

other foot." I was never quite sure of the connection between re-ligion and the spade but it was there, just like the rule book for the Benedictine monks.

And then we turned back toward the work at hand and I'd face the man with the spade and try to stay up with him as he tossed out each tuber. The spuds clustered in groups of about 12 at inter-vals of one foot. A good man with a spade could slice his instrument deep into the soil and spill out each top in one swoop. The back swing would knock off excess soil from the newly unearthed and toss out the rotten ones.

I'd scramble to gather the good ones into my tin bucket.

The ultimate sin was to slice a big potato. My Da worked with a surgeon's precision in a silence that valued a job well done and ques-tioned whether chatter was compatible with work. Man and tool worked in close harmony, and I was the surgeon's aide doing my best and keeping fingers out of the way. The monotony would be broken by the arrival of a head of whites instead of the traditional blues, and I'd giggle at the genetic disasters if 30 or 40 little ones were tossed out and not a decent one among them. But I'd still have to gather them all, thinking I was great with four or five in each hand. Now and then, I'd clean one off and pocket it for later.

Eventually Da would give up and we'd cover the pyramid of po-tatoes in the middle of the garden. The long green rushes would be laid on first, and then Da would toss on clay from a little moat dug around the pyramid—that way the water would run off the pit and into the moat and the potatoes would be kept dry, so he said.

Sunday was the traditional day of rest and didn't allow for the spade in an Irish work culture that is defined by physical labor. A man with a spade on Sunday caught the eye of the passersby on the way to church and chapel. It was OK to take the cattle in from the fields and pour Guinness bottles of medicine down throats for worms, but the spade stayed in its place. Other times we'd pile into the Ford and drive the 30 miles to Portstewart to play on the sand-hills and come back in time for the milking.

Sometimes after a family wedding or funeral, Da would go to the garden with the spade to turn over weeds or clear a drain to let the water away. The spade was the medicinal for dressed-up formality

that seemed like a waste of time to Da. We would watch him out
the kitchen window heading off to his retreat with the jacket and
cap and spade over the shoulder; then for a couple of hours he'd be
missing in action and we'd intrude now and again to borrow the
car at the peril of being asked to do something more useful. And
there in the twilight of the evening among the swarm of hedgerow
midges he'd take off the cap and flatten down the hair. Then he'd
spit on his hands to fasten the connection with the smooth shaft of
the spade. Sometimes the neighbors would stop for a chat and do
their business in the garden and plan a trip to another spade-man's
funeral the next day.

And on a wet evening the visitor would be brought in for supper
with the 10'clock news from Radio Eireann in the background. One
of the girls would serve hot tea and a plate of oven bread with butter
and jam. More than oft the tea was sent back to draw. At 11 o'clock
we'd kneel to say the rosary, leaning low over couches and chairs
with our backs to the fire. Da led the little ceremony and I turned
over *The Irish News* in front of me to read about the world that I
thought held more for me than anything I had here. I'd listen to
the instructions about saying the Hail Mary properly and throw
things at whoever was on the spot when Da wasn't looking. And
the man in the jeans and shirtsleeves kept the proceedings going
with the staple diet of work and prayer that constituted a seven-day
week.

Then the hobnail boots would be left out at the back door and
the socks hung over the firebox handle and the cap tossed up on the
plate rack above the stove. Then they hung the rosary beads over
the Sacred Heart picture and bid us goodnight, and we'd sit and
talk in whispers and listen to Elton John.

Come Easter Monday, the boys and perhaps one of the girls
would stand on the back of the tractor and we'd drive the three
miles up the face of the hill to the heather-covered boglands for the
annual turf-cutting. Each farm came with a turf bank on the common ground at about 1,000 feet, and it was the focal point of the
annual pilgrimage to win the turf which began on Easter Monday
when the children were off school. This was a primeval dig to expose
half-decayed vegetation from its air-tight bed of water and lay it out

in sods to dry in the westerly winds. The process involved the top
of the line in spades, so out of its cover came the "turf spade" to
take its sacred place in the spring rite. It had a narrower blade than
the typical spade and was two sides at right angles, so that it cut
back and side at once.

After the top layer of heather was removed the man on the spade
moved side to side and cut out French fries of peat in lines along
the face of the bank. One-million-year-old decaying Irish forests
were uncovered for the first time in this ceremony, the sticky black
fingers laid out to dry. They would be brought home in late summer
as the winter fuel that gave off the homey smell.

My position was always at the foot of the turf spade as I waited
for Da to slice out three or four slithers of moss. Then I'd pick them
up and load them onto barrows for my brothers and sisters to wheel
out to open ground and dump into heaps. With my sleeves rolled
up I'd bend over the operation and keep my fingers out of harm's
way until the agreed number of slices were made.

I always took the job of lifter because I told myself that I was
the quietest and most concentrated. The rest of the gang would play
games, naming cars and pop groups till no more could be remembered. Da and I kept quiet, and the slice of the spade marked time
in the silence and provided the background noise on a closeness that
wasn't articulated. This indeed was the school of life, and it would
take me 20 years to begin to value it all.

Back on the Notre Dame campus, the students gathered at the
student center for the speechmaking by the important people who
had driven around in sedans all day. I couldn't help but think that
they had missed a valuable lesson, the kind of lessons learnt along
hedges when Da and me struggled with a big dock-leaf, the worst
type of perennial weed whose root went straight into the ground,
and only an old hand could ensure that it all came out without the
little point of the root being left for another day's growth.

Sometimes in the long summer evenings after the milking we'd
cross to one of the hills away from the house. There we'd spend till
bedtime digging around the young briars that would spring out
from the hedges to tear at a cow's udder pressed full of milk. On a
good night we lit little bonfires and tossed on the briars.

We'd look down over the lights of the farmers who dug with the other foot in an act of defiance that something good was happening on the side of the hill, if only they knew it. I'd stand and warm my hands and look up at the stars and walk home to my Ma with the soot in my eyes and the satisfaction of a man at work.

And later, when the brother came home from college and 200-horsepower Fiats levelled hedges and filled drains, my Da would still grab that spade and unearth the stone or root that had been missed by the bigger machines. And no matter how well the foundations for the new shed were dug out by the big arm of the digger, there were still the corners to be squared off when the contractor was paid and dismissed at the back door.

For Da's machine was much more precise.

And I remembered the arguments about the value of the little garden of potatoes that wasted everybody's time and cost more than if they were bought at the market. Soon the fields were all the same and the little gardens leveled and dock weeds sprayed down with weed killer.

And now the men in fancy suits finished the speechmaking and I returned to my dorm room in Sorin Hall. And I thought of the need to pack my bag and go home to the man with the spade who knew about an art that wasn't covered at Notre Dame.

SEE DICK AND JANE,
SEE DICK AND JANE CHANGE

Mary Ruth Yoe

"TELL THE STORY about when you were a little girl," my 4-1/2-year-old demands at bedtime. Not pausing to hear my reply, her words keep cascading out, only slightly hampered by her thumb: "And your mommy got angry at you and said she was sorry but she was busy right now."

That's pretty much the story, although Mairead is waiting to hear how I left the brightly painted kitchen where my mother was cooking dinner and went into the living room, snuggled up against the family dog, and said into his silky black fur, "Midnight loves me. Mommy doesn't love me, but Midnight loves me."

Mairead's family has a dog, too, chosen by her mother because he, like the long-suffering Midnight, is an English cocker spaniel. But it's obvious that Mairead sees other parallels between life in her family and life in that family that used to be, a topsy-turvy world where her mommy was a little girl.

* * *

When I was little in the 1950s, I compared my family with families in Golden Books. It didn't take me long to realize we were somewhat out of step.

Children in Golden Books usually came in ones or twos, occasionally in threes. I had two brothers and two sisters.

The small towns in which the stories were set came equipped with all four seasons: maple leaves in October, snowy hills to sled down in winter, spring and summer sidewalks for going to school, visiting friends, playing hopscotch, selling lemonade. We lived on a Southern Maryland tobacco farm.

In the storybooks, childcare and housework were women's jobs, and houses were kept spotless. Our house was far from pristine, despite a maid who came in for eight hours each weekday. My mother, who never looked as freshly pressed as the storybook mothers, was always in the midst of projects—making duck aprons as favors for a birthday party, cutting out clippings of recipes and household hints that "might come in handy," mending books and toys and clothes.

The mothers in the books didn't have jobs outside the home. When I was 8, my mother went back to teaching school. Even then, I never saw my father change a diaper, set or clear the table, wash a dish, bathe a child, or pick up a fallen toy—nor did any of the fathers in my books.

On the other hand, my father didn't don suit and fedora to go, as one book put it, "into town to make pennies for Mommy and me." A building contractor, he drove off in a pick-up truck with a crew of men who assembled in our driveway each morning.

In the evenings, he helped my grandfather cultivate his tobacco. Storybook grandparents, I noted, were usually grandmothers and came in two varieties: those who lived across town and those who lived a car, train or plane trip away.

* * *

I compared my family to the families in books—and on television shows such as *Leave It to Beaver* and *Father Knows Best*—because I lived a childhood far more isolated than might have been expected in the '50s. Instead of a Levittown, we lived two miles from the nearest town. My parents, who had married late, had few friends with children my age. My mother didn't learn to drive until I was almost in my teens, and my father felt children belonged at home.

Reading was a way of exploring the world, and I pored over the stories and their illustrations; both seemed straightforward and simple, with none of the messy undercurrents—arguments, disappointments, rivalries—that ran through my own family.

As a mother of two little girls, I've found or bought all those books again, and as I read them now to my daughters I study the pictures I've remembered for so long.

Some things have changed. The family pictured on vacation in a new edition of *The Great Big Car and Truck Book* didn't quite ring true with the one I remembered, but until the original edition turned up in a friend's bookcase this year, I'd forgotten what I used to see. In the 1951 version, the mother is inside a camper, cooking a meal and minding a play-penned baby; outside, the father relaxes while two little boys play cowboys and Indians. In the edition I read to our daughters, mom is the one relaxing in the sun, while a little boy and girl play baseball (the girl's at bat). Inside, dad gets the baby up from a nap.

* * *

The books and the times have changed, and so has my family. After years of being part of the family into which I happened to be born, I'm now part of a family which I chose to form.

Like many people in the early stages of therapy (or in practically *any* stage of adolescence), I once swore that my own family would be nothing like my accidental family. Instead, it almost seems as if I have modeled my family after the '50s families of books and television. We have just two children. We live in a small New England town, with leaves to rake in the fall and a downtown that's easy to walk to. Mother stays at home, and daddy goes off to the office each morning (although he wears sports jacket and tie rather than a gray-flannel suit).

In the winter, rosy-cheeked and bundled up in brightly colored mittens, hats and snowclothes, the girls go sledding. In spring and fall, they fly kites, swing, pedal their tricycles around the neighborhood. They build summer sand castles at the lake. On Sundays, the whole family goes to church.

Once again, however, the storybook image leaves out important currents in our life.

Take the matter of work. My husband and I share the same field—one with sudden spurts of activity, writer's block, deadlines, and hours that go beyond 9-to-5.

"Working" was an early addition to both my daughters' vocabularies. It meant what mommy and daddy did when the girls were left at day care or when one of us couldn't join the family's weekend or evening plans. They accepted the word's matter-of-fact finality. At 2, Mairead finally caught a glimpse of me at a meeting, scrawling notes, and from then on, instead of drawing with her crayons, she did "working."

At 18 months, as she walked into day care on a Monday morning, Hanna announced: "Mommy working airplane." At least my husband was there to hear her first three-word sentence. All that week, whenever a plane flew overhead, she'd repeat the phrase. Despite her older sister's attempts at explanation, it took another six months before she understood that I don't spend my entire time away from home high in the sky.

Although I work at home most days, I spend about six weeks on the road each year—making me the business traveler in the family. Because their father normally takes them to day care, picks them up, gives them baths and reads them stories, dresses them and takes them to doctor's appointments, the girls don't find the basic outline of their days too different when I'm gone.

A large part of their life, of course, is day care. The Otter Creek Child Center is a white-clapboard dwelling that looks like the kind of place grandmas lived in before they all moved to condominiums—its wraparound porch comes complete with wooden swing and grapevine awning. Inside is the group of children and adults with whom Mairead and Hanna play, read, sing, talk, paint, eat and explore. On our errands in town, my husband and I sometimes run into our children and their friends on their own rounds. In Otter Creek, Mairead and Hanna have found a replacement for their far-flung extended family. (Their three grandparents live in three states; the aunts, uncles and cousins are scattered up and down the East Coast.)

Because of day care, the girls come home each night with news of a wider world: a visit to the horse farm, a new baby brother for Yuna, the broken water pipe on the way to the library's story hour.

Much earlier than our parents did, my husband and I have had to confront the fact that babies grow up and know things we don't teach them. So far, thank goodness, the extra knowledge has been benign: "Rice cakes!" Mairead screamed the first time we popped a package into the grocery cart; "we have those at Otter Creek!"

* * *

As a family, it seems we don't spend much time at home. Or much time in any one home. By the age of 4, Mairead had lived in four houses in three cities. (I lived in the same house until I went away to college; my father lives there still.)

Our car—its back seat littered with children's books, small toys and crumpled wrappers from fast-food places—is testimony to life on the go. Sometimes the car seems to double as a family room. The girls have their favorite tapes (from "Wee Sing" to Suzanne Vega), and their favorite activities, including keeping their eyes peeled for the highway icons of Wendy's, Burger King, Pizza Hut and McDonalds. One of the first words Mairead learned to read was "S-T-O-P."

When I was a child, family meals in a restaurant were, like family journeys, once-a-year occasions. Today we eat out once or twice a week, most often at a "family restaurant" called Rosie's where there are lots of booster seats, crayons delivered with the menus—and usually one or two of Mairead and Hanna's friends and their parents. Because we're part of a fairly large group of parents with small children, we often go to "grown-up" parties where children are invited. Adding in birthday parties, Mairead and Hanna are frequent guests in other people's homes.

Housework, like childcare, gets shared. Mairead thought daddies cooked and mommies did laundry until she was 4—that year we switched jobs. Household errands like grocery shopping get sandwiched in at odd hours, thanks to around-the-clock-stores, and the girls come along.

Because I'm at home, and housework is a way to procrastinate on tougher assignments, the house generally looks neat when Ed and the girls come back each night, and that gives me—despite my feminist convictions—a feeling of being a good mother. When the dust level gets noticeable, I feel guilty but remind myself that we're not home that much anyway.

* * *

I'm not really surprised to find that I'm sometimes uncomfortable in the family I've helped to create. For one thing, I married a man whose family differed from mine. My parents were cautious enough that none of their five children ever broke a bone or even sprained an ankle. Ed's family seemed always ready to take a flyer, certain that things would work out even when they were going wrong.

Ed entertains the girls by taking them places, letting them try new things. I'll stand in the background, trying to look unconcerned, while he sends Hanna's stroller hurtling down a hillside sidewalk; he runs beside her, Hanna shrieking with delight, as I imagine collisions with tree, lamppost or concrete. When Ed took the girls on their first Ferris wheel ride, I was away; Ed's father captured the moment on videotape: "Look at us, Mommy! My stomach felt funny!" Mairead says at each replay. As I watch my babies swaying in the frail seat, my stomach feels funny too. Soon they'll begin skiing lessons; I'm not sure I'll be able to watch.

My caution is one of several family resemblances I work to erase. My parents were uncomfortable with corporal punishment, but both were good with angry words. When I hear myself berating the two people I love best, I feel caught in a sharp-edged family trap.

Luckily, that feeling of despair is balanced by more benign inheritances, gifts I've been able to give Mairead and Hanna because my parents gave them to me: the games we play, the stories we read, the elaborate rituals with which we celebrate holidays, the jokes we share, the easy companionship of a pet—and the sense of life being a story whose next twist of plot is just around the comer. Within the stability of a relatively restricted world came an ability to be fascinated by minute changes and shadings.

I sometimes wonder if Mairead and Hanna will measure their family against images from '80s books—books with titles like *Katharine Goes to Nursery School, The Car Trip, Benjy Goes to a Restaurant* or *The Berenstain Bears, Too Much Television.*

If so, will they find our family was out of step?

Perhaps not. But more to the point, perhaps they won't consider the question important. They see into so many homes—so many ways of setting tables, setting rules, setting priorities—that they may have an easier time understanding that family differences, like family resemblances, are simply a fact of life. That's a lesson I'm still learning.

FAMILY MAN
Mark Phillips

MARGARET WAS SURPRISED when I arrived home from work two hours early. She didn't know I was about to become a househusband. At that point, neither did I.

Earlier in the day, my employer had slid his large belly under his large desktop and fired me from my paralegal job. He had already discharged two other employees and he wanted me to sit down and listen to a speech about his "cash flow" problems. I refused to sit, made a speech of my own and left his office dragging my pride.

Margaret was eight months pregnant with our first child and about to begin a maternity leave. For the next month I was a fitful father-to-be who paced restlessly through the house, took long hikes, jogged, lifted weights and drank too much beer. I worried about the health of Margaret and our baby, about how good a father I would be, about finances—and especially about not having a job. In bed each night I struggled for hours before finding sleep, and each morning I awoke exhausted and afraid, shooting up to a wide-eyed sitting position. I had no concentration for writing, reading or even conversation, and one afternoon, attempting to repair our car engine, I snapped off two bolts.

* * *

The lawyer asks the man with the foreclosure notice crumpled in his right fist to please sit down, but the man, my grandfather, declines. Once more he explains that he's an ironworker and he broke two ribs and bruised a lung on the first job he's had in seven months, but as soon as he returns to work he'll resume payments on the house. Who, he asks once more, is he actually buying the house from? Again the lawyer explains he's not at liberty to reveal whose estate he's managing and he regrets having to foreclose. Once more my grandfather reminds the lawyer that he has eight children and nowhere else to live. Perhaps the lawyer feels safe with an injured man because he stands up and breaks the gelid politeness by telling my grandfather he should have put away money for a time like this; then he asks him to leave and not return without two months of mortgage payments.

On his way to the lawyer's downtown Buffalo office, my grandfather had passed on the streets the Great Depression beggars, ragged wandering families, men selling pencils. Suddenly he's straddling the lawyer's chest, his hands squeezing the lawyer's neck, and the lawyer, face turning blue and arms and legs thrashing, is trying to spit out a name and address.

The next confrontation is with a butler, who informs my grandfather that Madam does not wish to be disturbed. Then she appears, an elderly woman in a wheelchair, and asks what the problem might be. He removes his hat, steps past the butler and quietly explains. She had no idea, she says; of course he and his family can keep their home. She offers him a seat in the plush parlor, which he accepts, and directs the butler to push her to the telephone.

Before leaving, my grandfather asks, "And, Ma'am, how many children did you raise?"

* * *

The birth, thanks to the Lamaze Method and Margaret's resolve, was nearly an anti-climax. Labor lasted nine hours before the doctor decided the baby was too large and a Caesarean was necessary, but Margaret had never cried out or wept. At 12:07 p.m. on September 19, 1987, healthy Hope Ann Phillips, nine pounds and one ounce, was lifted into the world.

While driving home from the hospital, exhausted after 23 sleepless hours, I carelessly passed a car that was making a left-hand turn; it struck my car on the passenger side and knocked me into a spin on the busy highway. No one was hurt, but in the midst of the spin I thought, *Poor Margaret, so happy with her new child and now she'll find out her husband is dead.* If we still had been merely a couple rather than a family, I suspect my thoughts would have been more selfish.

* * *

My father, tea steam and cigarette smoke clouding my view of his grimaces, sits with my sisters and me at the breakfast table. In front of him, between his cup and ashtray, are two bright red Darvon capsules and a piece of toast. At the counter my mother is placing two more capsules of the painkiller into his lunchbox, along with a Thermos bottle of tea, a baloney sandwich, a piece of celery and a piece of cake. He must work 93 more days before he can receive a small early-retirement pension. Ninety-three more shifts of welding in the power plant amidst the screaming of turbines, clouds of coal dust and clinging fly ash, and 100-degree heat. Ninety-three more days of climbing vertical steel ladders and squeezing into machinery and boilers with the cancerous pain in his lower back that seems to cut and burn as surely as the welding torch in his right hand.

* * *

Soon after mother and daughter's homecoming, I learned that infant-parent bonding can include fathers, if they permit it. I used to mock boastful parents: "Everyone's kid is gifted," I'd laugh, not understanding that every child is a gift. Now I was telling anyone who would listen, "She's already trying to hold up her head," and "She stops crying as soon as she hears my voice!" Indeed, my early paternal ego was such that occasionally, while Hope struggled to locate me in her days-old near blindness, I imagined that humans must appear that way to a benign God.

Margaret returned to her teaching position after a six-week rather than six-month leave. A few of my relatives—in particular my maternal grandmother who still thought of me as the 14-year-old who had permitted my grandfather's cattle to escape a fenced pasture just before one of the bulls charged her hanging laundry—warned of a child-care disaster. Among other things she predicted, "Hope'll learn to swear, will be drinking his beer and'll get stung by his honeybees."

Hope and I soon silenced the critics. I go to bed each night at

8, get up at 3 a.m., write until Margaret leaves for work at 7:30, and then abandon myself. Often, as 13-month-old Hope clumps into a room in her stiff-legged, stumbling run, I chant, "Enter the fairy, singing and dancing and shaking her wooden leg"—and we sing and dance: Dance to rock music, mock-conduct to classical, and sing badly to both. We explore a ground-level world, maul our patient cat, practice our animal sounds (cat, dog, rooster, cow, lion, bear, sheep, monkey), hike with Hope riding shotgun in a backpack, flip through picture books and family photo albums. Hope crawled at 5 months, walked at 10, could say 15 words by the time she was a year old and is almost always happy and affectionate.

Fortunately, Margaret returns from work anxious to spend time with Hope and mostly oblivious to my neglect of some household tasks. One afternoon the spoils of our offspring's forays into cupboards, drawers and shelves left the living room and kitchen floors littered with frying pan, pie tin, cooking pot, pot cover, partially spilled box of cornflakes, unraveled tinfoil, baby's rattle, doll, box of cake mix, jar of oregano. And three jars of baby food, can of cream of tartar, box of Jello, two packages of Kool Aid, gutted coffee pot, shredded grocery bag, coffee cup, shape sorter and shapes, one baby's sock, one baby's shoe. And furniture coaster, two crumpled sheets of typing paper, two badly wrinkled *Harper's*, shredded *Mother Earth News*, shredded *Buffalo News*, shredded Cabella's catalog, 39 intact hardcover books, child's plastic picture-book, child's brush, play telephone, jar of cloves and a harmonica. For most of the day I'd followed Hope around the house, amazed at her energy and happily accepting pillaged gifts. I wonder how many housewives and children whose cash-flow, head-of-the-household males demand immaculate homes and elaborately prepared meals would prefer to spend their days as freely as Hope and I.

I also wonder with alarm: If I were a cash-flow father, returning each evening tired and frustrated, would I by now be a stranger in my own home? In a study reported in 1972 by Professor Lawrence Fuchs, a group of suburban 10- and 11-year-olds was asked, "What does it mean to be a father?" A typical reply was: "Being a father means going out to work every morning, coming home at night, hearing all the problems at night, all the people yelling and scream-

ing. People asking for things. Getting headaches. Having to give
food money to your wife. Paying your bills. Trying to have enough
money for everything. Then some Saturday or Friday going out and
having fun with your wife. That's the best of it." No wonder a repeated lament in the anthology *Fathers,* in which prominent female
authors describe their paternal relationships, is that the daughters
knew their fathers merely superficially, as paternal strangers in their
own homes, not because of male duty but because of male self-de-
lusion.

Recently a friend of mine who works nights in a Chevy plant and
takes care of his two children in the daytime said to me, pointing
to the children, "This is what it's all about. Even if we're lucky, kids
are all we get for sure. These are it." Once I would have sneered at
such a cosmic conclusion, but now I nodded, not so sure that he
was wrong.

Yet while the other fathers worked, I played. Writing for maga-
zines is considered at best subversive and at worst effeminate, and
though I was also ghostwriting for individuals and businesses, I had
no shingle hanging out front and I punched no time clock, slaved
under no glaring boss, put in no long, inflexible hours and wasn't
saving up for a bigger house or even a satellite dish. As for my child-
care duties: What a wimpy cover for a life of leisure. Masculine dis-
approval chastised me daily by way of my postbox and the television
set; I know that, more fully and clearly than all of the churches
combined, Madison Avenue reflects American values. After a day of
hot toil, the blue collar worker earns a Bud Lite with the boys; following a day of outsmarting corporate sharks, the corporate businessman is served a Dewars on the rocks while rejuvenating in his
throne-like living room chair. Promising vicarious power, glistening
new cars zoom across the hostile landscape of American TV. And
if a man's job pays poorly, Mastercard is camouflage that's virtually
undetectable by the carnivorous landscape beasts. Jobless? Join the
army. Meanwhile, safe at home and in front of the camera, women
clutch boxes of Cheer and babies in Ultra Pampers Plus.

In weak moments I applied for jobs, and in Hope-inspired strong
moments I turned jobs down. Eventually, though, I was offered em-
ployment with evening and weekend hours, which meant that by

forgoing my writing I could both care for Hope and hold an outside job. I would be a so-called "youth aide" in a state institution for juvenile delinquents from New York City. I took the job and the state sent me to Rochester for a week of training in self defense, the use of handcuffs, use of shackles, physical restraint of violent youths, CPR, first aid and crisis management. "Why," asked one of my in-laws, "would you want to do that kind of work? Won't it be dangerous?"

*   *   *

Five stories in the air, my great-uncle rides an ascending beam, gripping one of the spreaders of the cable that the chugging and popping cantilever crane slowly wraps upward, the beam swinging slightly in the wind that gusts off icy Lake Erie. On days like this, metal cold and taut and stressed by the wind, he worries about joining his brother, who a year earlier in 1917 fell to his death—or, as ironworkers describe such accidents, "took the dive." One part of him fears and a different part of him reasons that it can't happen twice to the same family.

He puffs on the stub of a cigarette hanging from his lips and gazes out over squat Buffalo and shivers in the moist wind. Sometimes he wishes he'd become a blacksmith like the old man, but the old man said it was a dying trade and anyhow it was wrong for a father to expect a son to follow in his footsteps. My great-uncle must have heard the story a dozen times, while he was a kid, about the Phillipses who were horse traders in Wales and Ireland and about the hard feelings that never ceased after the old man ran away from the Irish farm. A man's first obligation, the old man always said, is to his wife and kids, not to the past. "And wouldn't you know it," as my great-uncle liked to tell the tale, "after fleeing halfway around the globe to escape a life with horses, in 1911 my old man got killed with a broken neck when a 'horseless carriage' backfired on Delaware Avenue and the horse he was riding reared up."

When the beam is eight stories in the air, wind rushes through the open steel skeleton with sounds like random organ notes blasting crazily. At nine stories he notices that his view of the city has changed direction and realizes that the cable is gradually twisting, and he crouches and curses that part of himself that made him choose to ride the beam rather than the elevator cage. And the slowly lifting beam has nearly reached the 11th and top story, where three of his buddies await, yelling down to him words that he can't make out in the wind, when he hears a sharp bang and knows no automobile nor the crane engine has backfired, understands, even in the split second before he is in mid-air, that the cable has snapped.

* * *

So by weekdays I was a mild-mannered househusband and by evenings and weekends I said "bye-bye" to Hope and held down a real man's job. My duty was to make fellow men out of boys, but the problem was that they had already lost their childhoods in environments that even Dickens and Hogarth would have had difficulty imagining. They'd learned to follow the rules of street gangs and the mores of the drug culture; considered women to be sexual objects at best; believed that through manly bravado and cunning they one day, like the neighborhood pimp or drug pusher, would own a Lincoln Continental. In the meantime stealing cars would do, and they considered their incarcerations mere detours. The state's solution was to "correct" them, 60 at a time in an old, mountainside YCC camp. Each lived and slept in one of four open rooms consisting of bunks and lockers, was expected to raise his hand to receive permission before speaking, found his days planned right down to bathroom calls, and was never away from either his peers or direct adult supervision. Much of my time was spent correcting boys who were marching in lines of 15 to the drinking fountain, bathroom, showers, gym, gameroom or school; no talking or humming, faces straight ahead, hands at sides and exactly two floor tiles between each marcher. I lasted in my dual existence, as nurturer of infant and drill sergeant of teenagers, for about two months.

One evening a boy angrily threatened to run away; with the knowledge of a shift supervisor, a worker pushed the boy outside and ordered him to leave. For 20 minutes the 13-year-old, clad only in underpants, stood weeping, terrified of bears and coyotes, until, presumably transformed into a man, he was permitted to come in out of the freezing fall night.

Several days later I was instructed to supervise a group of boys who had been assigned to write 20 times a series of statements that stressed the importance of respecting the feelings of others. One of the boys, who was medicated, seemed unable to concentrate on the task; a shift supervisor directed me to place a pen in the youth's hand, grip his hand and force him to write. I pointed out that the boy had a fractured arm and was wearing a wrist splint above his writing hand, adding that I believed physically forcing a resident to participate in an activity was illegal. "Don't worry," I was told, "you can't get in trouble as long as I tell you to do it. Your responsibility is to do what your supervisors tell you." I explained that following orders excuses neither lawbreaking nor unconscionable actions. As I spoke I suspected that I would eventually decide to become, once again, a fulltime househusband, but I had no idea that within days I would first become a hypocrite.

Fifteen boys were in the bathroom at the assigned time when one pushed another, then did it again despite my reproof. I grabbed his arm and moved him away from the boy he was bullying and he said, "Man, you're messin' up my dry cleanin' job." A tall boy, for the next hour in the living area he antagonized smaller, younger boys and mocked my interventions. Then I had him by his shirt, thrust him into a chair, stuck my face to within inches of his and profanely berated him at the top of my lungs. A different part of me, the part that loves my daughter, saw with pity that his body was shaking.

When I stopped, the other boys were motionless and silent until one raised his hand and asked, "Mr. Mark, do you like kids?" I almost spoke aloud to myself, *If I like kids, why am I working in a place like this? If I like kids, why isn't staying home with Hope enough?*

* * *

My great-grandfather, his eyes blackened and lips scabbed and swollen, watches from a steamer deck as Ireland fades beyond the sea and knows this was his last return to Drumbo. His heritage was boomed into him by his father and grandfather, and sometimes while swinging his black-smith's hammer he imagines he hears their voices. As far back as can be traced, the Phillipses bred and traded horses in Wales and then Ire-land, and the Drumbo farm was to become his older brother's but the brother ran away from home. Then the farm was to become his, my grandfather's, but he also fled, to a blacksmith's job at the Belfast ship-yard and then to Canada and then the United States. Yet wherever he fled he imagined he heard the voices beseeching him to return to the farm and breed horses as did his father and grandfather and great-grandfather, and as did the Welch "Philipps" family, as they spelled it, whose very name meant "lover of horses." And when my great-grand-father's father was close to death in 1910, his 85th year, feeling aban-doned by his five sons scattered around Ireland and the globe and none of them horse traders, who could blame him for deciding to bequeath the farm to the son of his daughter Sarah, a lad named William Davis, who lived with him and each spring, behind the two strongest of the work horses, plowed the fields?

My great-grandfather and his brothers blamed him; they challenged the will in court after their father's death, and lost. And then naturally, as Drumbo villager David Titterington would recall it in a 1967 letter to a descendant of my great-grandfather, the Phillipses and Davises "all came to Brown's Public House and had a free for all—I mean a good fight to the finish, women and all." So now my great-grandfather, gaz-ing out to sea and certain that he would live out the remainder of his life without again seeing his native country, wonders, Why would a man brawl with his own family over possession of something that he'd run away from to begin with? Why on earth did it matter to me? And he decides that the voices, which he loves and hates, made him a bit crazy.

* * *

Several fall evenings after I resigned from my job and tore up my resumes, Hope was standing in the dimness of our unlit kitchen near the picture window, pointing upward and exclaiming, "Bakah! Bakah! Bakah!" I walked out of our living room where I'd been reading a book and into the kitchen where I saw what she'd named "bakah"—a sky full of moon and stars. Margaret and I put a coat, hat, mittens and sneakers on Hope, and I carried her outside.

In the middle of our frosted lawn, Hope standing and I kneeling, our heads back, we gazed into the brightly silent sky.

THE ENDURING BONDS
Patricia O'Brien

M Y 12-YEAR-OLD nephew was hunched over the dining room table for hours one evening with his pens and crayons, struggling with a class assignment to draw a family tree. Finally, in frustration, he brought the paper to my sister in the kitchen.

"Mary," he said, showing her the chart filled with names, "I can't fit everybody on one piece of paper."

He indeed had a complicated chart to draw. His father has had three wives and five children. His mother has had two husbands, and now has several stepchildren in addition to her own. An aunt has been married twice. . . .

In other words, my nephew is a child of modern divorce, with all its new forms of extended family. It would be impossible for him not to feel connected with all of these people. This type of family exists all around us now and I no longer find it strange, because it involves people I love and respect.

But it can be a curious hybrid.

At Christmastime I see ex-spouses meeting under a single tree with new spouses, assorted children, new and old grandparents, and I sometimes have problems with it because it seems too civilized. I know it becomes part of healing for people to be polite and distantly pleasant when, perhaps, three years ago they wept and screamed at each other. I can accept that, but I don't think it is enough.

My sister and I can laugh over the story of my nephew drawing his family tree because he has come through it all with love and humor and is not cut off from his feelings. But there may be a price to pay somewhere down the line for many children of divorce.

Will they become so emotionally careful as they live with succeeding groups of "family" that they cannot commit themselves to
relationships with people they love? Will they develop easy smiles
and affectionate hugs but never really reach out and touch? Are they
adjusted, or are they simply survivors who don't cry on Christmas
Day when Daddy stops by at Mother's new high-rise apartment that
she shares with Jerry and his kids?

I don't know the answers. But I know that part of my instinctive
reaction to these concerns is to acknowledge and respect the continuities that do exist after divorce, if they are not denied. When a
man and a woman have children, they never fully separate—not if
they both continue to share the lives of those children.

Yet sometimes the emotional structure of these continuities sur-
prises us. I first realized that the night my eldest daughter, Mari-
anna, graduated from high school.

We were all there—her father, her mother, her sisters, and we all
shared the pride of watching this firstborn receive her diploma and
deliver a speech to her class.

Afterward my former husband and I took her to a class party,
she, all flushed in a white dress and giddy from the sense of victorious passage; we, feeling a sense of vicarious achievement ourselves.

We dropped her off and drove away in silence. "You know," I said
at a stoplight, "maybe we did a lot of things wrong, but we did
something right. We had that child."

He said nothing, just pulled on the car brake, turned, gathered
me into his arms and hugged me. I hugged him back.

It was our first realization that a bond existed that would never
be broken, one that had nothing to do with support payments, old
grievances or new life styles. No one else could share it with either
of us, because that child in her white graduation dress was the result
of our union, and it would never be any other way.

I remember the light turning to green and yet still we held on,
and I realized we would do this again in the years ahead. It was, for
us, the most natural response in the world to something we both
know is a hidden, unspoken comfort: If anything happens to our
children, good or bad, each of us is the only person who will share
the same joy or cry the same tears.

I know this isn't everyone's experience. Divorce is supposed to be the legal and emotional severance of all connecting bonds between a man and a woman. Emotional health is supposed to mean not looking back.

There is almost a mandate in our society to move on, keep up speed, forge ahead. We pick up our divorce decrees, sell our houses, move to new towns, meet new people—and then, somewhere along the way if everything works out "right," we reach that polite time when it becomes all right to invite one's ex-spouse over on Christmas for a holiday drink.

I think we take a great risk if we trust in our civilized adjustments to divorce too completely, both in terms of our own lives and those of our children.

Once, after visiting a friend of mine who was dying of cancer, I had dinner with my former husband to discuss a revision of our support agreement. I was prepared for a brisk, businesslike session, but I found I couldn't get my friend's face out of my mind. I felt cold and sad, and I couldn't stop wondering if there would be anyone around to help me when I was dying. Finally he and I put our lists and papers aside and began talking, cautiously. We each prided ourself on having learned to live without emotional dependency on the other. But this was different.

I don't remember who said what we were both thinking, first: "If you are ever alone and sick or dying, I promise you something. I promise I'll do what I can to take care of you."

For me, that was another affirmation of the unbreakable part of a bond that divorce, curiously, has not affected. It meant that we could still offer a gift of self to each other—in a different way than before, true, but it was real and we could trust in its reality.

When it comes to the children of divorce, none of the civilized patterns of response adults rely on are enough.

I know this is true, because children don't forget everything we would like them to forget. They may greet new people into their lives with poise and charm, but their hearts are not civilized enough to adjust too quickly—and the timetable for healing is locked inside each child.

I think the members of my family have been lucky to feel secure enough to exhibit their feelings, even though at times we were all groping with strange and frightening experiences.

But I don't believe for a minute that my third daughter wasn't hurt when the mother of a school friend saw fit to deplore the Neighborhood Divorcee—me—at a coffee klatch one afternoon, never bothering to lower her voice for the sake of the child in the next room.

Nor do I pretend to myself that my youngest didn't feel awkward when she could only have one parent at her fourth grade open house.

And least of all do I allow myself to believe that they easily reconciled their loyalties to two people they loved, but who no longer loved each other. I know they have been torn at holidays, and one daughter put it well: "Mother," she said, "when I spend the time with you, I feel guilty because Daddy is alone. And when I am with him, I feel guilty about you. Then I just get mad."

I understand, and I'm glad she told me. I have a friend whose son has not mentioned her divorce in four years, not once an expression of anger or a reflective comment or a question. She has problems ahead with that child, problems I am grateful are not mine.

I am in no way arguing that we should work to keep emotional wounds open, nor insist on our children sharing every pain they experience, but I know that it is wrong to work too hard at erasing the past.

Sometimes now my children and I put our feet up in the living room and laugh and joke about good times from years ago. Once we were remembering a wonderful golden afternoon when we all rented a powerboat on Lake Superior and set out to teach ourselves how to water ski. We spent hours out on the water, and each time one of us managed to get up and stay up, the rest of the family would cheer and yell and applaud. By sunset, we had all managed at least one wobbly trip around the lake. It had been a lovely family day.

"Does it bother you, Mother, to hear us talk about it?" one of my daughters suddenly asked in the midst of the reminiscences. "Not at all," I replied. And I meant it.

Yet I know many people would not feel comfortable with that

kind of conversation, perhaps because they can't allow such a day to be remembered as a positive experience without fearing they or their children would be hurt once again by the extent of the loss.

I am well aware that life moves on; everything changes. Once I lived in a big, rambling house with a husband and four small children, and now I live in a small townhouse with one child who is still in high school. Ten years ago I could not have dreamed where my life would take me after divorce, nor could I have had the slightest idea how differently my children would grow than I had anticipated back in the '50s, when marriage was forever.

Divorce is a profound human experience. It changes lives and reshapes them, and yet somehow many of us do much more than survive. We move on and build satisfying lives, learning from our mistakes, and that is the way it should be.

But I want to save the past. Its nourishments are rich and myriad.

One recent Saturday afternoon when she and I had nothing much to do, my 20-year-old daughter asked to try on my wedding gown. I was pleased. I pulled out that long-ago treasured garment of yellowed satin, buttoned her up, and watched her twirl in front of the mirror, tossing her beautiful long hair in the most basic female way.

"Oh, Mother," she said quietly. "I love it, and I want to wear it when I marry. What happy memories it must have for you."

How glad I am that she knows.

THE DEFIANT ONE
Barrie Maguire

Such memories I have of him.

When he was 9 years old we would go to the Flyers games and try to make each other step on the cracks in the sidewalk outside the Spectrum; then after we'd climbed all the way up to our seats in the highest row we'd argue over whose turn it was to go back down and get the pizza and Coke. I remember the time the Canadiens scored a shorthanded goal that put a crucial game out of reach and he was so mad he punched me in the stomach. And how we'd laugh at the guy with the neck veins down at the end of the row who kept screaming, "You turkey!" at the refs. And driving home together that delirious afternoon when the Flyers won the Stanley Cup.

I remember his first hockey practice at the Radnor Rink. He fell down a hundred times, and afterwards he looked up at me and said, "I *liked* it!" And the time six years later, during his little brother's father/son game, when he had been pressed into action on the father's team and he threaded that amazing pass to me as I stood poised in the slot on bent ankles—I swung at the puck, missed and fell down while everybody laughed. And I remember the feeling I got during his Bantam seasons when the other fathers would say, "If only all the kids hustled like Maguire."

And I remember that amazing moment the night I gave a music party and it was after midnight and I was playing "You Gotta Move" on the steel guitar; from out of the darkness came a high, clear, haunting blues riff that gave everyone in the room goosebumps. I looked up and there he was, sitting on the stairs, playing my other guitar. He was 14.

* * *

Whether it was just the normal urges of adolescence, or a long-delayed reaction to his parents' divorce, or some combustible combination of both, he changed. In his sophomore year his grades began to fall, and when we talked about it he got defensive and blamed his teachers, using language that shocked me. Whenever I offered to help with his homework or pressed him to get it done early, he'd blow his top, insist he didn't have any, and accuse me of never believing him. I'd wake up at 2 in the morning and hear him playing the guitar in his room; then the next morning I'd see his bookbag lying undisturbed in the front hall were he'd dropped it the previous afternoon.

To argue with him was frustrating. He was quick to anger. "Barrie," I would plead, "why won't you *ever* admit you're wrong? Why can't you just *once* say you're sorry?"

By early in his junior year it was taking me several attempts each morning to get him up for school. And whenever, in exasperation, I decided to make *him* responsible for getting himself up, he would miss the bus. Then I'd have to drive him to school and we'd argue in the car. By the time I finally arrived late at work my voice would be hoarse from yelling.

Even as our relationship darkened, the hockey rink somehow remained a sanctuary for both of us. Here we still shared an unbroken string of happy memories, the years of frigid pre-dawn practices and post-game Cokes and those priceless moments when, after a good defensive play or a goal, he would look up into the stands and make eye contact with me—in that instant a lifetime of love and understanding would pass between us, me grinning with my fist raised high, and he gliding slowly back to the bench, giving me an almost imperceptible nod of his head.

But by bedtime we'd be fighting again.

I tried being sympathetic, I tried placating him, I tried trusting him. I tried ignoring him, screaming at him, forgiving him, grounding him. I told him I worried about him, I told him I loved him. None of it worked.

I took a week-long business trip and left the kids alone, and during a Thursday-night phone call his older sister let slip that Barrie hadn't gone to school all week. I was furious, but he was not there to confront; when I called back the next morning, after the start of school, there was no answer.

That evening I rushed home from the airport with 24 hours of pent-up anger and frustration boiling inside. I went straight to his basement room. He was sitting in that mess of a room playing the guitar, and he smiled when he saw me. "Hey, Dad. How was your trip?"

"You didn't go to school this week!" I yelled. "Yes I did." "The hell you did!" "Who said I didn't?" I shoved him in the shoulder. "It's none of your goddam business who told me. You didn't go to school!"

I couldn't strike him but, oh God! I wanted to. I bore into him, provoking him, yelling at him, and he yelled back. I shoved at him and he gave ground, pushing my hands away, shouting, "Stop it, dammit, get your hands off me!" "Don't curse at me; I'll push you if I want to, goddammit!" "Stop shoving me!"

Then, from out of the tangle of our arms, he threw a punch at me. It hit me flush on my jaw. I thought, I can't let him get away with that. I took a wild, left-handed swing and he turned into it. I'll never forget the softness of his mouth on my fist.

His eyes went wide in amazement. His mouth and chin were covered with blood: his braces! He saw the horror in my face and put his hand to his mouth and looked down at it and saw he was bleeding. "I hate you!" he screamed, and bolted up the stairs. I yelled, "Barrie, come back here!" but he was already out the door. I staggered up the stairs in time to see him back my car down the driveway and, tires squealing, roar away down the street.

He went straight to his mother's house, thank God. But when she called, I told her in shame and bitterness and self-disgust, "I can't handle him. I don't want him living here anymore."

"I feel so awful for both of you," she said. "I told him I want him to live here with me. But he said no, he wants to live with you."

* * *

Barrie returned under terms better suited to a prison than a home. A tense truce had been declared, on my terms—terms as one-sided, as emotionally humiliating, as any victor ever imposed on a defeated foe. I treated him with distrust, cold anger lurking below the surface; I watched him for any sign of relapse and studied his face for hints of insubordination.

One morning during the second week he overslept. I lay awake, aware he was not up but damned if I was going to rouse him. The school bus roared past the house . . . *gotcha!* I leaped out of bed in a rage. As I stormed into his room Barrie was frantically pulling his clothes on. "You missed the bus again!"

His face contorted with disappointment, he said, "I know I did. I'm sorry."

I screamed, "What the hell good is it to say you're sorry?" But he would not fight. "I know," he repeated softly, "I'm sorry."

I drove him to school, frustrated that he wouldn't argue back.

It went that way for several weeks. Whenever I jumped on him for homework or making a mess in the kitchen or ignoring some household task, his arms would tense at first, his face would flush, but he'd deliberately calm himself and reply, "You're right," or "I will" or "I'm sorry."

The atmosphere in the house grew more tolerable as Barrie continued to return my aggression with passivity, my criticism with apologies. But still I couldn't—or wouldn't—let my guard down.

One night at the end of the hockey season Barrie's team lost a game, a tough one that eliminated them from the post-season play-offs. He had played well but had spent most of the third period on the bench as the coach kept only his very best players on the ice. When the game was out of reach, Barrie got on for two shifts near the end, digging hard right to the final whistle.

Twenty minutes after the game had ended, he emerged from the locker room. I watched him walk along the side of the rink, his equipment bag slung over one shoulder, two hockey sticks in his free hand. His face was flushed from the exertion of the game and his hair, wet with perspiration, still clung in curls to his forehead. When he came to where the parents waited, I went to him and put an arm around his shoulder and said, "Tough loss, Bar'. You had a great year. You made me proud."

He dropped his bag and sticks to the floor, and for the first time in a year he put his arms around me. I realized how tall he had become. Squeezing me tightly he said, "I love you, Dad." I put my arms around him and squeezed him back, and we both began to cry.

It was too late to salvage his junior year and it eventually took him an extra semester to graduate from high school, but graduate he did. After a year of work, he went on to music school in Los Angeles, 3,000 miles from home.

He's 24 now. I wish I could put him on videotape and show him to every father who's crying tonight over a "lost" teenage son.

Out in L.A., he delivers for a deli by day and plays his music by night. He's a member of a band that writes its own material, that's being "watched" by a record company, that's already performed at the Roxy. He's doing what he loves. Now his homework *is* playing the guitar.

I wish him luck. I send him my love and my respect. If he's lucky, before he's through thousands will have memories of him. Maybe even millions. But none of those memories will be better than mine.

THE ROAD TO MINDEN

Kerry Temple

I DIDN'T WANT to go; I never did. But my mother always said, "I don't think it's much fun for your father, either. But it's nicer to have his son along."

So on Sunday afternoons, about once a month, my dad and I would drive through the piney hills of north Louisiana to visit his mother, who lived alone in a little house near Dorcheat Bayou. She had raised four children in that house on that brambly acre of land, and now they had scattered to places like Houston and Denver. Her husband was long dead. My dad was the only one nearby.

If the trip was a burden to him, he never complained. But I'd let him know I wasn't happy by staring sulkily out the window. So we rode in silence, his large hands on the wheel, my legs dangling off the seat.

Sometimes, to break the monotony, I would sift through the official-looking papers in the glove compartment or punch the buttons on the radio we never played, asking what the numbers meant, spinning the dial. Mostly I stared out the window at the billboards and shacks and cotton fields flying past. The red clay earth. Raggedy frame houses with laundry on the line and chickens and loose-limbed dogs and trees—towering pines, dogwood and magnolia. There was a drive-in theatre on the way, and an army munitions plant but no bombs or cannons or tanks.

I watched the land and I watched my dad when he wasn't looking. It was years later, after I moved away, that I realized I can never think of my dad without recalling the scruffy Louisiana landscape, and I never see pictures of swampland or marshes or the lazy, rolling hills without thinking of him. In my mind, he and the land became inseparable. He grew up on it, he labored in its oil fields, then later, as an accountant for the natural gas company he worked for all his life, he drove all over the state till he knew almost every road and every good roadside diner. Sometimes he talked about my coming along with him. But I never did. Mostly I rode with him to Minden to see his mom.

I never knew what to say. It didn't occur to me to ask my dad what it felt like to watch your mother grow old and feeble. Like all children, I assumed she had always been old, that my father had always been an adult. I never asked about his boyhood in the country or what he had wanted to be when he grew up. My father didn't talk much either. Every now and then he would slap me on the thigh and say, "Howya doin', boy?" And I would say "fine" and look intently out the window—as if everything a boy could want was out there somewhere.

It was later, mostly through others, that I heard the stories: paralyzed from the waist down during the war in Burma, and the doctors saying he would never walk again; driving an ambulance in east Texas when a boiler exploded at a country school, the bodies, the burning; the time he accidentally killed his dog while shooting rabbits—he never hunted again. His father was a salesman, and one day when I was grown my father told me how his dad would strap a Singer sewing machine to each fender of his car and drive all over north Louisiana and not come home till they all were sold. Sometimes my dad got to ride along.

I think they were poor. The white frame house was small and shadowy—bare, empty, as if life had moved out. Dusty picture frames held faded photos of my dad and his brothers and little sister, and of Felix and Becky on their wedding day. They were country people; the ancestry could never be traced very far. The wallpaper was full of flowers; there were plastic bouquets here and there. There was no TV, nothing to do. She was not an especially warm or jovial grandmother, but a bony little person, hunched and wrinkled. Her long gray hair was pulled back into a bun and she used the furniture to steady herself when she moved from room to room. Mostly they sat in rocking chairs and talked in quiet tones, though occasionally my father had to repeat himself, speaking louder and more clearly.

As I recall those long and boring Sunday afternoons, I remember my dad being somehow different with her—a tone in his voice, a softness, something caring and attentive, filial, maybe vulnerable. She was the only person I ever heard call him Bev, a family name she had given him after she'd had too many sons. To anyone else, he answered only to Temp or B.K.

"Do you *need* anything?" he would ask, and she would ponder her response. Then she would tell him which neighbor had picked up some milk and which had been by the post office and which had paid some bills for her. "No," she would say in a voice that seemed to travel through dry reeds, "I can't think of anything." Sometimes she shared a letter from her daughter, Mary Bess; sometimes they just sat and rocked. There didn't seem to be a lot to say, and I would wonder why we had come.

So I moped around and looked at the calendars with pictures from far away. Or I would go outside and play imaginary football games or wander out behind the house where there were woods. When I was very little and the cousins were still around and she had chickens out back, we'd chase them. They'd squawk and run and we all would laugh. But there were no more chickens and the goats and sheep were all gone, and only a few good trees for climbing. So I would drag back inside and hope my dad would say, "Well, we better be goin'." But they'd be talking about her health and the medicine for her heart. She had cataracts and they got worse till she could hardly see. Then she had surgery, but they said only time would tell if it did any good. The years rolled from one to the next, and I remember thinking, "So this is how it ends."

In time I stopped waiting for my dad to get home from work. He no longer rode me around the house on his shoulders, and I stopped sitting in his closet playing with his shoes (lined up neatly like gunboats in a harbor) while he changed his clothes. I didn't go with him to Minden as much and, when I did, it wasn't the same sitting beside him. The car felt too small, and I didn't want to talk. And when I stared out the window, I no longer thought the land was pretty; I dreamed of all the places where those roads might lead.

I was 18 when his mother died. I was a reluctant pallbearer. I don't remember much of the service, except that there weren't many people there and the steel gray casket was lighter than I thought it would be. It rained like hell; the day was dark and cold. I rode in a hearse to the cemetery with the other pallbearers—all these men I didn't know—great-uncles and second-cousins, men with dark skin and narrow eyes and thick dark hair like my dad. They told stories about Uncle Millard and they laughed about Cousin Chris. As the little procession snaked out of Minden and up to the cemetery hill, they told me about my dad—the time he got snakebit and chopped an axe-hole in his knee and the time he carried a friend on his back for two miles when his friend had broken his leg.

The hearse got stuck in the mud in the cemetery, and we all got out to push. Black suits and white shirts, red carnations. Tires spinning like mad, whirling through the gumbo mud. Red clay splattering us, laughing, until the car swung free. Then the eight of us—all Temples—pushed two other black limousines through the bad spots so we could lay Grandma Becky in the ground. Then we stood in the rain, paying our last respects. I'm certain the whole world that day was gray and wet and cold. I don't remember if my father cried; I was thinking mostly of myself.

When I thought back to all these things later, I realized much of what was going on and how much of me came from people and places I hardly knew. But by then that road to Minden and beyond had carried me away.

My dad is a thousand miles away now and his grandsons are getting big. We get together once, maybe twice a year. I have a hard time knowing what to say. We talk some sports and about the little things. His eyes have gotten bad; he reads my rare letters with a magnifying glass. I think he's on medicine for his heart. He had cataract surgery not long ago; only time will tell how much good it will do. And as I sit beside him and fumble with all that's been left unsaid, I'm always afraid to ask, "Is there anything you need?"

POSSESSED

Walton R. Collins

A COUPLE OF YEARS ago my youngest daughter, then in her mid-20s, announced that she'd like to apologize.

"For what?" I asked.

"For having been a teenager," she said.

She explained that her husband's 16-year-old sister had just gone home after a week's visit. Apparently it was a very long week.

"It brought back all the things I did to you when I was that age," my daughter said. "And I'd like to apologize."

"Well," I grinned, "that's nice of you, but let me think about it."

In truth, this daughter's teen passage was not the smoothest of our three girls and two boys. What astonished us each time, though, was how nice these kids turned out to be once they came out the other side of adolescence.

A friend of mine who's the father of six boys says he's convinced something spooky happens to children as they approach puberty: "They become possessed by a dybbuk who takes over their bodies and suppresses their true personalities. For the next few years they're insufferable. Then, somewhere around 21, the dybbuk steals away and the kid wakes up one morning his old self, a little bemused by foggy memories of the intervening years."

My friend just may have something.

The dybbuk seems composed equally of raging hormones and a need to become a person independent of one's progenitors. In recent years I've had a number of friends tell me—sometimes out of the blue—that they'd never want to re-live their adolescence. There always seems to be more than a little denial in these remarks, as if the speakers were wincing at the memory of what they were like at 15 or 17 or 19.

Some wincing is understandable. At those ages they probably were self-centered, self-conscious, self-dissatisfied and vacillating between braggadocio and embarrassment. One of my sons went through a short stretch in his mid-teens when he refused to accompany the rest of the family to a pew toward the front of church at Sunday Mass; he'd duck into one of the back pews as we started up the aisle. Generally it's the better part of wisdom for a parent not to get too nosy about such behavior, but after a few weeks I asked him why he wasn't sitting with us. "If I walk all the way up front," he explained, "everybody'll be looking at me." Suddenly, just for a moment, I remembered.

Adolescents are prone to bouts of paranoia, and it undoubtedly has something to do with the fact that they're simultaneously fascinated and frightened by sex—and members of the opposite sex. As a result they experiment with different roles in their several circles of friends, and sometimes they feel there's no real "me."

On the home front, they want and need their parents' approval but take no small delight in outraging them, or at least looking down on them as hopelessly out of date. And even as they push the boundaries of their independence, some part of them craves limits and rules.

Small wonder that we wince at the thought of a return to that decade of life.

When it came to dealing with our children, my wife and I complemented each other pretty well. She preferred them small—the smaller the better. She'd get weak in the knees at the very sight of a drooling 1-week-old; come to think of it, she still does. By the onset of adolescence, however, children lost most of their allure for her. She suffered our teenagers as a duty, if not a penance.

I did my share of infant diapering and spoon-feeding and driving the small ones to swim lessons and ballet school, but I found the absence of intellectual engagement in those years dull. With each of our five, I waited not so patiently for the age of reason to dawn. I had a pun I'd trot out when the kids got to the age of 8 or 10.

"How do you get down off an elephant?" I'd ask. Pause. Then I'd deliver the punchline: "You don't; you get down off a duck." If the kid looked puzzled, I'd know her time hadn't yet come. If there was a flinch of pain at the pun, I knew it was the moment for engagement to move forward.

So the early years were my wife's territory, and I took the teen watch. In spite of all the barriers adolescents erect, at least there's intellect there, and sometimes you can get through to it. Our dinnertable conversations, once the chairs started to be occupied by teens, were often fun. Except on their worst days, they could be lured into bantering, they responded to wit, and it was possible to find interests and topics that bridged the parent-child gap, though we carefully avoided discussing music or the condition of their rooms.

Crucial to parental survival of a child's adolescence, I'm convinced, is a hardy sense of humor. If both sides have one, so much the better, but it's useful if the parent at least remembers once in a while that much of what transpires between parent and teenaged child is more the stuff of humor than of conflict.

Not that laughing is ever easy. But when one of my sons, sporting a fresh driver's license, banged up the family car twice in a matter of a few weeks by sliding off the same winter-slick curve near our house, it struck me as absurd enough to be funny. Fortunately, he didn't do it a third time, or my amusement might have given way to something grumpier.

Not all teen mishaps are benign, of course. The last of our children passed out of adolescence in the middle '80s, thereby missing the more vicious recent years of the drug era. I'm thankful for that. Peer pressures are such a major influence on youngsters that parents may find themselves helpless in dealing with a child who runs with a group that's into serious drug use—or other self-destructive behavior.

When the time came to deliver the first of our children to a distant college campus at the age of 18, I felt a mixture of pain and relief. We bought an old-fashioned steamer trunk at a garage sale and rented a U-Haul trailer to carry it 200 miles to the high-rise dorm where our daughter settled into a room on the fifth floor. The trunk weighed about 30 pounds empty, and the following spring we suggested that she leave it on campus for the summer. To my relief, we never saw it again.

What we saw, as the Thanksgiving holiday was followed by Christmas and spring break and sophomore year and our daughter's junior-year move into an off-campus apartment, was a maturation process all the more discernible because we viewed it in episodes rather than as an unbroken drama at close quarters.

Soon there were two children out of the house, then three, and eventually my wife and I appreciated the gag, "Life doesn't begin at 40; it begins when the last kid moves out and the dog dies." We had weathered the teen passage, and so had our offspring.

Despite the bad rap given those years, they have their moments of triumph and joy as well: the thrill of getting a driver's license, the excitement of going to a high school prom in a rented stretch limo, successes in extracurricular activities, election to the National Honor Society.

I happened upon one of my daughters one day in a hospital where I was visiting an ill friend. She was a Red Cross Candy Striper, and I hadn't realized that she was on duty. I spotted her coming toward me down a long, sterile hospital corridor, and even at a distance I could sense her desire to be of service and her quiet competence. I felt a flush of pride.

The thing about grown children that's most startling to a parent is a demonstration of competence. The parental role is so focused on teaching that it comes as almost a shock to see a child showing adult skills—mechanical, intellectual or interpersonal, and especially parental. The moment can be a culmination of the fundamental parental goal, which is to nudge the fledgling out of the nest fully equipped for flight and survival.

For my money, the best part of adolescence is its aftermath. With luck, the parent-child relationship can move at last out of the authoritarian mode and into one based on real friendship. I remember sending one of my daughters a note one January after she had returned to college for her final semester. "Even if you weren't in the family," I wrote, "you're someone I'd really like to know." She later confessed that she cried a little when she read it.

On the other hand, I'm not above feelings of revenge once in a while. My oldest son is now the father of three teenagers himself, two of whom are pushing to take driver's education, and I can't help feeling it serves him right. As for my youngest daughter's offer of apology, I'm still pondering whether or not to accept it.

MY BROTHER TOMMY

J. Martin Green

MARY WAS 23, penniless, homeless and seven months pregnant. She had just been kicked out of the apartment by her boyfriend, who told her he didn't want her around anymore. She was wearing a green maternity jumper and four-inch stiletto heels. She'd had no prenatal care or vitamins. She looked scrawny.

My wife, Peggy, a volunteer at the soup kitchen, was concerned. The heels—Mary's entire situation—might have given Peggy a clue, but she was scrambling to locate an obstetrician when she got the call.

It was Tommy on the phone. She recognized his cough. He was 45 years old, schizophrenic and—my brother. *Oh, God,* she thought. *What now?*

Tommy was distinguished by the cobra he'd had tattooed on his forehead when he was discharged from Rusk State Hospital after a nine-month involuntary commitment. The cobra covered Tommy's entire forehead. He said the artist was paid to depict a king cobra's head, fully spread out and poised to strike. Tommy didn't think the artist had quite gotten it. Peggy thought it looked like a bat caught in a spider's web.

When I asked Tommy why in God's name he had gotten a tattoo on his forehead, he told me, "So the next time someone tries to screw with my mind, it'll reach out and bite them." Sounded reasonable. It *did* tell anyone who could see that the man would not be deterred by social convention.

Before the snake, Tommy had gotten other tattoos. On his right arm was a small angel with a tilted halo, and on his left was a small red devil with a pitchfork. He also had two five-inch vertical lines tattooed on his back, one on each side of his backbone, about shoulder-blade height.

Tommy said those marks were openings for his angel wings to grow out of his back. I told him that was crazy. Tommy said it just verbalized what many people thought but were too chicken to say. I pointed out that tattoos were non-verbal.

Anyway, I said, if he wore a shirt, no one would see the tattoos on his back; and if someone did, they probably wouldn't know they were slits for angel wings. Unless Tommy told them. And the topic might not even come up. But you couldn't miss the snake on the forehead. It was there to bite you.

Tommy had a way of finding Peggy—or Pat, my younger brother—when he wanted something. Pat kept Tommy's money and distributed it as frugally as he could. The 90 miles between Beaumont, where Tommy lived, and Conroe, where Pat lived, provided some distance between Tommy and the drugs he wanted, rather vehemently at times.

Tommy used Dilaudid, a synthetic form of heroin, but insisted he could take it or leave it. One night when he was strung out, I talked him into voluntarily committing himself to the drug abuse unit at Beaumont Neurological Hospital. I came by the next morning to check on him and to bring him his comb, toothbrush, mouthwash and cigarettes. As I handed him his kit, I asked, "Do you need anything else?"

"I need a hit," he said.

I shot back, "I thought you told me you didn't need it."

Tommy took a long drag, looked me in the eyes, blinked very slowly and said, "I lied." We both laughed till we cried.

Tommy didn't have a job or much money. The money he had saved when younger he had given away to the church during a mental breakdown, and he hadn't asked for it back when he came out of it. He hadn't worked steadily since he'd burned his feet walking barefoot through chemical drilling mud near Port Bolivar. He had tried a little longshoreman work but thought it was too hard. And they wouldn't let him smoke when he wanted to. A little royalty income made him independently lower-middle-class—if he could get to Pat or Peggy.

"What do you need?" Peggy asked.

"I have a toothache. I need a dentist."

Tommy's driver's license had expired during his stay at Rusk State Hospital, and neither Pat nor I had helped him renew it, hoping to diminish our search area if he should bolt again. Prior trips to New Mexico and California to retrieve Tommy and his wrecked cars had made us eager to restrict his mobility. Once he'd given his car away in a bar in San Diego and been found later in the desert, naked and hallucinating.

Tommy's danger to himself was not always inadvertent. During one psychotic episode back at the old house when Mother and Daddy were alive, Tommy had rammed his Ranchero into the cars we had strategically parked behind his in an effort to block him in while we tried to convince him to go to the hospital. He had banged his way to freedom, crushing one taillight, his front right fender and a couple of azaleas. Later that night the police picked him up for ramming a car from behind while driving down the Galveston freeway. He explained to the cop that the car in front of him wouldn't get over and let him pass. He had also attempted suicide by cutting his throat with a safety razor. He hadn't done much harm, but every time he mentioned John the Baptist after that, I'd think about it.

* * *

So Tommy had a toothache. Peggy tried to put him off, but she knew Tommy's forethought was measured in nanoseconds and his patience in cigarettes.

"My teeth hurt."

"Stay put and I'll pick you up."

As Peggy headed for Tommy's apartment, she wondered if Mary would keep her doctor's appointment. The image of the young pregnant woman in stiletto heels wouldn't go away. Who would be so mean as to kick her out of her apartment? "Jerk!" she thought. He hadn't even let her pack. Women don't normally walk around in spiked heels when they're seven months pregnant. Gradually, the word formed in her mind: pimp. He was a pimp. Mary was a prostitute whose pimp had discarded her when she got pregnant and couldn't work. It fit.

After dropping Tommy off at the dentist's office, Peggy stopped for groceries before coming home, exhausted. As she began putting up the food, the phone rang.

"Can you come get me? I'm at the dentist's office."

"That was quick. I'll be right there."

Tommy got into the car holding his jaw.

"Does it hurt much?"

"Yeah."

"What was wrong?"

"Abscess."

"What did he do?"

"He started to drill. It hurt, so I left."

"You what?"

"I left," Tommy repeated with some detachment.

"You mean you didn't get the tooth fixed!"

"Well, it hurt," he explained.

"It hurt! I know it hurt!" she exclaimed. She began to spit out the words. "That's why we went there to begin with. Now it'll hurt worse and I'll have to do this again."

Tommy took a long slow drag on his cigarette and looked out the window. Peggy stayed furious all the way home, then called the dentist to explain and apologize. He said it was all right and didn't mention the tattoo. He just said, "So that's Marty's brother." Three days later Tommy called and she took him back to the dentist's.

* * *

Tommy's mental illness tended to disrupt family plans. Once, as my brother Pat and I stood in the ticket line at Hobby Airport to begin our long-awaited hunting trip to the Yucatan and Cozumel, we were paged. Pat hurried to the phone. It was Peggy.

"Tommy's been arrested. What do I do?"

"Is he hurt?" asked Pat.

"No," she replied. "He's been drinking, and may be getting sick."

"OK."

"Who should I call? Tommy's in the Beaumont jail."

"Don't call anyone."

"You don't understand. He's in jail."

"I do understand. He's locked up. He's safe. He'll be fed. He'll be dry. He'll be sober. And we'll know where he is."

"Oh," said Peggy, having gained a new perspective on jail.

When Tommy was psychotic, he would communicate—or block communication—with the world by using his own private code, composed of references to Catholic religious figures or devotions, card games and suits, and rock'n'roll songs, mostly Elvis and the Beatles. It was not really possible to stay with him in his free association, but you could gather some meaning from the symbols. Drunk, he would sing bits and pieces of songs:

When I find myself in times of trouble,
Mother Mary comes to me,
Speaking words of wisdom,
Let it be.

That song would inevitably lead Tommy to reflections about his relationship to our deceased mother, Mary Lou, as well as Our Blessed Mother. His merger of mothers named Mary was reinforced by the fact that Tommy really had been born on Christmas Day.

Attempts to talk him into getting medical help during the later stages of a flareup would be met with code responses.

"Tommy, you know you need help."

"You're playing clubs now. But I've got the queen of hearts."

"Tommy, you're talking code. Cut it out. Will you go with me to Beaumont Neurological before it gets any worse?"

"You've got the queen of diamonds, but the queen of hearts is your best bet. It's hard to be born. John the Baptist had a hard time being born. And the chicken didn't have a chance to get borned."

Sometimes Tommy would characterize himself as the two of clubs. "I tried for the ace of spades, but I'm only the two of clubs." He'd remember the time Vaughn, Daddy's foreman, killed a chicken for supper at the farm by twisting its head off. Tommy watched with astonishment and horror as the chicken ran around the corral, rhythmically gushing spurts of blood from the neck hole. Tommy talked about the chicken not doing anybody any harm and compared it to John the Baptist. Vaughn thought Tommy was crazy for carrying on like that about a chicken. That was the way he had always killed chickens.

About nine months before he got his forehead tattooed, Tommy was getting sick, but he refused to go along with a voluntary commitment for his usual four- to six-week stint. So with Dr. Rao's blessing and willingness to testify as an expert, Pat and I filed for involuntary confinement.

A jury trial was scheduled in Judge Buford's court. When the assistant district attorney in his opening statement referred to some of Tommy's bizarre driving activities and hallucinations, Tommy stood up and interrupted. He told Judge Buford that his lawyer was going to talk for him, not this other lawyer who was talking. Judge Buford looked over his glasses at the defense lawyer and spoke in his courtroom gravel voice: "Counsel, if you can't control your client, he'll be removed from the courtroom."

Tommy responded, "I just wanted y'all to know he's not my lawyer."

Since the jury could not see the angel-wing slits along Tommy's back, his breach of courtroom decorum gave them some indication that there might be a case.

On the stand, I testified about Tommy's history of mental illness. To show that Pat and I were not just two lawyers trying to control the estate of our eccentric brother, the assistant district attorney asked me if I loved my brother. We had not previously gone over that question and I was stopped cold. My heart and my eyes filled up. When I finally mumbled "Yes," Tommy stood up and said, "I love you too, Marty."

During Pat's testimony, the same dialogue occurred. Tommy added, for the jury's illumination, that Pat loved him more than I did because Pat had not turned his cheek when Tommy went to kiss him on the lips, but I had. And I remembered that I had indeed turned my head to receive Tommy's kiss. Sometimes Tommy would refer to this when angry at me: "You gave me a Judas kiss on the cheek. You wouldn't kiss me on the lips."

When Tommy took the stand, the jury heard him refer to himself as John the Baptist with his head on a plate, and to the Blessed Virgin Mary as his mother. He called her the queen of hearts, not the queen of diamonds. He then gave his name as Aloysius, his confirmation name. By the time he got to the chicken, the jury had broken the code.

The jury stayed out for five minutes, long enough for a cup of coffee. They found by a preponderance of evidence that Tommy was a danger to himself and to others. Judge Buford ordered him committed indefinitely to Rusk State Hospital. Pat and Tommy and I hugged each other and cried in the courtroom.

* * *

Indefinite commitment did not mean that Tommy could not get out of the hospital. He could leave on furlough, but there would be no need for a retrial if his family or his doctor felt it was time for him to go back in. He might still have been there, forehead clear and head full of lithium and Raleigh Filter Kings, if the doctors at Rusk had not tired of his disruptions and discharged him.

Anyway, as Christmas approached, Tommy called Peggy and said he needed some groceries. Rather than give him money, which tended to go for drugs, Peggy usually got groceries for him. As he listed his groceries, Tommy threw in a request for Pampers.

"Pampers?" Peggy was surprised.

Once before, Tommy had attempted to follow the Biblical injunction to be fruitful and multiply by attempting to get married. He had met a rather tough young woman at a country-western bar during one of his pre-tattoo breakdowns. Pat and I got it annulled, although the girl's mother had demanded $1,000 to sign the annulment papers for the unconsummated, drug-booze, one-night mis-deal. So Tommy never married, had no children, and had no need for Pampers.

"What for?" Peggy asked.

"For Mary and the baby."

"What?" Oh God. Christmas. The Nativity. His 46th birthday. He's going off again.

He repeated, "For Mary and the baby."

Peggy drove out to Tommy's house to see how bad he was. When she opened the door to his apartment, Tommy was sitting in his blue La-Z-Boy recliner, smoking. Near him on the couch sat Mary—of the stiletto heels—holding her baby, with a friend named Debbie alongside. There really was a baby. There really was a Mary. It was Christmas time and there they were. The Mary she had helped in October had found a place to light with Tommy.

Over to the side was his Christmas tree. Mary and Debbie had bought and decorated it with beautiful red ornaments. Tommy's smoke hovered in the air like acrid incense. Peggy paused long enough to hold the baby before she hurried to the store to get the Pampers. She decided to get them a turkey, dressing, some Christmas cookies and a birthday cake as well.

After Christmas, she called the welfare department. She was anxious that the baby get some postnatal care. The mother and friend did not appear to be up to a lot of healthy stuff. There were needles around, and Mary was getting Tommy drunk while Debbie was turning tricks in the other bedroom.

Tommy's last birthday was spent taking in Mother Mary and the baby, and being taken in by them. He died the following May in his apartment. Debbie and Mary moved on. Peggy and I were in San Antonio when he died. Pat arranged for the funeral at Holy Rosary Church in Houston, our old family parish. We had an open casket and Tommy's tattoo was clearly visible. We had Father Joubert's organist play "Let It Be." Back in Beaumont, Father Bertrand told Peggy that Tommy was God's way of taking care of the street people. I didn't notice any street people at the funeral in Houston. I guess they couldn't get over or didn't know about it.

We've hung the leftover Christmas ornaments on our Christmas tree every year since Tommy died. They're fragile and they've broken one by one. We only have one left now. I look at it at Christmas and think about Tommy and many of the events in this story.

Just three weeks ago, Pat told me about a song Tommy loved to sing, and how it was all there: the cards, the drugs, the loneliness and the hope. I went to my son Joe's record collection and put it on. *Desperado*. The Eagles. "Why don't you come to your senses?" It fit. I hadn't made the connection before, and I cried as I remembered him singing the phrases.

You better let somebody love you.
Let somebody love you.
You better let somebody love you
before it's too late.

*   *   *

So yesterday I showed this story to Peggy. She asked me what it was for. I told her that Sherry, our oldest daughter, had asked me to help her with a gift for our youngest, Mary Jennifer. Mary Jennifer had asked Sherry to be her sponsor for confirmation and had also asked, "Who is the Holy Spirit?" and "What is an experience of the Holy Spirit?" So Sherry asked a few people to write some responses, which she would put in a little binder to give Jennifer at her confirmation.

So I wrote this and Peggy sat down and read it. She said it was close, but that I hadn't really said what I wanted to say. Like the tattoo artist, I hadn't quite gotten it.

What I wanted to say was that Tommy's life was made loving and helpful by the Holy Spirit despite, and maybe even because of, his mental and physical illnesses, weaknesses and sins, and that God had used Tommy to love and care for the poor. He was as screwed up as those he suffered alongside of. Since Tommy was crazy, he could see things we could not see, do things we couldn't do, and go places we couldn't go. She said that because Tommy had taken in Mary and Debbie, he wasn't alone when he died. She said it was providential that we were in San Antonio when Tommy died. God protected me from finding my older brother's body two days after he had died, after Mary and Debbie had cleared out.

Peggy said we should have had the funeral in Beaumont at Saint Anne's where Tommy, tattoo in plain sight, would occasionally scare the hell out of Sister Collette or some half asleep parishioner by taking up the collection. If Tommy had been buried from Saint Anne's, the street people, the drug pushers and users, the whores and the pimps, could have shown up, and Father Bertrand could have led the just and the unjust in prayer together. Then we still could have gone to Houston and buried him near Mother and Daddy. And she said that not only did Jennifer need to hear the story of her uncle and godfather, but that his brothers and sisters needed to hear it too because we had been too distracted, too busy, too angry, too frightened, or just too weary to listen while Tommy was alive.

And when I came back to type in what Peggy said, I realized I had forgotten even to mention that Pat, kneeling and praying after communion, saw a vision of Tommy last year. He still had his cobra tattoo, the stigmata of his suffering, and he was smiling and peaceful. Mother and Daddy were standing off to one side.

No one said anything, but Pat was glad to see them. A communion vision, sent by the Holy Spirit, is a blessing. Let it be, on us and on our children.

BEHIND CLOSED DOORS
Carol Schaal

THE FIRST TIME she came to visit her children, I sneaked a long look at her. I wanted to see what a monster looked like. She sat on a chair in our living room, a tall, trim, brunette, attractively dressed in red. No matter how hard I looked, I could spot no sign of evil, no hint of wickedness in her pale face. That was the day I learned that monsters can come in perfectly ordinary human packages.

Throughout my teens, the lesson was repeated over and over. My parents cared for foster children, and I soon stopped being surprised by the shocking stories the children carried with them or by the harmless-looking parents who were sometimes allowed to visit them in our home.

The faces still come back. James, blinded in an incubator, had been shut away in a back room of his family's middle-class home. The literally starving toddler was discovered only after worried neighbors finally reported to welfare officials that they had not seen the family's younger son in many months. When he recovered from malnutrition, James turned out to be smart and curious, an absolute joy. Three years later his parents were allowed to take him back, and I decided through a haze of disbelief and grief that the legal system was not to be trusted.

The monster woman I'd studied so carefully was the mother of 5-year-old Stephanie and 6-month-old John. We called Steffie "chatterbox"; she talked constantly in a high-pitched, nervous voice, her mother's dark eyes flashing in her thin face. Once, while I washed and she dried the dishes, she told me about an argument between her mother and grandfather. They started throwing dishes at each other, Steffie said softly as she looked down at the plate in her hand, and she had to crawl behind the sofa to get out of the way. Steffie and John eventually returned home, too; I still wonder what became of our frail, dark-eyed chatterbox.

Many, many others came to us, accompanied by a social worker who often carried only a grocery sack, the sum total of the child's clothing and toys. Some came from hospitals, bearing the marks of their parents' abuse. A few would never be cured by love or affection or proper diet: The rows of black stitches in Pat's head were the visible sign of a brain that would never again function normally; the hearing aids in Doug's ears were mute evidence of several home "accidents."

Years later, as a newspaper police reporter, I covered my first murder. As the cold night darkened, the indisputable facts began piling up. A 15-year-old girl, good student, well-liked, had blown her mother's head off with her father's shotgun. Many months after that I stood in the lobby of the county jail, sneaking glances at a pale, thin, 15-year-old boy who was soon to admit that he'd killed his mother and father with a hatchet. In his face, I also could see no sign of the monster.

A cousin of mine, who works at a center for mentally retarded teens and adults, told me last Thanksgiving that the center was dropping some programs because of funding cuts. For some of these people, she said, the center was their only social outlet. Their parents were ashamed of their handicapped children and rarely took them out in public.

When people talk about The Family as though it's a sacred unit, these images run through my head like a shiver. A family can be a wonderful thing, but our national insistence on its right to privacy, its assumed perfection, is not so wonderful. Politicians shout down laws that might invade that privacy, courts award unsupervised visitation rights to incestuous fathers, neighbors ignore a child's constant bruises. What goes on in the house next door, the apartment upstairs or the trailer across the way, our nation seems to believe, is really none of our business. We forget that the holy walls of home may enclose a starving, sightless child.

The blind eye society turns to The Family's stresses, to its potential for viciousness, also results in social and economic policies that offer up occasional punishment but little prevention. We see no contradiction in leaders who tell us they want to Save The Family and then cut nutritional programs for poor pregnant women.

But The Family knows best. And the monster may lurk behind a perfectly normal face.

THE PRISON OF HER DAYS AND NIGHTS

Barbara Turpin

SHE DIDN'T SO much sit down in the chair as collapse into it, and when she removed her sunglasses, I was suddenly grateful for the inconspicuous booth I'd chosen in the corner, in the dark.

"There was a little . . . scene . . . at my house last night," she began cautiously. "Nothing really serious."

If it wasn't really serious, then why the panicky phone call and the invitation to dinner?

My eyes were drawn to the purple and blue discoloration above her left cheekbone, directly below the eye, which looked glassy and didn't quite focus on my face.

"What happened?"

She sighed, her face stony. "Tony got mad at Tommy," she said matter-of-factly, as if reporting on someone else's experience. "He hadn't done the dishes. Tony has a temper. And he likes things neat."

He slugged his son over dirty dishes? I was surprised, though I shouldn't have been.

I've known Alice for almost 25 years. We met in college. She dropped out in junior year to marry Tony. I never really liked him— he had a certain wired quality about him, like a tightly wound spring—but for years I pretended I did. I stopped pretending a few years ago at a party at their house, when he publicly reprimanded her for forgetting to put the vodka in his drink, and then for not stirring it. I can still hear the screaming silence in the room and see the eyes of the guests fall to their plates. I still feel her humiliation.

"Stir it yourself, creep," I wanted her to say—after she spat in it. But she didn't. She didn't even flinch. Like a robot, she stirred the drink.

Later, I asked her about what happened. She laughed it off: "He's Italian."

"So am I," I reminded her.

"Well then," she replied, "you ought to know what Italian men are like."

I did. I understood. But understanding why someone does something wrong doesn't make the act less wrong. I told her so.

Ever since, things had been cool between us; polite, but definitely cool. I had trodden where I wasn't wanted. So I couldn't figure out why she wanted to talk to me about this.

A waitress appeared and we ordered a couple of Cokes. "So Tony went after Tommy," I said. "But what happened to you?"

"I got in the way."

How hard should I push for details? At what point would she get defensive or, worse, clam up?

"Has this happened before?"

Her face lit up. "Tony's a great guy," she said animatedly. "He does some of the cooking, takes care of the yard and works very hard. Even on weekends."

Her animation dissolved as quickly as it had appeared. "It's just that he holds things inside for so long that after a while he just . . . explodes, like a volcano." She smiled. "It's funny," she went on. "He and Tommy are so much alike."

"Tommy's . . . explosive? At 15?"

She fidgeted: "He's had a good teacher." She knew this behavior is learned, is cyclical.

"If only I had an education like you," she said, her voice heavy with regret. "If only I had a good job." She fixed her gaze out the window, the way a man dying of thirst in the desert fixes his gaze on an oasis, not yet aware it's only a mirage. "I should have known better."

But how could she have known better? At what age had she learned her true destiny—that her life was not to be what she made

of it, as it would be for her brothers, but was determined by biology?
Was she 15, 10, even younger? Or maybe she was simply born knowing that if she was to be a woman, she would have to marry and
have children.

How long did it take her to realize the fundamental incompatibility of that imperative and her ambition to be a doctor, a lawyer
or a teacher? When did that ambition collapse under the weight of
the incompatibility? When did she draw the logical conclusion that
life would be much easier if she just settled for what her mother
had, and her mother before her? Protection. Who could blame her,
then, for asking herself what possible use an education would be to
her? If her fate was sealed at birth and she would always be taken
care of, why bother?

She couldn't blame herself for the unfortunate results of the dependency she imbibed with her mother's milk and the air she
breathed as a child. She could not have known that protection
doesn't come free of charge. Besides, would an education and
money really change anything? They wouldn't give her what she
needed right now—self-esteem. They wouldn't erase a lifetime of
brainwashing. How many women doctors tend to battered women,
how many women lawyers defend them when they kill, how many
women professors teach feminist texts—and then go home at night
to be flung about the room?

"This isn't about education or money, Alice," I told her. "It isn't
even about Tony." I reached across the table and took her hand in
mine. "Tell me about you. Tell me how you feel."

Tears flowed in a thin stream down her face and her chin fell to
her chest. "Awful," she said softly. "I feel like . . . like a slave."

Like the ones on the Southern plantations after the Civil War
maybe, who wouldn't, couldn't, leave their masters, who'd been en-
slaved for so long, grown so used to it that they didn't know what
to do with freedom when it was handed to them. They were scared
to death of it. Slavery was at least familiar; there's comfort in the
familiar.

"There are options," I said. She shook her head. "We're Catholic," she reminded me. "For us, there are no options."

I tried to imagine the prison of her days and nights, a moral quagmire in which there were no options, only the primal need to survive. I imagined her awakening each morning with one thought in her head: Avoid an explosion at all costs. I saw her furiously vacuuming the house, leaving no dishes in the sink, having his martini-with-vodka stirred and ready for him the moment he walked in, holding supper until he finished drinking, keeping the children quiet—all in an attempt to give him no excuse. Was there no indignity she wouldn't suffer to preserve this porcelain peace?

And her nights, what torments did they bring? Did she have nightmares in which her entire body was cast in stone, in which she couldn't move a muscle, could not even breathe, in which only her brain functioned, telling her she was about to die, her mouth open in a frozen silent scream?

Did she lie in bed, her stomach in knots, desperately trying to silence the small voice in the back of her head that told her something was very wrong? Was the voice silenced by those others, the voices of her mother or the Madonna or Jesus on the cross? Did she listen to them tell her what her proper role was, what she was supposed to do, and that she had to carry this burden with her to her grave because pain was the price she had to pay for eternal life?

"Have you spoken to a priest?" She nodded. "And?"

"He didn't tell me anything I didn't already know," she said, trembling as if on a tightrope. "That I was responsible for saving our marriage. It was my duty."

Sure. And afterwards, when it was all over and she would confront him, wanting to know why, he'd tell her the church never sanctions self-destructive relationships. And he'd actually believe that, because he wouldn't know that she and he grew up in two different churches.

The tightrope went slack and she sobbed, spitting out the words in fits and spasms. "If only Tommy weren't so ornery! If only he'd behave! If only I'd been a better mother, Tony wouldn't have to. . . ."

If only.

If only she were a better housekeeper, he wouldn't have to yell at her so much. If she were more sociable, he'd want to take her out more. If she didn't always say the wrong things, he wouldn't have to monitor her phone calls, read her mail or embarrass her in public.

He wouldn't have to drink so much, or call her names and swear at her. He might stay home at night or on the weekends. And when he was gone on business trips, she wouldn't have to pray to God to make his plane fall out of the sky, or to make him wrap himself around a telephone pole in his car, or think about how much worse she would feel, how'd she kill herself, if God answered her prayers. If only she weren't evil incarnate. If only . . . she were someone else.

If she was miserable, Alice knew, it was her fault. She deserved what she got. The question wasn't why she stayed but how she'd ever find a way to leave.

She collected herself. "All I want is to be happy," she sighed. "Why can't I be happy?"

It was meant as a rhetorical question, requiring no answer. But there was one.

I asked her, "Who is 'I'? Who is the 'I' who wants to be happy?"

Suddenly her face was an empty page.

"What are your limits?" I prodded. "What are your needs?"

She observed me quizzically. "I can't answer that," she replied. "I don't understand. Good people don't have limits. Or needs."

It wasn't Alice's voice that spoke. It was the Madonna's, the one that told her happiness was to be found outside herself, to be bestowed upon her by a man and children; if she wanted to be happy she had to be good, and goodness was self-sacrifice. I had to find Alice's voice again, before she woke up one morning, looked in the mirror and saw the fruits of her training—that the only good wife, the only good mother, was a dead one.

She was so far gone. How long would it be before she never spoke of the violence done to her, before she no longer saw the violations? It happened to six million Jews, after all, who were so numb to the violence that they could be led like lambs to the slaughter, praising God's name even as they entered the gas chambers; it happened to generations of blacks too, until Martin Luther King Jr. pried open their eyes.

How long would it be before the violence became as normal and predictable as the rising of the sun; before her marriage became a tiny pocket of evil, a black box impervious to light; before she became as blind as those fish found in pools of water in blackened caves, who grew so used to the darkness that they no longer needed eyes? How long before she ended up, like so many of her sisters before her, on a slab in the morgue?

I wanted to find Alice's voice. It was in her somewhere. She was there, talking to me. You can't talk about something you don't see, or give words to feelings you don't have. As long as she was seeing, feeling and talking, the voice was there.

"You can do this, you know. You can leave. There are places you can go, and people who can help you." She fought back the tears and struggled to find the words. "I can't. I just can't. I'll lose a lot if I walk out."

"Not nearly as much as if you don't."

She gazed out the window again. "He'll apologize."

And he'll send her flowers in the hospital. And he'll beg her forgiveness. And she'll remember how it used to be, and she'll forgive him.

"Maybe it won't happen again."

And maybe the sun won't rise in the morning.

I wanted to take her by the hand and lead her to a safe haven, but Alice still prayed to God for the strength to take it. She'd have to stop praying first; not easy for a woman trained from birth to look outside herself for salvation.

"I can't fail," she said. "I can't."

"Sometimes leaving isn't failure," I told her. "Sometimes it's success. It'll mean you've found in yourself what you looked for in Tony."

"Do you think so?" she asked wistfully, her voice lifting as if carried aloft like a bird on currents of air.

"Yeah, I do. It took a lot of courage for you to talk about this. I couldn't have done it. Tell me something. What made you want to talk, and to me of all people?"

She shrugged. "I don't know. Maybe because I felt like I was going crazy. Maybe because a little voice told me I needed a reality check. And maybe because I knew you wouldn't tell me what I wanted to hear."

I felt my face redden. "You know what I think?"

She shook her head. "No, what?"

"I think you'll be just fine. As long as you listen to that little voice—and keep talking."

She smiled, her eyes twinkling, reflecting the play of light off the living water of the oasis within her.

YOUR FATHER'S CURSE

Philip Milner

WINNING THESE WEEKLY games of racquetball gives me no particular pleasure, Daughter, and seeing you tie yourself in knots trying to beat me makes me wonder what either of us is trying to prove. Victory over your father will come, Daughter, and when it does, it will not be as sweet as you think it will be.

I want to tell you a story. It happened long ago in another country. The hero is 30 years old, and he has three children under the age of five and a wife at home taking care of them. There may never have been a more earnest father than the hero of my story.

My hero is a writer. He writes articles for the Chicago papers, rates vehicles for *Camper Coachman,* investigates trailer deals for *RV Retailer,* does annual reports for any school board with a thousand dollars to pay him. Editors don't always want his articles, and when they do want them, they don't pay what they are worth. So the writer drives a 1964 Chevrolet that roars when he starts it, smokes when it climbs a hill and keeps on running after he cuts the engine. He fills the tires with air every day; he is so poor he can only nod humbly when gas station attendants tell him he owes it to his family to buy new tires.

Four evenings a week, from 11 at night until 7 the next morning, the writer puts on a blue uniform and a hat with a badge above the bill and becomes a security guard. Sometimes he puts drunken students to bed. Sometimes he tells crowds of people to stand behind the rope. Sometimes people tell him to go to hell.

Most people think he is a security guard, but he tells himself and everyone else that he is a writer. And since the world doesn't let him get away with many pretensions at this time of his life, we won't take that one away from him just yet. We'll call him the Writer.

Let's give the Writer in our story some blue sky, a single billowing white cloud, a warm sunny day and a perfect magazine assignment. He will boat down the Yellow River on a gorgeous summer day, photograph the sights, catch a carp, sleep in a tent, and write about the experience for the two million readers of a Sunday newspaper. The Writer borrows his father's aluminum boat, and over the next two days he floats the boat 25 miles down the lazy river.

When he lands, his father backs his pickup up to the river bank. The Writer pulls the tailgate down and tries to lift the back end of the boat onto the pickup. He pulls and he puffs, but the boat falls, each time, onto the muddy bank. He cannot lift that aluminum boat onto the pickup to save his soul.

"God damn it, stand to hell back," the Writer's father shouts, using a special voice full of contempt that only his wife and children ever hear. The father steps into the water in his shined street shoes, grabs the handles on the back of the boat, and flings it onto the pickup.

"See if you can run the God-damned rope through the bow and throw it over to me," the father says. "See if you can do something right."

On the drive home, the Writer sulks. He keeps his thoughts to himself, but I will tell you what those thoughts were. The Writer cursed his father and wished him a thousand misfortunes. Not knowing the Writer had put a curse upon him, the father talked about the weather, about the Cubs' chances of winning the pennant, about a fellow he knew in Wabash.

The story jumps forward 15 years and moves to another country. You know some of the rest, Daughter. That nice old man you always tell me I should be nicer to, whose diabetic eyes light with love when you walk into the room, who tells you stories about me that make me sound like Einstein and Gretzky rolled into one; well, that old guy is the father in the pickup. That old man who tells you all those stories about his love for his son never said "I love you" to his son. Not once.

And the seething 30-year-old Writer who cursed his father with an adolescent's powerless passion? Well, some money and human kindness, 15 years of good luck and a job that gives him some respect have changed him, Daughter. He'd like to think they've changed him beyond recognition. But you know that man, too.

There are some morals to this story, Daughter. I know you'd rather be somewhere else, so stop twisting the handle of your duffel bag around your hand or you'll cut off your circulation. I'm almost finished.

The first moral is that curses do work. All the curses the Writer uttered against his father came true. The Writer's father pees with pain, can't turn his head without wincing, and it's all he can do to push himself out of his chair. Today, he couldn't lift that boat if his life depended on it.

The second moral is that beating your father is the work of the first third of your life. Once you beat him—and you will, Daughter—you won't lose to him again.

But here is the strangest moral. The Writer would lift his curse if he could. He would like nothing better than to see his father wade up a river with a fly rod in his hand again or drink six bottles of beer on a Sunday afternoon again.

In fact, the Writer would like to throw his arms around his father, tell his father he forgives him, and ask his father to forgive him a few things, too. But that is not how the Writer and his father work.

There's another moral here, Daughter; I'll say it and you can be on your way. The Writer loves you as he loves the air he breathes. And even though words are his bread and butter, he can't seem to say that to you any better than his father could say it to him.

The time is coming when you'll win that racquetball game and some other games, too. The Writer won't mind. He knows who he is, after all, and winning racquetball games is not where it's at for him.

But he's scared. He is afraid he will lose you the way his own father lost him.

MOTHER EARTH

Virginia Tranel

THIS MORNING'S MAIL brings an envelope from my son Dan, my eldest child. Warmed by the familiar handwriting, I tear it open to find a hurried note: "I know you have certain ideas regarding this, but the enclosed article calls attention to several issues of concern. . . . "

The title of the enclosure is *Environmentalists: Ban the (Population) Bomb*. A mix of anger and dismay grips me. Is this an indictment of my life, my work of 35 years? Or a fantasy of retroactive birth control?

I know that retroactivation of another type is on his mind. Last week he sent me an article about the focus of his research—synchronous multiregional retroactivation, the term his scientific team uses for their theory of how the human mind works. I teased him that it sounded like another name for family reunion. He snickered. He knows my pride in him, but he also knows that I sometimes fail to worship at the altar of science.

We have a little game: His mind stands guard like a cat under a tree while my words flutter, bird-like, among the branches. Sometimes an errant word swoops low. He bats. Other times they fly wide circles and tantalize his scientific grounding. He snatches. He makes menacing jumps toward wisps of thought. He pounces on wild generalizations, intuitive theories. He hungers for clarification. I quote books I've read, none of them with footnotes.

Ultimately we retreat in mutual respect—the cat to curl up on the grass, the bird to rest in the tree. But this morning he has caught a wing and I fall wounded. I can't fly from this reality: I am the mother of 10.

I pick up the article and begin to read: "Ask almost any environmentalist the underlying cause of the world's major environmental problems and the answer is likely to be—too many people." The coordinator for population affairs in the State Department declares that "overpopulation is not a stabilizing factor, whether it be political stability, developmental stability or environmental stability."

I feel compelled to justify my life, to explain my choices to my son, to rebut his Malthusian attack. I want to tell him about the idealism of my youth, about the challenge and value I sensed in my creative work. But I imagine his face taking on the skeptical look science has trained him to use. He tilts his head as if to turn his brain a certain way, arranging the critical input receivers for the best filtering of information.

I am trapped. I've done the deed. I fantasize about the cultural ideal—two "replacement" children. Which would I choose? Undoubtedly Dan claims first-born exemption from his own advice. Michael is the second child. Two sons. I visualize life without the third child, Elizabeth; the fourth, Ned. Surely two talented, healthy adults can't be classified as environmental problems.

Suppose my husband and I had spent our first five married years nurturing our relationship rather than children? Our children then would be Alane and Monica, in real life numbers five and six. Never could they complain of being the "neglected middle kids." What if there were no seventh child, Paul, who arrived in 1968, the same year as *The Population Bomb*? Undaunted by that book's gloomy outlook, Paul's response as a 2-year-old to "I love you" was, "I know." The world *needs* people who know in that uncalculated way.

I want to tell my scientist son I'm glad for Paul—for all my children—but I would sound calloused, unconcerned about ozone depletion and global warming. Is this the despair priests feel—their life's work considered not only obsolete but also dangerous?

Aha! Priests! I see him pounce: *The church told you what to think and do*. I can't deny the comforting shelter of the cultural cave where candles, flickering and dancing to the chant of litany, lulled me to listen without question. Smug with certitude and fortified by the optimistic consumerism of the '50s, I responded with enthusiasm to the biblical injunction, "Be fruitful and multiply." Even as the national birthrate declined, we kept having children. Far removed from the raucous unrest of the '60s, I spent days making bread, sewing, pushing strollers, reading Dr. Seuss, answering simpler questions:

"Why do caterpillars have sticky yellow stuff inside them?"

"Does God wear cowboy boots?"

"Why do I have to nap and she doesn't?"

Let others wrestle with questions about war and race and justice. Did the survivors of the '60s emerge with anything more than memories of smoking pot or awesome sex with someone whose name they've forgotten? I tell myself I'm not sorry I ignored that tumult.

But I don't want my son to view me as a mindless slave who bore children as a means to salvation. I wanted each one. Each revealed a fresh dimension of life. One day as we waited, motor idling, for a traffic light to turn to green, an elderly couple shuffled across the street in front of our car. Jennie, 4 years old then, studied them from her back-seat perch: "Who are they?" One of us replied, "Some old people." Her eyes grew somber. Finally she spoke: "Are we new people?" Yes, yes, new people. I liked looking at life through this clear lens.

These thoughts bring me up short. Was it instinct that prompted me to bear children? Carl Jung said the first half of life is a "state in which man is only a tool of instinctive nature." Children, he claimed, "are driven unconsciously in a direction that is intended to compensate for everything that was left unfulfilled in the lives of their parents." My dad was 52, my mother 42 when I was born; there was little chance to jump and shout and revel when I was young. Maybe childbearing was a remedy for the aging and death that hovered over my childhood.

Or perhaps I was trying to empower myself through a greedy use of the limited options available to women then. Or embodying society's ideal—and my church's theology—of woman as mother.

(Bishop Fulton Sheen in his book *Three to Get Married* described
the divine triangle—man, woman and God—and stirred my youthful hopes.)

Perhaps I was rebelling in a socially acceptable way against my
mother's overprotective tendencies. I moved far away and set up a
life of challenge, thus proving my independence—no need to be a
"flower child."

Was it *all* unconscious reaction? Was there no element of rational
choice? My husband and I did, after all, have a vision: a place where
it would be good to be a child. We found Montana, where land
rolled endlessly and teenagers could gallop full speed across prairie
seas. "There's nothing like it," Monica once said, "no words to describe the feeling of being out there on a horse."

Sensing that children needed real work and not just busy-work,
we built a life involving necessary chores—hay to stack, gardens to
weed, fences to paint. And we tried to nurture play. An enormous
sandbox occupied a shady corner in our yard. Children could bull-
doze roads with Tonka trucks, turn sand into hills and hills into
mountains. Each spring our children transformed another corner of
the yard into a rodeo arena, with ropes to define the chutes, old
brooms for horses and five-gallon cans for the barrel race. A 2-year-
old child who wandered onto that scene soon found herself plunked
into one of those cans to play clown, a strategy that simultaneously
involved her and kept her out of the way.

Coulees were distant lands where young explorers strayed, and
they sometimes provided lessons in biodiversity: Encounter a rattle-
snake and you faced a choice—killing the snake would mean more
mice in the barn.

This memory prompts another. I think of the afternoon I saw a
bull snake twist up the trunk of a pine tree, watched it wind around
branches and through stiff needles to its destination, a nest of baby
birds. Flinging its head into the nest, the snake grasped a newborn
bird and devoured it. Another thrust of head, another baby gone.
Bird by bird, the snake emptied the nest. The mother bird flew frantic circles overhead and cried out in beseeching chatter.

I am that bird. Today's cultural mindset winds like a snake
around my life, intruding upon my nest of certainty. Lately I hesi-

tate when people ask, "How many children do you have?" "Five daughters," I say and wait. They digest that response. Then I add, "Five sons, too."

Usually they ask if I am Catholic or Mormon. On their faces I read the same questions my son Dan raises. What I fear from the jaws of the cultural snake is judgment, negative judgment upon my choices.

I would like to be flippant, to toss back arguments: People don't just gobble natural resources, they *are* a natural resource. Must each child be measured against global warming? I would like to quote Princeton demographer Ansley Coale: "If you had asked someone in 1890 about today's population, he'd say, 'There's no way the United States can support two hundred and fifty million people. Where are they going to pasture all their horses?'"

At other times my best defense is arrogance. I propose a plan—designated parents—based on the reality that not everyone possesses the financial, psychological and physical resources needed for parenting. Those with the resources could have four, six, eight children, rather than the two recommended by the culture, while those without resources would remain childless.

This approach would be efficient and environmentally sound: cribs and high chairs recycled from child to child; groceries bought in volume (less packaging); clothing handed down instead of thrown away; less water wasted (no 20-minute teenage showers twice a day because a younger child would be beating on the door and screaming, "I have to go NOW"); more discernment between necessity and luxury.

Another benefit would be the preservation of the wisdom that siblings have to share. Older brothers and sisters relate in ways impossible to parents. I think of snippets of advice I've overheard in our home:

"Nobody asked me to dance at the freshman social, either. I thought the world would end. But it didn't. I lived. And look, I'm even married!"

"Don't worry too much about not having a best friend. Sometimes it's better to make lots of friends you like for different reasons."

"Your football coach wants you to lift weights all summer? Get big enough by fall to do some real damage? My coach wanted me to gain 20 pounds, too. Three months later my wrestling coach wanted me to lose 20. Finally I figured out who was getting hurt."

A selective-parent plan would also salvage seasoned parents, mothers and fathers taught by experience to detach their egos from their children. We discovered that even if a child wasn't potty-trained by 2, he would be eventually. We were embarrassed when our oldest son grew "Afro hair" at 16; last year his youngest brother, Ben, spent good money having a basketball shaved into the back of his head. "This too shall pass," we thought as we saw the basketball soar over the crowd on the head of our 6'4" son.

Last summer my husband taught Adrienne, our youngest child, to drive. At 13 she was too young to be licensed, but experience told him that by 14 she would no longer listen to fatherly advice.

Dan would sink a claw into my preposterous plan. *Mom, you sound like Hitler.* But how *do* we know when we're on the right track? We spend our energies on a dream and awaken to find it disdained. Today's attitudes ask me to squelch my hard-earned joy in my children, to see them as some giant oil spill or destructive path slashed through a rain forest, to see myself as the perpetrator of an ecological crime.

Yet Dan's concerns are real. For a multitude of reasons, human communities can self-destruct and often do. But when I observe Dan's compassion for our world and its welfare, I wonder: Did it germinate long ago as he leaned over to teach a younger brother how to tie shoelaces, boosted a little sister to his shoulders for a "high sky ride," or gathered a group of siblings for an afternoon of fixing fences? I imagine a trace of wistfulness in his eyes. His questions may not be about *my* life, after all, but about *his.*

Perhaps he wishes he could follow his dreams, as I did, without so much concern for the larger world. His letter may be a plea for understanding, his way of explaining why his choices are different from mine. Now I realize what we *both* clamor for: respect for the sincerity and context of our choices.

Each of us, standing alone at the edge of uncertainty, tries to balance beliefs and desires. Then, swallowing hard, we lunge, hoping our decisions will bring satisfaction. My desires pulled me to necessary places. They were, in a sense, *my* environmental truth, planted in me for a reason. If I had ignored them, I might have wandered through life lost. My children have challenged me to dig in and let go, to call them by name and know they aren't mine, to live life as process, sons never finished, daughters never solved.

Now, in this morning's mail, Dan has confronted me with another truth: the truth of change. For a moment I'm afraid. I want to hang onto my ideas, defend my choices. I want assurance that my life has earned the rational respect of the scientist. But I treasure far more this envelope full of questions and the irrational love of a son.

A NEST FOR ONE

Sonia Gernes

O N NEW YEAR'S DAY of 1992, a friend's home burned. The
house was a two-story brick structure with a view that is rare
in this town: an expanse of windows directly above the Saint Joseph
River. I had not been in the house for some years, but the Saturday
before it burned, my friend and I talked over coffee of the remodeling project that had occupied much of his attention in 1991 and
would (he thought!) do the same in '92—of the staircase that would
connect the living room to the deck above the river—of the new
bathroom with the latest in whirlpool tubs. "I figure this may be
the last bathroom I ever do," he said. "I want to get it right."

I learned of the fire the night of January 2nd, and on January
3rd, compelled by the need to offer help in some way—to run errands, make an emergency loan, produce a home-cooked meal—I
drove along the river to the little cul-de-sac that now looked tired
and tarnished in a January mist. How else do you connect with
someone whose phone lines are melted, I thought? How do you contact someone who no longer has a home?

The brick walls were still standing when I got there, as were the
white pillars of the porch. The windows all wore rough particle-
boards behind fringes of glass, and what I could see of the roof was
littered with little pockmarks of blackened debris. Ninety-five thou
sand dollars damage to a $110,000 house, the newspaper said, and
I believed it. But then I did a curious thing: I got out of my car,
stood staring at a facade that could not quite conceal its scorched
secrets despite all the boards denying entry, walked up the drive and
began rounding the garage on the left of the house. Two cars and

a pickup were parked on the premises, and I thought to call out my friend's name—to see if he or anyone who knew his whereabouts would answer—but I didn't. I couldn't. Halfway round the garage, I began to sense that the damage was much worse on the river side, and I stopped. Charred rafters protruded into the sky beyond the garage roof, scorched lumber spilled in various directions, and bits of debris mingled with leftover leaves on the lawn. On the riverbank, a sled with blackened runners lay like a turtle on its back. I stood in silence for a moment. I gazed out at the water—at a river that was bleak and unfrozen in this strangely mild winter—then I turned, walked back to my car and left.

It was a sensible action, and I knew it—at that point, I would only have been in the way—and when I got home I did something more sensible still: I sat down, wrote a note and mailed it to my friend's professional address. But common sense was not the reason I stopped on that lawn before I had a full view of the damage, and my leaving had very little to do with my friend. Despite curiosity, despite concern, what was twisting in my stomach as my eyes moved from those black rafters to that hapless tortoise of a sled was a recognition of my own need not only for shelter, but for privacy—a recognition that for me *home* is so intimately connected with *self* that to look on the rawness of that fire damage would be the equivalent of ripping back a bandage to stare at someone else's wound.

Has it always been like this? I wondered as I drove through the mist toward a hilltop cottage that has been "home" for me since the fall of 1989. *Have I always been so invested in the four walls that surround me?* It seemed unlikely. Since I left the home farm in Minnesota, I've had 14 different addresses (not counting summers or the three times I've lived abroad), and only once or twice did I leave them with regret. And when I left that farm, eager and callow at the age of 17, I had no idea of ever owning real estate. I was entering a convent; I was adopting Teresa of Avila's motto, *The world is thy ship and not thy home.* It seemed a good way to live at the time: In 14 years I sailed through 10 addresses with little more than one suitcase and a good-sized trunk.

But then something happened, as things happen in everyone's life. I turned 30; my health broke down; I left the convent after a wrenching interior struggle, and a year later the South Shore Railroad deposited me in South Bend, still with my black suitcase in hand, still with the same sturdy trunk. Now, however, the whole idea of housing was different. Loosed from the cocoon of communal life and feeling my aloneness, I needed a shell to protect me. I needed more than a mailbox and roof—I needed a home.

It would be easier to write about making a home without a family if I'd ever made a conscious choice to do so, but I didn't. When I left the convent, I assumed a marriage was somewhere around the bend. Like most of my single friends, I live alone because none of the other options seemed workable as they presented themselves, one by one, year by year, event by event. At some point I saw a pattern forming, however; at some point I *did* make a conscious choice: Between throwing my energies into finding a mate or pursuing all the other goals I wanted, I'd choose the latter. Between putting my life on hold in a singles' apartment or feathering a nest for one, I'd make myself a home.

I regret neither of those choices. Like John Huston, the great film director, my priority has turned out to be not romance or wealth or fame but "an interesting life." And happily enough, at some point in the process I found myself needing the quiet and solitude that living alone gives me, enjoying the freedom, liking the fact that things stay where I put them, that no one else's taste determines the color of a room.

My first home in South Bend was a high-ceilinged apartment in an old Victorian mansion that fulfilled my fantasies of living out the Mary Tyler Moore show. My fellow tenants fit the fantasy too—we were young, urbane, congenial. We thought we were droll. We had Halloween parties in the attic; we pooled our food during the Great Blizzard of '78; when Elvis died we dubbed the place "Presley Towers." All in all, we achieved a nearly perfect combination of private lives and companionship, but in the fourth year of this camaraderie, the mansion was sold to new owners. Within a month or two, we all received notice that our leases wouldn't be renewed.

I reacted with both sadness and rage. I sensed—correctly—that friendship depends partly on proximity, and that our lives would drift apart. (I was right—all the others eventually left South Bend.)

But I was full of fury too: The home I'd worked four years to make was being pulled out from under me, and there was nothing I could do. "You seemed so depressed then—so vulnerable," a friend told me later, and indeed I was. Counting my assets didn't help: I had a scant $3,500 in the bank and not a financial clue.

When all else fails, I tend to read—to lose myself in books that have nothing to do with the current crisis—and that's how I dealt with dispossession: novels, poems and a new book by Nancy Friday called *My Mother, My Self.* I remember hunkering down on the sofa while Friday explained how women internalize their mother's attitudes toward sexuality and men—attitudes which may have been appropriate for the mother's generation but not necessarily for the current one. It made sense, I thought, but my mind kept wandering to more acute problems: Where was I going to live? How could I keep this from happening again? My male (and usually married) colleagues had all bought houses from which no one could evict them, but men knew about money and mortgages and investments—I did not. My financial training was all from my mother: how to find bargains; how to scrimp and save and re-use and stretch.

Suddenly it hit me: My mother had handled money only on the consuming end because it was appropriate to her time and situation; financial planning was the *husband's* domain. However shrewd she might have been if given a chance (and I suspect plenty), she chose not to threaten the relationship, and chose rightly, I think. But I *wasn't* married; I was a generation later and about to lose my home. "That's it," I said, sitting up. "I'm calling a Realtor. I'm buying a home."

The house I bought was not a marvel, but the decision to buy it was. And implicit in that decision was a knowledge that for me *home* was now *place* as much as *people*. If I accepted that—and I saw no other choice—I was determined to make it a good place, to surround myself with as much of beauty as I could afford.

Even in 1979, $3,500 didn't go far, but with a $2,000 FHA down payment and new set of tools, I became a sudden homeowner, remodeler, restorer of wood. Old carpets disappeared, cheap paneling came down, calomine-lotion pink turned to creamy white, and missing woodwork went back up. After I'd spent a full summer in physical labor, a colleague said: "You've changed. You seem more secure somehow—more confident that you can deal with the world." He was right. I had a home now. I'd also gained a reputation I never bargained for: the petite professor who tackled plumbing; the poet who bought a crowbar and tore down a wall.

That house served me well for 10 years, but I was never quite content there. The street was busy; the traffic noise went on all night. The many rooms were small, confining, and the back yard as level and boring as the top of a cut-rate desk. Having grown up in hills along the northern Mississippi and gloried in Seattle's mountains during grad school, I found the move to Indiana a disappointment. I've never liked flat land; I never will. For almost 15 years I craved a view, a prospect, a sense of height. I wanted to live surrounded by nature but still within the city. I wanted a cozy cottage, but I also wanted spaciousness and light.

The house I found two years ago seems something of a miracle. It stands on the cusp of a hill above a little park. Neighboring treetops spread out below me and catch the autumn sunsets. Groundhogs sun in the front. In summer I can sit among the fireflies at the top of the 44 steps that lead down my hill. In the winter I can stand at the French doors and watch children sledding in the park, their bright snowsuits like flags of joy in the snow.

For me, home is now a sort of second skin, an expression of self, a canvas on which to paint and draw and decorate—to work out an exterior harmony in which inner harmony can grow. It's a buffer against those who would infringe too much, a place of regeneration from forces that suck me dry, a comfort for the odd moments when loneliness still catches in the throat. I'm well aware that it's a house to share—for such gifts are not given to us solely—and I've resolved to do so. A Chinese friend stayed for two months last year while she finished her dissertation; a grad school roommate is coming for a month's visit.

The problem with a home like this is that it tempts one to attachment, and that's a danger. It's one of the lessons I learned the day I left the fire site. I've made, sewn, refinished or lavished attention on almost all of my possessions, but I don't want them to own me. Should I too return home someday to char and ashes, I don't want to be missing too large a piece of the self.

I saw my friend the other night. He says his rebuilt house will be better than it was before the fire. He has blueprints to prove it: a new roofline, better use of space, fewer interior walls. He says the old adage is right: There's something good in everything. I make a note of that and add it to the other antidotes I keep against my own possessiveness, my tendency to hoard.

For some reason, I think about the old, sturdy trunk I took to the convent in 1960. It sits now in my basement next to the workbench, and I use its surface when I'm sawing or painting or clamping things with glue. In other words, I've kept it because it's useful, but I suspect that I keep it for symbolic reasons as well. Embedded as I am in my little house on the hill, I need to remind myself that it's not forever—with all those stairs, it's probably not even for the rest of my life. If I'm to negotiate whatever decades remain, "home" must be more than place, and "self" must be separate from furniture. The old trunk reminds me: The world is a ship; I must be ready to sail.

YOUR PLACE OR MINE?

Rebecca A. Code

A S A GRADUATE of Notre Dame's first class of women, I believed I could have it all: successful career, marriage and family. Most of my fellow graduates, male and female, felt the same. But a rigorous academic education did not prepare me for the harsh realities of a marriage in which both spouses actively pursued careers.

The choices we made resulted in numerous lengthy separations. We should have seen it coming, since we had established a commuter relationship even before we were married: When we were first dating, I was finishing my last year at Notre Dame and Jim, a Naval officer, was stationed about 3,000 miles away. After we were married, I was the one in the Navy and Jim was in graduate school in another city—we saw each other, on average, twice a week over a period of two and a half years.

When the Navy transferred me again, Jim stayed behind to finish graduate school. Our meetings dropped to two weekends a month. For 13 years we leapfrogged like that—living together only about half of our married life due to career-related separations. Thinking that we could maintain a marriage and an intimate relationship under such circumstances was pretty naive, yet we put ourselves in that situation over and over. Whenever a good career opportunity arose for either of us, we'd grab it and work out the living arrangements later. "We've done this before," we thought confidently; "we know what we're letting ourselves in for. We're pros at this."

In addition to the financial strain of trying to maintain separate households in two states (tax preparation season was particularly nerve-wracking), there were also the long-distance phone bills and the cost of airfare for our rendezvous. In one 18-month period, I clocked enough frequent-flyer miles to earn two round-trip plane tickets to Australia.

Those little "honeymoon hops," however, were far from relaxing or satisfying: physically, emotionally or sexually. I would barely arrive on a visit to my husband before I had to reverse gears, pack up and catch a flight back to loneliness.

Friends who chuckled, "Well, at least living apart saves on arguments," obviously never experienced a commuter marriage. No matter how many long-distance phone calls are made, more arguments develop than in the traditional marriage. "I thought that you were going to pay that bill from your checking account," one of us would say; or, "Why can't you fly to visit me this weekend? What's more important, your job or our being together?"

Uncertainty about what a spouse is feeling, thinking and doing from day to day easily drifts to extremes: becoming frantic because his scheduled phone call is overdue, imagining him seriously hurt in a car accident or even lying dead in a ditch somewhere. When I finally did reach him, my relief would often come out distorted by frustration: "Where the hell have you been? I've been worried sick about you!" Then I'd feel foolish when I realized he was supposed to call tomorrow night, not tonight.

Years of a schizophrenic lifestyle take a toll. Lack of companionship was not a major problem for me, since I worked with active and enjoyable people; parties, picnics and sports were plentiful. But the fun and laughter at a get-together were difficult to convey over long-distance wires. The excitement of watching the local football team win a close one was hard to relay. The brilliance of a shimmering summer sunset was dulled by trying to describe it later.

Things we had enjoyed doing together I was now doing solo, with no end in sight. Could we ever recover the lost time apart from each other? Would we regret being married 20, 30, 40 years and having few happy memories of times shared?

It would have been simple if I'd hated my job; it would be easy then to quit and follow Jim. But I truly enjoyed the research I was doing and the stimulating, challenging lab where I worked. So it was no big sacrifice to spend nights and weekends there, especially since no one was waiting at home.

Work became a means of filling a void, yet the more I focused on my work, the more I developed tunnel vision: I came to think that the sun rose and set on my research, on my project, on me. I tended to forget that I was not single, that there was someone out there who needed me and my support, someone who needed a surprise phone call or letter to show I was thinking of him.

Eventually my career became the most important thing in the world, so much so that when I learned Jim was to be transferred even farther away than a monthly visit could remedy—and that the time and money I'd have to invest in maintaining our commuter marriage were escalating again—I took it as a personal insult. Why couldn't he give up his career and come join me?

Since he was the major breadwinner and always will be (research does not pay that well), it was logical that he accept the new position, take the transfer and do what was necessary to advance his career. Unfortunately, he was being transferred to a rural area where I would have no opportunity to continue my research. If I went with him, I'd have to find a new line of work.

At previous crossroads, I did not have as much time and effort invested in my career as I had by now. I was established in my research field and had acquired a reputation as a hard-working scientist. I was viewed as an "up and comer." What my colleagues thought of me was important not only as a matter of self-esteem but also to ensure the future letters of recommendation I'd need to obtain fellowships and grants.

This was the pit I had dug for myself: If I decided to follow my husband, it would mean abandoning my research career and disappointing all my former mentors and their faith in me. Equally distressing, my decision would provide further evidence that women should not be supported in science, since they eventually follow their husbands, have babies and become housewives. My colleagues, all dedicated scientists, would not understand my "throwing it all away" to go live in the boonies with my husband. In fact, I was putting so much emphasis on what I believed my colleagues would think that I did not stop to consider what I really wanted.

The scientist in me tried to reach a logical decision: I would compile exhaustive lists of the pros and cons and debate them endlessly. Sleepless nights were punctuated by suffocating nightmares and drenching night-sweats. By day, any casual bystander might fall victim to my outpourings, since I hoped that by talking out my dilemma the clouds would part and I'd see the right choice.

Finally another woman scientist, sensing the psychological gymnastics I was undergoing, confronted me point-blank. "Who do you want at your deathbed?" she asked.

My interpretation of that question was, "Will all the accomplishments of a successful career amount to much if you die alone because you decided that your marriage was not as important to you?" It was the slap across the face I needed.

From that perspective, the choice was obvious: Jim and I had been separated for too many years already for the sake of our careers. Enough was enough; nothing would be gained by proving once again that we could survive separation. It was time to try something new: a marriage in which we actually lived together.

We moved to the rural area, and in less than a year my husband was transferred again, this time to a place where I could resume my research career. I know that I'm very fortunate: How many other people get a second chance?

I often wonder whether the fact that I'm building memories with my husband again isn't related to a more fundamental decision: to make my marriage a higher priority than my career and to have faith in God to take care of the rest.

PLUNGED INTO FLUX
Brooke Pacy

THE DEFINITION makers of the Oxford Universal Dictionary describe adolescence as "youth, the period between childhood and maturity," and bravely assign it a time frame, "from 14 to 25 in males, from 12 to 21 in females." Scholarship and life often diverge, however. An elderly friend of mine has a cushion in his living room on which someone has embroidered neatly, "The American male matures only when he has exhausted every other possibility." I, in my 50s, find myself thinking, "when I grow up . . . " (I actually *think* in terms of reaching a certain stage, but I *mean* "grow up"). There's no need to nitpick over a few years; it is the concept of "between" that lies at the heart of the adolescent experience, giving it both its misery and its radiance.

Enough has been written about the pain and the pimples occasioned by puberty. It's not only hormones that rage as the child stretches toward adulthood, but the whole person, muscles, mind and spirit, is plunged into flux. What's more, as everyone in contact with at least two adolescents knows, that flux is in no way orderly or predictable. With rare, smooth exceptions, adolescents are not in synch, not with each other, not with themselves. Bones forget one another and grow idiosyncratically. A wiry little boy will come through a door and be suddenly, alarmingly, all hands and feet. A girl whose passion is backyard football wakes up to find a new earth-mother figure obstructing her easy lateral.

The experimental encounters with adult life have the painful/funny raw quality caught by an occasional movie like *Flirting* or by insightful writers: J. D. Salinger's quintessential '50s Yale student waits on the station platform for a date to arrive, giving the impression he has five lighted cigarettes in each hand. Somewhere between yearning and spacing, abstract thinking kicks in—occasionally.

The whole experience is disorienting. One day, your trusty treehouse buddy has grown three inches and is muscled like Schwarzenegger, but he can't understand a word of the brilliant psychological theory you evolved the night before. You have been catapulted from a familiar world divided comfortably between adults, who stay up late, and children, whose sunlit days are bounded by bedtime as the fireflies come out, into a cloudy border zone without a guide.

In a story called "The Aquatic Uncle," about the early evolution of species, Italo Calvino evokes this adolescent vertigo. His not-quite-yet land creature squirms with malaise, caught between an embarrassing elder, the fish, and his new-age beloved, a young dinosaur, both definite beings, certain of themselves. They abandon him together, bored with his self-conscious evasions and intrigued by each other's differences. The main character recognizes them as superior in some way but prefers his own fluid, undetermined nature to theirs. He is a comic, awkward figure, unsure whether he is fish or lizard, but he has within him the magic potential of choice, and he is an adventure to himself.

Is that your 15-year-old? Most want a driver's license dated early enough to satisfy a bartender, but none would be his father or her mother—with good reason. Adolescents aren't saying any longer, "Don't trust anyone over 30," but they see that most of their adults have made sad bargains for definition.

Alice Munro writes in a recent *New Yorker* story, "Having children . . . gave you the necessary stake in being grownup, so that certain parts of you—old parts—could be altogether forgotten and abandoned." She suggests later that those parts are: "to be careless, dauntless, to create havoc—that is the lost hope of girls—" also of boys who take small children and mortgages on their shoulders. Who doesn't cheer when the stockbroker-parents-of-four sell their rooms full of furniture, abandon the firms, and hoist sail for a year to learn with their children what wind can do? All those disappointed, gray-minded grownups who have lost the elan of adolescence, that's who.

It is easy to forget that a personality unfurling itself can be glorious as well as inconvenient. No doubt Jesus was considered a pain by his elders, as was Gandhi. The young need to check out their wingspreads, and adults need to be adult enough to withstand the onslaught of beautiful hair, terrible noise and challenge to every sensible norm, remembering that these people are great fellow travelers as long as there is room for their 400 pounds of stereo equipment. They can tie knots that hold, muscle out the mired car, ski uncomplainingly in sleet and ask provocative questions. If they can't be counted on to see any connection between current behavior and future goals ("How can you blow off U.S. history and expect to get into Cornell?"), to make a plan or respect a schedule, no need to despair. A pizza will usually assemble them in one place at the same time to get a job done.

In dealing with the young, we have to remember that they too have lost something, and not just the keys to your car or their contact lenses. In adolescence, we—those lucky enough to have had a childhood—reenact the Fall of man. An innocence ends, a trusting harmony of spirit remembered later as light from the beckoning world, Wordsworth's "clouds of glory." The sense of having misplaced something golden, perfect, haunts the dreams of children on the verge.

One summer before junior high school, I dreamed the same story again and again. I dove from the steep bank of a colorless place into a brilliantly sunlit underwater world of blues and greens, and swam freely, ecstatically, along a path lined with round stones. As I swam toward a familiar house at the path's end, the light dimmed and I knew that I had to open up the shed behind the house, find and capture the golden spider hidden in the far corner. Before I could enter the shed, dark, nameless creatures spewed from the house and came for me. I fled, swimming in panic back down the path, feeling them close in. At the last possible moment, with wrenching grief but knowing no other way, I escaped into a large metal pipe like an upended storm drain. Next, I was sitting with anonymous others on a dark wooden bench in a school principal's office, where a severe-looking woman handed out purple envelopes to us. I woke each time shattered with longing, that shimmering underwater world gone and lost.

Lost and at sea in newly alien bodies, is it any wonder the young are often inconsistent, faddish and—in the face of adult righteousness—solidly united behind glazed eyes? They band together in groups as homogeneously dressed as lima beans, the length of their hair a wry comment on the spontaneity allowable in their homes or on parental norms of beauty. Without a clear inner directive on what they are supposed to do with their phenomenal energy, they generally wait to see what's happening and stay as noncommittal as possible—hence the popularity of "like" in their speech.

That invaluable expression, loathed by anyone over 28, answers a deep-seated need to be vague and is spreading like a virus. A dialogue which 10 years ago would have been reported in definite terms ("Mom, first he goes, 'What's happenin?' then I go, 'There's a party at Louanne's . . . ' ") now comes through in similes: "I'm like 'Where were you?' and he's like 'I was at Jeff's. What happened to you?' " Elusiveness is all.

Can a girl decide where she wants to be next Saturday at 9 p.m. when she doesn't know who she is? She knows only who she is not: not her mother, not the dork next door, not the baby she was last year, not (sadly) her glamorous cousin modeling for magazine covers in Austria. . . . Leaving Eden means embarking on a long, uncertain climb toward self-awareness through the murky jungle of self-consciousness from which only the bravest emerge—ever—as real grownups. It means shaky steps, again and again, that break us free of external authorities.

Most of our familiar, societal, religious and educational training denies our right to find sanction within ourselves, but, until we claim our own lives, we haven't the power to give them, not to others, not to God. Maya Angelou speaks in her autobiography of recovered "innocence" when she emerges from a period of hell to trust herself anew and perceive a world in which harmonies are possible.

In *Iron John,* Robert Bly examines an ancient folktale for clues to the demands of growing into full humanity. He describes a moment early in adolescence when the hero catches sight of his reflection in a pond, and the mirror experience separates the self he perceives from a shadow self, an unknown being within. In that new, suddenly external perception of self, wholeness and wholeheartedness have been lost. Each of us, catching a stranger's glance in the mirror, misplaces the small child's ability to experience from the inside, purely and timelessly, the building of a village with blocks or the motion around an anthill. We start getting in our own way. In Russell Baker's terms, we become "solemn" rather than "serious," humorless and without delight.

Introduced to Baker's distinction, my 17-year-old students grasp it instantly and can, with laser-like accuracy, divide the rest of us into two uneven lists. As Baker points out, it is the rare adult who has the integrity to be serious; that is, to ignore corporate pressure, media hype, mockery, opprobrium and commandments in order to connect simply and naturally with his own desires. It is the even rarer adolescent since, with all that sprouting going on, desires tend to flip-flop or cancel one another out.

Still, the young know seriousness when they see it, and they lust after it immoderately. That is why Arthur, in the days before he pulled the sword out of the stone, allowed Merlin to turn him into a hawk or a fish and initiate him into the natural world. That is why young black city boys respond avidly to educated black men who have chosen to teach them how to be men rather than pursue more lucrative pursuits.

Bly's focus is on male development, but insofar as we are androgynous when completely human, his story speaks to us all. Its pattern is older and more instinctive than political correctness: It invokes the need to abandon parents (as ultimate authority); to free and accept as mentor a hairy creature found at the bottom of a pond, a creature that is frightening but capable of leading the young boy to marvels through which he changes and acquires powers; and to find the king one must serve in order to come into vigorous wholeness. The initiatory wounds the boy incurs in freeing the Wild Man/mentor are turned to gold in his domain. Bly says these wounds are the source of the boy's own peculiar gift, and, *seeing them in the mentor's presence,* the boy will receive hints about where his genius lies.

The story says something about the adolescent recklessness that dares death so lightly. Several years ago, a former student wrote to me in unconsciously felicitous phrasing, "Don't worry—I'm still the same wreckless person!" Given her 90-mile-an-hour, six-pack-driven pursuit of college life in Georgia, the letter itself was a miracle. Why tempt fate?

The young breathe the ether of immortality. Not even the death of a close friend penetrates the shining, illusory armor of that conviction. Their physical blitheness is an outward manifestation of, or perhaps a substitute for, the courage they need to accept spiritual wounds—the rage or indifference of a father or mother—and examine them. In the absence of an elder who has gone the distance with the wild creature and become wise enough to lead them into a world made coherent by insight, the young men or women turn up the volume on the tape deck, put the pedal to the metal and let sensation fill the emptiness.

The young are betrayed by adults who have betrayed themselves. In revulsion at "cant" and avoidance, many adolescents revolt with their own forms of the same dishonesty, the only language they have been taught. Results are catastrophic: Bly speaks of the depressed and the "grandiose ascenders," those who give up and drift with the prevailing current and the others who keep to the high ground in a search for purity, constant spiritual elevation, self-esteem. These last are the anorexics or the superachievers whose anxious, airy egos often collapse in the second year of college or law school. Both groups are crippled in their inner lives and easy prey to fanatics, all the prophets of imbalance that assault this century's hazy air. When the pupil is ready, the teacher comes, for good or ill.

For the ascenders, Bly's story recommends work in the kitchen among the ashes; Cinderella is not only prettier than her pampered stepsisters but also more virtuous, in that she is wiser. For those on the upward spiral, time out, an exit from the prescribed pattern, can

be the saving, grounding grace. Young Americans used to ship out
on freighters and see the world. Now they take bikes and backpacks
on the road, washing dishes to eat, or hike through foreign coun-
tries. Or they head to the Rockies and balance the winged euphoria
of skiing with jobs cleaning condos or tending bar—a year, two
years of lateral living, neither climbing nor descending the ladder of
achievement that dominates their education.

If they are lucky in their contacts with other human or animal
beings, with great rivers or poems, with the slope as they land after
"catching air"—or even if they're not—they may learn more of
value than in all the years of formal preparation for life. However
randomly, they are searching for a serious education. For fun—
meaning involvement, connection, an occasional "Aha!"

If education eludes them in school, perhaps the efforts to instill
it have been too oblique, too trivial or badly timed. If nothing they
read speaks to their own lives and concerns, if their disconcerting
questions are quashed as interruptions to the obligatory flow of
facts, if they must master trig this year, ready or not, because it is
taught in junior year, then they are going to miss out.

The best of them, the most serious, may drop out. A teacher I
knew used to say, "It isn't the race, it's the pace that kills." Most
will finish the course but they won't break the ribbon together. In
the fantasy world of curriculum planning, however, the daffodil
blooms with the aster regardless of season, and young people are
fed an artificial diet of academics, TV and youth culture during the
years when most of them need work they perceive as relevant: ap-
prenticeship or service.

Growing is an experimental business that cannot be done on an
unforgiving track. The young need time and space to stretch in
weird directions. They need to survive disasters of their own making—that kitchen work again—or they will never know anything
about themselves. My youngest son decided, when he was all bones
barely covered with skin, to be a swimmer. He had all the flotation
of your average V-8 engine, but he suffered for two years the contempt of coaches, the condescension of teammates, and the igno-
miny of losing regularly in order to swim with the varsity team. The
place he made for himself was never glorious, but it was respectable

and honorable. He learned that nothing is entirely beyond his capacity if his desire is strong.

I have students whose minds work like shotguns, delivering blasts of unsorted, occasionally brilliant ideas. If they have never known elastic time, encouragement and strategies for revision, they see themselves as hopeless writers. They are not. They are, like me, merely slow writers, but a system that requires a finished essay every week rather than the unpredictable process of writing one—of trying the impossible, failing and fixing it—will never persuade them to reach for words . . . or the shape, the concept, the stride that covers territory as they see it, clearly and honestly, themselves.

Instead, they will gravitate toward some lesser, easier task that a piece of their minds can accomplish while the rest remains anesthetized with cheap fantasies, snoozing along with a laugh track as a lullaby. In spite of themselves, they will harden into their disappointed parents, or dream away their energies in shadowy tiltings at windmills, unless a lucky bolt of reality chances to jolt them out of triviality.

The glory of each adolescence is the ready potential for grandeur as the child reaches awkwardly, circuitously for the Key, or the Ring, or the Secret Door—learns to kiss the Frog, sympathize with the Beast, take the hand of hideous Iron John—and begins walking toward the adulthood out there in front of us.

To grow up at all is to know viscerally what physicists tell us, that there is nothing certain but motion. It has to do with retaining the soft, flexible bones of growing life, with using them to poise ourselves, balanced like gymnasts on a particular stage for a leap or a slide to the next one, from whatever direction it may appear.

I walk the steep hill behind my house watching a plane, a tiny arrow in February's blue sky. A friend who lives in flat country would want to be up there, knowing the air, flying. Not I. At 30,000 feet, the pilot has only air, and this jutting landscape flattens to a disc below him.

On my hill, with its precipitous, clear sweep of space down to my farmhouse, I inhabit both earth and air. When a cold front stood up to a southern storm last spring and brought us a rare feathery snow, I skied the hill. My legs remembered mountains, flight, the weightless drop through pines and aspens down the sheer white edge of space. There is a natural happiness in traveling the edges of things, sailing coastlines. Things become quintessentially themselves, apparent, where they come up against their complements—rock to sea, woman to man, feeling to form.

In poem after poem, Richard Wilbur muses about ambiguous human nature, the restless, "difficult balance" we must keep, caught as we are on an edge between matter and spirit. In "Water Walker," he writes of the caddis fly newly hatched on a river, "There is something they mean / By breaking from water and flying / Lightly some hours in air, / Then to the water-top dropping," and he compares the fly to "Paulsaul the Jew . . . Walking the point where air / Mists into water, and knowing / Both, with his breath, to be real." The words conjure moments of mystical duality akin to the delicate magic of adolescence, easy to overlook as a room fills up with sneakers, borrowed sweatshirts, and kids clothed mostly in provocative, shining hair.

The young walk a point where their being mists into becoming. They are as vulnerably human, as malleable, as mysterious and paradoxical as they will ever be. If their youthful vagaries are irritating, anyone who has ripened a melon knows that total maturity is the beginning of rot. Anyone who has lost an adolescent knows the bottomless, rimless void they leave behind.

It is adolescents who remind us of our true natures, of the nature of things in this universe. They are unstable, but why not? On the most basic level, our very building blocks are fluid and indecisive, wobbling like teenagers between their contradictory functions as inert matter and active energy. If the entire universe is waffling, it says adolescence is the way to go.

If we can't grow up in time to be Merlins to the young Arthurs in our children's psyches, we could at least try hanging loose longer. We could be more lithely alive and serious, leaven confusion with a little courage, and show the watching young that our difficult balance is easier to keep when we lighten up.

WHEN HOME BECOMES
A PLACE TO FLEE

Kerry Temple

HE WAS NEVER really the same after his mother pointed out the way to New Orleans. He was 11. He watched his world out the car window. His mother was taking him to get a haircut and they stopped at the red light. He knew the intersection: Creswell School and Glenwood Drug and the old Broadmoor Theatre where he went each Saturday to watch the Tarzan matinee. The drugstore had cherry Cokes and penny-pack baseball cards, and Jim Jordan lived over behind the school, on Preston Avenue. He knew the shortcuts, the hiding places, the best trees for climbing. He didn't know why she said it, but it made a deep impression: "If you take a right turn here and just stay on that road, you'll wind up in New Orleans."

She pointed toward the new shopping center and the new junior high and the new subdivision full of brick ranch-style houses on the outskirts of town, out toward the two-lane highway that led out of town and south between the long, even rows of cotton, between the splintered shacks whose corrugated tin roofs were rusty and brown.

He had been that far. He had picked some cotton; he had been in the homes of the colored people, in the shanties where little boys like him but brown stared at him with their chocolate-drop eyes. Barefoot, they wore his hand-me-downs. The homes were dark inside, the sunlight slashing through cracks in the walls, through the slits where the hand-hewn planks were no longer plumb. They had pictures of Jesus on the walls and wood-burning fires and ticks. But he didn't know what lay beyond that. Where did Red River go after it flowed through here? Or Bayou Pierre after it moseyed over the edge of that flat horizon? He had never thought to ask.

He gazed down the road until the light turned green, down to where the asphalt disappeared. What his mother said, he turned it over and around in his head: "You don't even make a turn. Drive all day, you'd be there tonight." He looked over his shoulder as the car pulled away from the crossroads. What he couldn't understand was this: He had seen maps before, the squiggly red and blue lines, the yellow splotches of far-away cities. The ones in the books. The ones with baseball teams. Just places on a map, connected by mysterious lines.

But the light went on inside him now because he saw the road—LA 1—that could take him from one splotch to another. He could get there from here. Even *he* knew the way. And suddenly New Orleans, glimmering New Orleans, was a part of his universe. It wasn't so mysterious after all.

He was never the same after that. The whole world lay at his feet. But days and months and years would pass before home became a place to flee.

What happened in those days and months and years he did not understand either. Once upon a time he had basked in the glow of the hearth, nestled into quilted evenings, curled next to his mother while the family watched TV. Sunday nights, when he clung to the lap of his own before Monday-morning school. When the whole family, sitting in the shadows, was bathed in the radiant silver glare of the black-and-white screen. Rainy nights, when he slept to the sound of water drumming on aluminum awnings. Velvet nights, when nightmares drove him to his parents' bed, the musky sheets and giant, cradling bodies.

On winter mornings his father got up in the cold black air and lit the gas stoves. Room to room he would go, filling the house with warmth and the scent of gas burning. Then he'd rouse his son hiding beneath the sheets. Grudgingly the boy would rub the sleep from his eyes and come out into the world, emerge as from a snug cocoon. He drank coffee then, full of cream and sugar, dipping his buttered toast into it, and no one talked, although he felt wrapped in the blanket of his family's embrace. It was the world that was hard.

Once back home, he went to the kitchen and sat at the table while his mother was getting dinner on. Another cookie would spoil his supper; he had her to himself and they'd talk. While she snapped beans and he inhaled the aroma of chicken baking, they talked. She was full of wisdom, and there was light in her blue eyes, and he told her what he wanted to be when he grew up.

For a time, that home, that harbor, was enough. A place from which to stand and view the world. A watchtower. A parapet where he could gaze out upon the dragoned landscape. On sick-days he created battlefields for his toy soldiers from bedspreads and shoe-boxes. He ran his electric train and read of heroes. Refuge and fortress: Strong hands could lift him to the ceiling there; his mother's smile brought him sunshine there. And the house was a port amid his grand imaginings. A porch on which to sit and tell stories on summer evenings after the games were over and the fireflies were gone and the moon shone in the starry sky. He leaned against the white-washed shingles and watched the leafy trees blow until his mother's voice and the crickets' droning blended into a single murmur.

He would sit there forever, he thought then, in the days before home became a place to flee.

Although he was never the same after his mother pointed toward New Orleans, time passed before he realized something new was in his blood. All he understood was, the yard was too small. The alley was a bore. Columbia Park was too familiar. And so his bike carried him away. To the farther reaches of his ever-widening universe. To the frontiers of adolescent exploration. To the private clubhouses in forbidden locales. And the world that beckoned him, that called him to its wider fields, made his home look small and boxish, as confining as a package wrapped with paper, string and ribbon. He wanted to break out, to loose himself from the grip of their proper expectations, to leave their questions unanswered.

Was it then that he began to withdraw from them, didn't want to be seen with them at the movies or in church? The more he avoided their company, the tighter they clung, the more questions

they asked—until he would not tell them where he'd been or why
he no longer wanted to be at home. Their gazes caressed him too
tightly, their hugs enfolded him too snugly, their smiles felt invasive.
Even the house, when he returned from fields afar, seemed to examine him too closely, watching him from its front windows, meas-
uring his approach, too eager to gather him into its smothering
bosom.

When he was around, he stayed mostly in his room. With the
music turned way up loud, and a scowl upon his face, to show he
wanted to be alone, to show disdain for their peculiar habits. He did
not know what venom was coursing through his veins, but he felt
the watchspring in him wind tighter until it was coiled to blow. And
the walls that once offered refuge and seclusion now became a suffocating prison. He had to go; he could not stay. He needed distance.

So one late Saturday night, after a week of being grounded, a
week in his room for not coming home on time, he bolted. He got
out of bed and pulled on his jeans and slipped his tennis shoes on.
He crept downstairs and sneaked out the door. Then he stood a
moment with his back to the door and held his breath and let the
nighttime air wash over him. He started walking and he walked
faster, not on the sidewalk but out in the street, in the middle of
the nighttime street, under the streetlamps, beneath the arching limbs of oak and sweetgum trees. He began to run, jogging at
first until he got a head of steam, and then he really began to run.
Legs churning, feet flapping on the pavement fast as they could go.
He ran.

He ran straight out, flying down the streets where no car ever
came. He was young and strong and fast, and it didn't matter that
his heart was pounding, that his lungs burned and his stomach
burned. He ran, driven by the engine of some internal fire. And
then, on one downhill stretch, his legs flew, took off without him,
out of control, spinning like windmills in a storm. And at that point
he felt, he really felt, that if he would spread his arms, open them
wide, they would become wings and flight would be his. He would
take off over the houses, over the schools and parks, over the build-
ings and into the open spaces that called him.

But he didn't. He ran hard, puffing, gasping, then slowed to a cruising speed and ran like that for a long time, longer than he counted. It was a feeling he would never forget: to go unbounded. He would later wonder, when he recalled that night, if his feet were actually touching the ground. Or if, in his heart of hearts, he was soaring.

There would be other escapes after that first jailbreak, flights made freer and more exultant because they came from behind the wheel of a car. But none in which he came closer to flying.

In the years that followed he took the road to New Orleans and found where Red River went and swam in its waters. He played in the woods around Bayou Pierre and stood on the trestle that spanned its swampland until the train had blown its whistle three times. Barebacked and brazen, he and his friends would dare each other into showing a foolhardy courage: They would stand close to the rushing train, the rumbling monster boxcars, feeling the wind, tasting the acrid oil-and-iron fumes as the ground rattled beneath them. And in the muddy red-clay cliffs they carved out caves and sat on their perches drinking beer and bragging about the girls they would bring here.

Sometimes they hunted snakes, slung rocks at glass bottles, and cracked open the wild pecans whose meat tasted fine. And they stole away here in the mystical shield of darkness, when the moonlit woods had a spooky cast to them and the owls called their names. And on late summer days they talked to the blacks who lived in their shanties nearby—the ones with holes in the walls—and who picked the cotton and found those marshes to be a good provider of food: crawfish and catfish, coon, turtle, possum and squirrel. And somehow all these things—the smell of pine on rainy days, the sluggish brown water going nowhere, the look in a Negro's eyes when he met you face to face—got into his blood and made him who he was.

But it occurred to them all, these restless boys born and raised in a staid Southern city, that they had to get away, that life awaited them far away from here, that this place held nothing for them. Familiarity bred contempt; their hometown would only hold them back. So in time he moved away, leaving the words unspoken, the distances uncrossed, the splintered home unmended. There were no apologies for things said in anger, no hugs, no explanation for the barricades between them, no words to heal the wounds. Only an awkward goodbye, his shuffling feet, his eyes averted from their faces when he said he had to go.

Years later, when he was back there on a visit, he was asked if he were ever homesick. And he said no. It was later still when he realized his answer might have stung—to tell those who had once wrapped him in their love that he was happy a thousand miles away from them. And, in all honesty, it was only a part of the truth. Because there were times, when the world was cold or mean, that he thought how nice it would be to go home and curl up under his blankets like he did on sick-days, or sit on the porch again and talk until the voices blended with the sounds of twilight in the summer; to come home to his mother in the kitchen, to ride on his father's shoulders, his head scraping on the ceiling as he dreamed of all the places he would someday go.

But he knew he couldn't get back home, couldn't be that way again. Too much had happened, too much time had passed, too many changes had taken place to go home again. Not the way it was. You can never get all the way back there, no matter how hard you try. What you once had, you lost, and its touch is irrevocable.

I *have* gone back to the house that boy once lived in. I have stood in the knotty-pine den and seen again the owl and the alligator hiding in the wood grain and whorls, as mysteriously as the constellations twinkling in a jeweled sky. I have stood again in his room and looked at his stuff—the childhood books and school pictures and toy soldiers. And at the other books and pieces of wood and rock, and out the window that spoke to his longing.

I have walked around in there and sat on the couch and drunk milk in the kitchen, all the while wondering what it is that makes home, once so embracing, a place we need to flee. As if the poles of some internal magnet get reversed, so that what was once so appealing drives us away.

I have also gone back to the woods there by the trestle that flank the marshes of Bayou Pierre. One Saturday night I bought two quarts of Pabst and I drove out south of town, past the subdivision that once was new and is now shabby, past the newer suburbs that surround the city in layers like rings in the trunk of a tree. The old shacks were gone, the cottonfields too; there were condominiums all around, and big, fancy houses where the woods once stood. Bayou Pierre had been paved; four-lane highways with exit loops and entrance ramps now dwarfed the trestle. But I found a red dirt road and followed it to the end, and I pulled out a quart of beer.

I could hear the night and smell it—breezes laced with the scent of a wood-burning stove. There was a full moon, its light filtering through the pine and cypress trees draped with moss. And in the distance, nestled among the trees, I spied a ramshackle cabin. Its light glowed soft amber in the windows. A stream of smoke rose from the chimney. And clothes still hung from the line like apparitions in the wind. There is comfort in such settings, a soothing tranquility. The beer was cold and bracing. The red-clay earth, carpeted with pine needles, felt good beneath my feet—as if the soles of my feet belonged there.

And I thought how curious it is that the longer I am away from this place, the more faded is my accent, the less I see these streets, these woods—the more I am drawn back here. The more it feels like home. The more peace I find in this landscape, as if it and I are inseparably joined in mysterious, subterranean ways. And I realize that, although I have spent years getting away from here, this land, these people, this city are embedded deep inside me. And so is that little boy.

Once he saw the road to New Orleans, he knew he would some-day go away. He never suspected that he would carry all this away with him wherever he would go.

A BROKEN ANGEL

Breyman Schmelzle

I SAW THE quarter-shaped blemish on my newborn daughter's lower back, but I didn't comprehend it. Then I sensed my wife's exhausted joy turn suddenly to instinctive agony.

When the doctor said, "There is a problem," the message didn't register in my truth-proofed brain—not even when he added the chilling words a parent equates with hell: "Birth defect." Months of blessedly pink plans and dreams of frills and lace had cocooned me.

Jill had spina bifida, exposure of the spine. It causes severe nerve damage, and often the nerves are splayed and strung outside the back like a gutted old radio. The specter on her back was the lesion, covered by a shadowy-thin membrane.

We couldn't beat million-to-one odds.

Spina bifida is the number-one child crippler in America, but 10 years ago it was news to me. I was a person who gave no more than guilt-induced sighs for lame or starving children and for all the bad things that happen to good people. Now, suddenly, my wife and I needed to know something on which to anchor our faltering, numbed emotions. But nobody could give us a clue as to what was going to happen to Jill.

They kindly told us to expect the worst: She probably would never be able to walk, and maybe she would be paralyzed. Then they whispered the grand coup of despair: possible brain damage.

The world had suddenly called in its chips on me; I felt a leaden weight of stain and nameless guilt, and my paranoia shouted at me that I was the most persecuted wretch in existence.

Then something saved me. Maybe there really are guardian angels. It occurred to me that my problem was not a damaged-goods baby, but me. I saw it in an eternal instant, a life's epiphany: What had been given to us was the most precious blessing imaginable. The only emotion required was ecstatic joy. Jill was Jill, and nothing else mattered. "She is what you wanted," I told myself; "take her and love her."

As they wheeled her into an ambulance to go to another hospital for specialized surgery, she smiled at me. The impractical nurse said it was gas, but I choose to believe what I believe.

Nine and a half years of unconditional joy and 10 major surgeries later, Jill—of normal intelligence and a high pain threshold—stood on a podium and widened that smile that had never gone away. She was about to receive a silver medal for the softball throw in the Tucson Special Olympics, and the same kind of revelation came to me as on the night of her birth. She was experiencing a grand rite of passage calling out her hidden selfhood. Standing on leg braces and leaning on a walker, she saw herself and loved herself and all her exciting possibilities. My baby had come a long way.

On the night of her birth a neurosurgeon took six hours to fold over skin from her sides to cover the lesion, and inserted a shunt in her brain for hydrocephalus. For three weeks, I only saw her asleep and pitifully wired. Then another divine nod: She was home for Christmas. I finally got to hold her.

I remember her first kick; her foot hit my hand as I leaned away from her crib, distracted by something, and my spirits soared. I remember her first step after she had stood terrified for months in clunky metal braces; I didn't see the step but I sure heard about it—her mother came running down the street screaming.

So the lesson was being witnessed, one I had always thought trite and illusory: Never give up. Never stop believing in your impossible dreams. Today Jill can hop-step on scaled-down calf braces and swim the length of a pool, kicking with a whirlish vengeance. She must divide her time between a wheelchair and, to her dismay, the leg aids and a godawful trunk brace. The contraptions win out most of the time. Every day at her school, through the deserted halls, one can hear her catchup clip-clop.

Genes have given the two of us—father and daughter—a special affinity; we are both dreamers and miracle believers. My task now is to convince Jill that miracles don't just happen; you have to work and sweat to make them occur. I must be tough with her, even draw tears and risk my own.

She must accept her affliction completely; she hasn't yet. She must learn to release the anger that simmers when her friends treat her as a curious toy, or when she stares forlornly out the window at little girls running.

She is battling to stay out of diapers and has a huge, unsightly kyphosis on her lower back from the original surgery. It's scheduled to be removed this winter in surgery number 11. It will be the riskiest operation of all, and we may be back where we started.

"Why am I handicapped?" I had been waiting for the question, but the first time she asked, it froze me. "Because you're an angel and you must be special in order to better help people." I do her a disservice with this con; she doesn't relate to any specialness yet.

And what of myself? How do I grow with her? "Dad, I'm 9 years old," she reminds me with the stern admonition to stop seeing her as a baby. Despite her tardiness at life, she is growing away. That scares me, but woe unto me if I try to pull her back.

I'm not happy at what happened to my daughter, but the joy that is Jill has enriched our lives. I look at her and thank God for the honor of being privileged to "borrow" her for a little while—and for the undeserved chance to grow myself, with a special, holy love.

Handicapped children. Such pity is wasted on them. What they are about is the soul of life itself . . . the right to life and dignity. The larger the handicap, the greater the smallest step and the more triumphant the victory. And from that—for us, for them—comes the ultimate victory.

Blessed indeed are the meek.

WHAT ARE FATHERS FOR?

Thomas M. Mulroy

ALTHOUGH I WAS a bit shy of 5 on the bright September day when my father died, I remember details of that day with distinct clarity. These are not the memories of family legend, refined by frequent retelling; death was an awful secret in our house after that late summer afternoon when my father went to catch up with the lawn work and died instead.

The boy next door found me at a neighbor's house and said I was needed at home. The atmosphere there was confused. Friends and relatives had appeared out of nowhere. I skirted the yard where my father lay dead, my aunt holding me back not in a forceful way but to let me know it was no place for a small boy. Neighbors buzzed as we waited for the red and white ambulance. There was no particular rush. The sentence of death was recognized and accepted.

Inside I found more evidence of tragedy. My mother, 39 and suddenly a widow with three young children, lay prostrate on her bed where she remained until days after the funeral. My younger sister lay on a rollaway bed that had inexplicably appeared in my mother's room. My older sister, 13 then and fully able to grasp the events of the day, had retreated to her room, where she knelt by her bed, crying. I took my place next to her, not certain why I should be sad or yet recognizing what I had lost.

My mother, angry and hurt, said little of the husband she had lost. Somehow she managed to convince us that we were better off without him, implying that her hard work and ambition far surpassed his limited vision. Theirs apparently was not the happiest of unions.

Through the years I stumbled past the embarrassing questions of new acquaintances ("What does your dad do?"). I came into adulthood thinking I had not lost much growing up without a dad. I started my own parenting intuitively, never feeling a need for any paternal lodestone. I finished law school and became what lawyers euphemistically call a "family" lawyer—a divorce lawyer.

Increasingly I suspect it is no accident that I ended up here, trying to patch up the marriage in my own life that ended in tragedy. And now I suspect Mom was wrong: I may have lost something of value when I lost my father. But as I survey the landscape of my compatriots who shared their formative years with their dads, their own discomfort unnerves me.

Every day I sit across the desk from men and help them define new limits to a concept—fatherhood—that I have very little knowledge of, at least on the receiving end. Day after day I attempt to define something I cannot describe to the client, but which the client and I both think we know well.

Peter is a typical example: married for 12 years, two kids, a marriage that has not worked out too well, a new apartment in the city, and a lot of time on his hands on the weekend with the kids in a strange new land of part-time parenting. "He's so fakey," his daughter complains as he adopts his father role for their weekly rendezvous.

"This is not the same as being there to tuck them in every night," he complains. "I don't know what they expect of me." We cover all the old territory again: how it's better for the children to stay with their mother during the week so school schedules won't be unduly disturbed; how, when we look at the division of time, he spends more time with the children now than before. Sometimes I recite empty platitudes about quality time. "You're still their father," I conclude. He gives me a blank stare.

In this era of failed marriages and joint custody, men are trying to redefine fatherhood and, more importantly, trying to figure out how to relate to their children in the fluid relationships that are replacing the nuclear family.

The problem is one of significant proportions. First, the numbers: The divorce rate has exploded in the last 20 years, and the statistics are amazing even to those of us caught in the fray day-to-day. The census bureau suspects that almost two-thirds of the children in this country will experience divorce at least once in the family before they reach adulthood. The question of defining the relationship of fathers and their children will certainly affect most children in the country, especially if children continue to reside primarily with their mothers when marriages fail.

All of this comes at a time when the concept of American manhood and fatherhood is taking center stage. Robert Bly, and others like him, have apparently touched a national nerve. Bly's book, *Iron John,* posits that much of our national malaise revolves around the issue of male definition. Modern men, he says, have lost touch with male myths and mentors, are impotent in their attempts to pass on maleness to succeeding generations and are suspicious of their own masculinity and of each other.

Bly's insight may tap into more than we feel comfortable admitting. Groups have formed all over the country which attempt to provide experiences that relate to Bly's theories. Men camp out together, create male bonding rituals and attempt to find and define their common ground through a lot of hooting and hollering and smearing mud on their chests.

It is not as silly as it sounds. What a lot of these men do is cry uncontrollably over their own sense of inadequacy and their perceived lack of worth in the eyes of their own fathers, whom they saw as distant and unloving critics. Whatever definition of modern fatherhood we come up with, many American men would not want it based on their fathers' versions of the role.

Many fathers who face the question of fatherhood after marriage has failed are really facing questions that all of us are uncomfortable about: Who is dad and what is he good for?

Our grandfathers, those men who raised the generation of fathers that no one wants to emulate, came out of a world where dad's place defined everybody else's. He was the one without whom there were no others. He literally owned his wife and children, and their very survival depended on his efforts and good graces. He may not have been liked, but his children knew who and what he was. In many ways, he controlled their fates.

The next generation is not as easy to get a handle on. These men left the farm to work in the city, and they apparently left behind things we treasure in our national heart (spawning the endless barrage of contemporary sales pitches based on good ol' down-on-the-farm flavor, values, smells). Life changed rapidly for these men, as wars and the Depression leveled all the things they thought would prop them up in times of trouble.

The roles of women changed too, but those changes were mostly changes of addition. Their sisters told them that they could have it all. Their husbands, meanwhile, entered an era of subtraction—they lost the respect and dignity of being the *sine qua non*. While men of previous generations may have gloried in preparing their sons for their own age of dominance, these men faced sons they could not face, perhaps out of a sense of shame over their own diminished role. If my thesis is correct, as evidenced by the attention the "male" question is receiving in the media, it appears that these men left a blank page where their legacy of manhood should have been.

Apparently their sons, who grew up sensitive to the needs of women and who embraced the sharing of parenting with their super-achieving wives, were wearing a thick veneer over their deep sense of loss. Now they face their own children, often amidst the rubble of failed marriages, and they question the essence of who and what they are. Too often they find no answer and just give up.

Statistics show that we are raising a generation of fatherless children and, from where I sit, I can assure you that many of them are not the offspring of young unwed black girls, as so many of us presume. The question must be asked: Do we need fathers anymore?

In this fungible generation of breadwinners where mothers can do it all in terms of motherhood and careers, what do men really bring to the family formula beyond their baby-making abilities? Our most publicized example of a population without fathers is our large urban black population, where an overwhelming majority of children are being raised by women labeled by the government as "female, head of household." While it would be foolish to blame all of the devastation affecting that population on the absent fathers, it would also take a strange case of myopia not to see the correlation between absent fathers, family disintegration and the alarming increase in problems among these groups. Fathers apparently contributed something good, the absence of which is bad.

Now divorce is spreading the "father loss" like wildfire through the mainstream American population. Moreover, if Bly and his followers are right, it is not just the children of divorce who are suffering, but also many of the children and dads who are grappling with who they are to one another.

I know, I am one of them. Although my relationship with my father was cut short, I was blessed with the friendship of a few older men who mentored me and taught me a little about the gifts of fatherhood. Their influence has affected my fathering in a positive way, and their gifts were uniquely manly, unavailable from women.

I also depend upon the example of my friends who had great dads; I watch them being great dads in turn (as it should be).

Yet, despite all this, I have no definitive answers. But I do know the question. When I asked my children to define the difference between mom and dad, they gave me the same blank stare I get from my clients. Somehow, we have to find some answers.

THE IDENTITY FLIP-FLOP

Barrie Maguire

D O YOU HAVE a son in a rock band?" the clerk at Borders Book Store asks as she studies my credit card.

I stare at her in disbelief, then answer, "Yes. How do you know about that?"

"I read something in *The New York Times* last week and the name kind of stuck."

* * *

I better sell that novel quick.

My son—and namesake—is the bass player in a new band called *The Wallflowers*. Their first CD has been released, their songs are running on the radio, and yes, their video has even appeared on MTV.

My son and I have swapped polarity; he used to be Barrie's son, now I'm Barrie's father.

I sometimes wonder if the other *Wallflowers* fathers are going through the same emotions I am. I suspect they are, even the band's famous father, Jakob Dylan's dad, Bob.

* * *

My wife receives a letter from her 78-year-old mother who lives in Conway, Arkansas, and a newspaper clipping falls out of the envelope. It's a two-column ad from the *Arkansas Gazette* announcing that the Bob Dylan National Tour is coming to Little Rock. In the margin next to a photo of Bob Dylan a note has been neatly written in pencil: "Is this the father of Little Barrie's friend?"

* * *

The identity flip-flop. Sooner or later, all parents go through it with their kids.

It usually happens in the late teens or early 20s, after the Rebellion is over and the Reunion has begun. The earlier warning signal often comes in the form of a joke; you make a very funny remark and instead of laughing like he's supposed to, your kid comes back with an even funnier line, and before you can catch yourself you've laughed out loud.

Uh, oh.

Or one night during dinner your oldest girl starts talking about how the big weakness with democracy is that individuals always vote their self-interest, which isn't necessarily the best thing for society as a whole.

Huh?

Or little Skippy comes home from school and drops a videocassette of his freshman projects into the VCR. As you watch in amazement, you make a mental note to destroy all those Super-8 epics you made of the peace march and the beach vacations.

Flip.

Or Daddy's little angel calls excitedly to tell you that she went down to the AutoMall armed with a *Consumer Reports* printout and bought a new Civic for $90 over dealer cost.

Flop.

As embarrassing and humbling as it is, eventually we all become our children's groupies. I'm not talking about being their number-one fan. I'm not talking about the pride we felt when they learned to walk or talk or read at such an early age. And I'm not talking about what we felt when they brought home straight A's or won the Most Improved Player award. This is something totally different.

No longer is it enough that they love and respect us. Now we need them to *like* us.

We start pursuing them, pandering to them. Because 11:30 p.m.

is way past our bedtime, we tape *Saturday Night Live* and watch it on Sunday so we'll be able to demonstrate that we're hip to Hans and Franz and Dieter and Deep Thoughts. (We even resist the temptation to fast-forward through the Red Hot Chili Peppers.) We swell with satisfaction whenever our kids agree with us about a movie or TV series. We listen intently to Gergen and Shields so we can have our own insight into the political scene. We want our kids to take us seriously.

* * *

"Get your banjo. Let's play something," Barrie says when I walk into the room. He's settled comfortably into the far end of the couch next to the Christmas tree, my guitar on his lap. The house is full of family, and Barrie's been noodling around on the guitar for the last half hour. I've been listening, marveling at how well my old Martin sounds in his hands. "Naw, I'd rather just listen to you," I say.

* * *

Sometimes I tell people that the reason I don't sit around and jam with Barrie is because I want him to remember me as the guitar-genius who taught him to make his first E chord, not a cute old guy who can only play folk songs. But that's not the real reason. It's that damn identify flip-flop; I'm longing for the days when I sheltered him, worried about him, even argued with him—all from my vantage point as leader of the band, our merry band, *my* family.

Those days are history. He and his sister and brothers own the family now. Nothing our kids achieve will really surprise us. We just hope they still like us.

THE GIFT OF BEING A GIVER
Elaine Cripe

IT WAS A big apple and, for a 6-year-old, a big job to cut it in halves for sharing. The halves didn't come out equal, of course, and I was greedy enough to take the larger for myself. Mother came along just in time to notice and to scold: "Elaine! When we share, we always give the larger part to the other person." I looked at her, at the fruit, and at Barbara, my cousin. Then I shoved both pieces in Barbara's hands and said, "Here. You share it."

Since that childish burst of ingenuity, I hope I've learned a little about the adage, "It's better to give than to receive," but you'll never convince me it's not great to be in the receiving line for gift-wrapped packages, compliments or recognition.

Americans are fortunate to be able to give many gifts, often. The proliferation of gift-giving occasions, however, has cheapened the concept. A gift tends to be judged by its cost, not its value, by its size rather than by the feeling that prompted it. Take Aunt Mabel and Aunt Gert.

Aunt Gert is a dear. She loves anything you get her, but she loves you just as much if you come empty-handed. Given a gift, she exclaims, "How did you know I needed this?" or "Oh, I always wanted one of these." When you simply call, her joy at being remembered infuses you with a pleasure of largesse.

Aunt Mabel, on the other hand, has a serious problem of pickiness. Whatever you get her will be the wrong color, size, shape or brand, or else she already has one. Her thanks always begin with: "You shouldn't have. This is very nice, dear, but. . . . " Try a gift certificate: "This is very nice, dear, but it's so hard getting out to the stores." Try taking her to dinner: "This is very nice, dear, but I don't know what I can eat on this menu. . . . "

What you give either of them doesn't matter. Aunt Gert deserves the best; Aunt Mabel is never satisfied. So for whom do you think you'll spend more time and money? In the Christmas crush, who will get more consideration? Mabel, of course. It isn't fair, but it's human.

One of the best gifts I ever received was in the second year of my marriage. My husband was still in college; my own studies had earned an unexpected sabbatical with our first baby, and now we were going to have another only a year later. Besides taking a full class load, my husband worked at a local dairy a mile-and-a-half walk away. The cash was low and there were no reserves. One hot day when my spirits were as low as the cash, he came home with a great bouquet of petunias, the pale-lavender, wild kind, that he'd found growing in an empty lot. He brought them roots and all. We planted them in the windowbox of our rented duplex, and they perfumed my summer.

We remember presents that were special to us not because they were things we needed, or perhaps even wanted, but because they made us real. They made us understand that we were important to somebody.

That sort of getting is a wonderful thing, but it has its requirements, too. Getting implies a symbiosis of sorts. Getting is as good as giving if we recognize what the giving means.

My mother knew about giving. She always gave the larger half. One of my most prized possessions is a recipe book she used as a bride during the Great Depression. On a blank page at the back, she had noted a week's purchases: bread, 10 cents; lunchmeat, 18 cents; lettuce, 7 cents; church, 25 cents; Harry's insurance, 20 cents. Harry wasn't my dad, he was my dad's mentally-impaired brother, whom no one in the family would claim. When he died, it was my mother's hard-saved insurance that buried him.

She didn't have a fancy house or clothes but she usually seemed to have money to give—she called it a loan to make us feel better—when we needed it. For potlucks and church bazaars and senior-citizen bake sales, she made the best and the most. But she didn't know about getting.

Mother was the hardest person in the world to buy for. Her drawers were full of gift sweaters and slips and dresses that she wouldn't use "until the old ones wear out." She wasn't comfortable in restaurants. She liked to cook and she preferred having people, especially grandchildren, lick the pans and "eat up!" There was nothing she needed or wanted. She didn't use new-fangled contraptions like electric mixers and she didn't pay attention to things we thought she needed—such as blood pressure monitors. If you gave her money, she gave it to somebody else or put it away "for a rainy day." For some reason, she didn't have those, either.

Mother always said thanks, but she didn't understand the art of receiving. It doesn't exist in "thanks, but. . . . " People look for more than words. I can understand why some nations despise America, especially those that owe us the most; the desire for equality is eminently human. No one can keep receiving and saying thank-you without beginning to feel obligation—like a crust of hives and lesions—beginning to form. It's a kind of Golden Rule; when someone does for you, you want to do back.

Months before Mother's birthday, I would listen and watch for gift clues. One year, I heard her mention one of those picture frames that hold several snapshots. She should have pictures of all the grandkids on the wall, she said, instead of pinned to the bulletin board, curling at the edges.

That was it! Not too expensive for her to accept, related to family, something that she herself had said she'd like. Perfect! A few days later, we stopped at the Kmart, and I made a fatal mistake: I asked her which size frame she preferred. She answered, "No, no. I don't need that. You put the money away, you need it more than I need a picture frame, my birthday isn't important. . . . "

I exploded in anger and hurt. The money was insignificant. I wanted to do something for her, give her something she'd like . . . but once again she was refusing my offering, rejecting me. I was so angry that I spoke too loud, right there in the aisle. "All right. I was trying to think of you. I wanted so much to please you. I guess I can't. The hell with you. I'll never try to buy you another thing. Never. Not even a card. So Happy Birthday!" And I walked away, leaving her dumbfounded and embarrassed and humiliated.

Somehow we finished our shopping, we went through the check-out line, we drove home. We got through the next day in a stilted, lame sort of way, and the day after that was easier.

Mother was a traditional sort of person: She took care of us, told us what was wrong with us, didn't often say she was sorry. She didn't apologize this time, either.

A few weeks after the Kmart scene she said, in the imperious, haughty tone she sometimes affected to mask a self-conscious nervousness, "You know, Mother's Day is coming up. I have a list here, and if any of the grandkids don't know what to get me, well, maybe this will help."

I looked at the list. Clothespins. A flashlight and batteries. Bubblebath. She was giving me the gift of being a giver.

WHEN WE HAD IT MADE IN AMERICA

Mark Phillips

WHEN MY COUNTRY was the land of opportunity, its clattering factories and smoking mills used electricity generated at the power plant where my father worked as a welder. He wore a hard hat and belonged to the union, and I believed he was more mighty than even our young president who had stared down Khrushchev. Dad was still at work when my sisters and I climbed off the safe school bus in the afternoons, but Mom was there to greet us, in her sparkling kitchen, and I believed she was as fulfilled as a saint. In that time and that place, our family was protected by steel parentheses, made in America, from a hurtling, changing story that we couldn't yet understand.

Graced, we believed our American lives would never change.

* * *

Although my immediate family believed in forever, even back then—when the shelves in the stores weren't yet packed with Japanese and Korean products, the factories weren't moving to Mexico and Malaysia, and "downsizing" wasn't a word—my grandfather knew better. Because he was old, Barley Phillips no longer believed in forever.

By the time I turned 7 he had retired from his job as a foreman at the power plant, sold his house in Buffalo and was living with Grandma in the countryside. Along with a small house, his property included a chicken coop, workshop, empty barn and 11 acres of abandoned crop land.

Because I spent so many evenings and weekends with him while Dad worked overtime at the power plant, I felt closer to Grandpa than to my worshipped but often absent father. Once, when Grandpa was preparing to smoke wasps out of his workshop, he pointed above the workbench to a large framed photograph of a man with thick frosty hair and bushy eyebrows, a long nose, a handlebar mustache, a stern expression. He told me that was his father, who had been "a hardworking blacksmith." Although Grandpa didn't keep the photograph in his house, he hadn't discarded it; he kept it in his workshop, as if his memories of his father were inextricably tied to labor.

In the yard on warm summer evenings, sitting in metal lawn chairs or stretched out on the grass near the pear trees and the hand-operated water pump and the metal pink flamingos and the free-ranging chickens stalking worms, Grandpa sipped beer and I gulped pop and we talked until dark. He gently teased me, encouraged me to talk about my life and listened sincerely. But because I was far too young to believe it, he never told me what he had learned about forever. And so together we drifted lazily over sunken family legends that I had yet to learn and that he was trying to forget.

You know the legends. Substitute your own surnames and ethnic backgrounds, change some other details, and you know them. The Welsh horse-trading ancestor, his name now forgotten, who settled in Ireland. The Welsh-Irish great-grandfather who ran away from the farm to work in the Belfast shipyards and then, when work slowed, sailed to North America and became a successful blacksmith in booming Buffalo. The grandfather who became an ironworker in Buffalo even though two of his older brothers had fallen to their deaths on the job—but who, after helping to build a power plant, took a safer and better paying job there. The father who became a welder at the same power plant. All of them always chasing work, capturing it, becoming better. In these legends, equal-opportunity laws don't exist, the wife stays home, the kids do their homework, each generation buys a bigger house than the one before and the economy grows stronger forever.

One evening while he was driving us home from the power

plant—where I was working during my summer break from college—my father looked over at me and said, apologetically, "When you knew your grandfather, he was old. He wasn't the man he used to be." By then the factories in Buffalo were beginning to close, and Dad had cancer.

I'm reminded of my father's longing for past, for the days when working men were real men, each time I hear someone reminiscing about that lost paradise in which a blue collar worker didn't need—or permit—his wife to work. A friend of mine who'd been laid off by a steel plant once said to me about the rust belt, "Our grandfathers wouldn't believe it."

But I think Barley Phillips would believe it. I think he'd shrug and say sadly about the loss of paradise, "Things change."

* * *

For many of those who lost paradise, the hardest part was that they believed they had earned a permanent stay.

Eighteen years old, my father was assigned, as was each new employee at the power plant, to the Utility Department. Whatever messes occurred around the plant were cleaned up by the Utility laborers. The other workers called them "the shit crew." In the Coal Department, to which most Utility laborers hoped to be promoted, the work was just as dirty but the pay far better; so the Utility men waited and hoped for someone in Coal to retire or die.

On his second morning at the plant, my father climbed up a steel ladder to a cramped four-foot-high area above a boiler. Most of the sweltering space was deep in leaked fly ash. Crouched on his hands and knees, he surveyed the space. A long vacuum hose, connected to the stack system of the plant, lay in fresh ash that had accumulated since Monday, when he left much of the area clean. He put on goggles, then a respirator. Immediately his perspiring face felt uncomfortable within the rubber, and he began the labored deep breathing necessary to obtain a sufficient air supply. Pushing off his hard-hat, he crawled farther in and picked up the eight-inch circumference hose. He handled it gently but the light ash began to fill the air and adhere to his sweaty work-suit and skin. A few minutes later another

Utility worker, with a shovel, joined him, and the air quickly became saturated as the two men, shoveling and vacuuming, worked blindly in a gray cloud of hell.

After several months in Utility, Dad was trained to weld and was promoted directly to the Maintenance Department, where his father was a foreman. Dad worked in the same noise and heat and dirt and crawl spaces as he had in Utility, and his ankles and wrists were severely burned whenever molten metal splattered into his shoes or gloves, but he was now a skilled laborer and problem solver, with job security and a fair paycheck.

Now he was "set for life." And although he and she would need to live with his parents for a year before they could afford a house of their own, he proposed marriage to Eva Wagner. As he perspired at the wedding reception, fly ash and coal dust, embedded deep in his pores, gradually turned his white shirt gray.

Dad always took one of his two weeks of vacation in November to hunt deer, and the other during the summer to work around our home. He worked too much overtime at the plant to accomplish substantial household repairs and improvements at other times. In 1958, so that my sister Kim and I need no longer share a bedroom, he used a week of vacation to convert our small living room into a bedroom and to begin building a new and bigger living room. In 1959 he finished the living room and poured sidewalks. In 1960, he put on a new roof and remodeled the bathroom.

Separately we were so busy—he with work and I with the childhood that I felt was eternal—that at times we seemed, despite our love, to be mere acquaintances.

* * *

Without knocking, his clothes and skin blackened with coal dust, a man walked into our home. Laughing at my frightened failure to recognize him, Dad explained that the showers at the power plant were shut down for repairs.

Eight years later, when I was a college freshman majoring in English, I thought for a moment that I knew who that man was. He was dying and I asked him if he would change anything about his life if he could live it over. Without a pause he replied, "No."

I then asked another, malicious question: Suppose that the coal dust, fly ash or welding fumes had caused his cancer, wouldn't he, if he had it to do over, go to college, try for a better job? "No. All my friends work at the plant." Suddenly, I thought I recognized him, in *The Hairy Ape*—Eugene O'Neill's play about an uneducated, misled and fanatically proud laborer named Yank.

But then Dad, who had lost his prostate and adrenal glands and testicles to the knives of surgeons, who took Darvon for the pain in the inoperable places, who was still welding at the plant, my father, smiling mischievously, said something uncharacteristic of a Yank: "Well, there is one thing I'd change. I would have raised you different."

* * *

What was it all for, the toiling, sacrificing and saving in an imaginary paradise that would be lost?

On a sticky summer evening Dad and I, in the middle of the front lawn beneath a maple tree with lusterless leaves hanging still, sat in lawn chairs that rocked slightly on curved, springy legs. Nestlings chirped and robins hopped across the lawn. Throughout the neighborhood men and children, and women after the kitchen work was done, all full with food, came outside. Children in bathing suits ran shouting through the cool arching spray of lawn sprinklers, fell, jumped up laughing with blades of grass sticking to their skin; others, including my sisters, migrated barefooted up the shoulder of the road, stepping gingerly on the gravel, carrying towels to visit friends who had small swimming pools.

As the shadows grew and the angling light became syrupy, the shouts and laughter reverberating off the encircled water of the above-ground pools faded into the chatter of children hiking home with bathing suits dripping and wet hair tangled. Adults carried lawn chairs into the garage, coiled their garden hoses, walked laggardly into sweltering houses.

One by one the living room windows filled with yellow light. The heavy sky rumbled in the distance, the leaves rustled, and the air began to fill with the earthy odor of an approaching storm. Dad and I, who all evening had said no more than a dozen words but felt contented, stood up to go inside where Mom and my sisters had settled in front of the television.

It was all so that there was a brief time and small place where the endless toiling, sacrificing and saving could be forgotten.

*   *   *

Today I have a good enough life. I'm a househusband and freelance writer, and my wife is a schoolteacher. We have a roof over our heads, food on the table, and our children seem as happy as any. Yet sometimes I feel that everything has gone permanently bad: the economy, the government, the American family, the morals of the young, even the weather. It's in the newspapers and—everything is changing, going to hell—and it's been in the newspapers since our nation was founded. It's our perpetual regret to discover that no amount of work can preserve the present or bring back the past.

Several months ago, my graced 6-year-old daughter began requesting a new type of bedtime story on evenings when I'm not busy writing. She studies the several framed photographs hanging on the living room wall before pointing to one and asking, "Tonight will you please tell me a story about that picture?" And after she is tucked in I tell her a legend inspired by the photograph of her great-great-great-grandfather gripping the handles of a horse-drawn plow in Ireland, or her grandfather wearing grimy coveralls, or her mother holding her in front of our new home when she was a newborn.

And recently, after I finished telling her the legend of the sacrifices her mother and I made before we could afford to build our small home, my daughter asked, "Do you think I'll live here when I grow up?"

"Maybe."

"Forever?"

DIVIDED WE STAND

Ann Egerton

MORE THAN A year later, I still have regrets about my son's wedding. Oh, all went well, even though it poured rain. The bride was lovely, the groom (I thought) was handsome; everyone knew where to go and what to do; no one flubbed his lines. It was a happy day for the couple.

But I regret that I wasn't standing next to my son's father, beaming with unmitigated pride and happiness. Because of our divorce five years ago we sat apart; I with my new husband, he with his new wife. Don't misunderstand me. I'm glad I'm no longer married to my children's father; I'm thrilled I found a new husband. My ex surely feels he took a positive step too. Had we stayed together even longer than the 30 years we were married and put up a united front at our son's wedding, it would have been a perverse sham. The title of John Updike's collection of short stories about the dissolution of an old marriage describes our situation perfectly: *Too Far To Go*.

Still, nothing dredges up the pain of divorce for parents like the wedding of one of their children. Perhaps my pain was deserved punishment for our failure, but such parental separateness seems to throw the celebration of a new union in the family out of kilter. It creates a disquieting and ironic undertone, almost an omen, at a child's wedding.

While my ex-husband and I are civil to each other, our divorce did cause awkwardness, especially at the bridal dinner the night before the wedding. We gave the dinner together; he paid for the meal while I covered the flowers and invitations. I planned the menu and arranged the 30 or so guests at the three round tables. Everyone was polite and jolly, but arranging the seating, especially of my ex and me, veterans of a failed marriage, and our new spouses, was delicate. Typical repressed WASPs, we welcomed each other with curt nods and monosyllabic greetings and then stayed far apart during the evening. Next day my ex and I were no better; we exchanged hellos once, and we certainly didn't dance at the reception. I wondered if my ex-husband was sad, too. I wondered if he felt the same void I did at our son's wedding.

Parents who sit apart at an offspring's wedding symbolize the larger issue of the breakdown of the family that is plaguing this country. The symbols are there at holidays, birthdays, graduations, such religious ceremonies as first communions and bar mitzvahs—all those special days that constitute important milestones of a young person's life and that assume celebration and family togetherness. When the family is in pieces, the spontaneous pleasure of the occasion is often diminished and the event becomes something to get through instead of celebrate. Everyone, especially the young, is robbed.

The divorce rate has slowly and steadily been going up since the 1960s, and by the 1980s only half of the marriages that took place were projected to stay intact. The number of strained weddings and other family occasions must be going up too. Certainly many of the weddings I've been to lately have been fractured affairs like my son's, outwardly festive, but with an undercurrent of tension. I assume that many other parents in similar situations have felt as torn as I.

Or am I just being old-fashioned and mawkish? Is it more hip to shrug off these feelings of sadness and failure? How sophisticated must the divided couple at a child's wedding be? Maybe the times call for indifference to the past on the part of the parents and of their children. Maybe emotional coolness is a required corollary to the breakdown of the family, a defense mechanism that we've acquired in the latter part of this century—a mechanism that helps us not to show, perhaps not to feel, if we've become really good at it, the hurt and the guilt.

I suppose this is why many divorced people hate the big holidays so, even if they have remarried and created a new nest. It's not just the crass commercialism of Christmas, for instance, that we dread.

It's that we must feign gaiety and conviviality, and everyone in-volved—above all, the children, whether they're 7 or 27—know it. Of course, if an intact marriage is miserable, the children suffer from that too. But the gatherings of reconstituted families, of stepchil-dren and assorted stepparents, can be strained and serve as a re-minder of the initial failure and loss. As for sharing the children on holidays, my son has told me that he and his wife aren't going to spend their time going from her parents to my house to his father's. "We're going to alternate," he says, quite firmly. "Otherwise it's not a holiday for us."

We're a funny culture, increasingly tough when it comes to in-your-face language, music, clothes or conduct, but still with a wist-ful faith in the sanctity of big occasions and their implicit family togetherness, even when the family isn't together. Family weddings involving parents who are torn asunder represent a dichotomy be-tween the fresh vows to be together until death do us part versus the failure to do so. They smack ironically of idealism on one hand and practical realism on the other.

There are no solutions to this. Life does go on, and the passing of time after a breakup makes the big occasions easier to bear. With luck, the reassembled family makes new, happy memories of its own in time. However, I can't help but notice that a large segment of the 20-something generation is waiting a long time to marry and, it would seem, picking and choosing more carefully, although the birth control pill and mass entrances of women into the work force have as much to do with the postponement of marriage as wariness by the children whose parents were divorced.

In the meantime, I learned something at my son's wedding: I'm not so hip.

THE FIXER
Regina Blakely

I WAS 11 years old on the day my father retired from the bank where he'd worked for 45 years. My mother made a big dinner and a frosted cake, and I remember that when the front door opened she did not wait for him to wend his way into the kitchen but took a few steps away from the stove and craned her neck to watch him come in.

And he did not stop to look at the mail on the dining room table; instead, he kept his eyes fixed in the direction of the kitchen. Even when my brother intercepted him to shake his hand, my father only barely acknowledged it—his eyes were full on my mother and the two of them, my parents, seemed to be having a conversation they'd waited 45 years to have, all in the look that went between them.

It probably wasn't half a minute before somebody said something loudly cheerful like, "So, how does it feel?" and my father answered something confused—"Yeah! How 'bout that?"—and everyone gathered around him to see his new watch while my brother examined the liqueur they'd given him. The phone started ringing then, with calls of congratulations from his three college-age children, who had wanted to be there but couldn't, and from all his friends in the neighborhood.

My 11-year-old mind got stuck on that look though, and I could not, no matter how hard I swallowed, move into celebration. Instead I took the big mahogany nameplate my father had brought home with him down into the basement and curled up with it in an old armchair. I held the heavy authority of that nameplate in my hands and fingered the thick brass letters that spelled "J.D. Blakely." As I listened to my father laughing with the crowd above me, I thought about how official he wasn't anymore and started to cry, until my mother came down and assured me that *she* had plenty for him to do, and that if she ever ran out of ideas he would just have to find another job.

Whenever I remember the day my father retired, I remember my mother, and how ready she seemed for it all to happen. My father was a bit overwhelmed, and as I watched him come in I should have recognized that my own overemotional response toward life was inherited from him, the balding but forever boyish-looking man with the flushed cheeks and the watery, expectant look.

The sense of moment could hardly have been lost on my mother, whose lifestyle would be changed as much as his by this event, but no matter, if there were to be an episode of passionate upheaval inspired by the situation then she could handle herself, and she could handle my father and me too. With the compassionate firmness genuine care inspires in women of strength, my mother had a way of letting her brood know when we had despaired enough, when it was time to "stop being ridiculous," and most importantly, when it was best to "get on with things."

The ethic of "getting on with things" played an important part in the lives my parents crafted for themselves in retirement. During the first months of his apparent joblessness, my father kept busy by fixing things, and often he would attach himself to a worn-out something that my mother thought beyond repair. For a while he ran a halfway house for ailing household items out of his workspace in the basement. "There's a couple of good years left in that," he would say as he dragged a broken chair or a tool without a handle back from the garbage to keep until he could restore it. If my mother would refuse to admit the piece to its former place of dignity in the house, he'd put it to work in his territory for the time that he had promised to extend its usefulness.

Some things he "fixed" did serve him those "couple of good years," though sometimes in a more limited capacity: A child-sized card table chair that had rusted was low to the ground and thus "good for gardening," screwdrivers with taped handles stayed on his inventory of tools "to open paint cans." Once, he took on a huge dining room table that seemed to resist his best restorative efforts, but before it could be carried out it lay legs-up for six months on the basement floor. At last his son with the carpentry experience came in from Canada for Christmas, and the two spent hours together working on it, my brother noting with empathy that it was indeed made of "good wood," my father finally conceding that while it had three great legs, the last one was "a stinker."

Eventually he did go back to work. He took a part-time job taking care of the banking and other special errands for some Walgreens executives. At 10 a.m. he left the house each day and drove to company headquarters, where he picked up the banking paperwork and was then driven downtown in a chauffeured limousine. For two hours or so, he would walk through the Loop "taking care of things"—making large deposits, arbitrating complicated loan agreements, stopping in at Tiffany's to pick up a diamond for the vice president's wife—trivial stuff for a former bank officer, but he was hardly interested in advancement. He became a kind of corporate wise man to the people he worked with—he was one bold step of disinterest beyond those "seasoned professionals," and they trusted him. One day he came home particularly pleased that he'd consoled a worried junior executive by explaining that the company was "grooming the fella for management." And "sure enough," the following month the promotion came through.

In the meantime, my mother made plans. Regularly and playfully, she added to her list of things she always wanted to do and coaxed my father into doing them with her. They'd never been to Europe—three of us took a dizzying tour of the continent. She efficiently handled their elaborate schedule of bridge dates and golf outings and dances, and always managed to be sure that "the folks" were home whenever their more casually organized children drifted in for the holidays.

Gradually, my father began to accommodate to the rhythms and pleasures of this new lifestyle. By the time he retired for the second time, his fix-it work had become less painstakingly carried out and more outspokenly clever in appearance. There was the eyebrow tweezer that hung precariously in a dashboard groove of our car where the knob to control the heater had broken off. If you wanted heat, you reached into the groove with the tweezer and turned the stem. And there was the bright blue tile from his collection of odds and ends that he grafted onto the smooth pale gray of a kitchen counter to hide where the coffeepot had burned the formica.

His resilient optimism about the utility of time-worn things made the house a place of contented amusement for all of us—the corners that marked his work area seemed particularly charged with this air of almost ridiculously high-spirited antiquity. Few of his strictly make-do repairs coordinated well with my mother's decorating scheme, but if she argued against them he'd defend his craft with vigor. Inevitably, she then would caution him about how "eccentric" he was getting in old age.

Indeed he was and is, but my parents now see "eccentricities" as a kind of old-age index that they check regularly in their playful teasing of one another; it is one in a whole list of fears about old age that they make it a point to laugh about and then "get on with things." They moved to Florida a few years ago, where they bought a mobile home in a community of their peers. It is a place full of people who, like them, live bravely and, despite fears about eccentricities or physical frailties, pursue relentlessly the game of "shuffle" or the dip in the pool or any other number of "daring" things they do to bring themselves joy.

It's there that my father will celebrate his 90th birthday this December. If I know my mother, there will be plenty of Bailey's Original Irish Cream on hand for the celebration, as well as family and close friends and telephone calls from the working children who wanted to be there but couldn't.

I will be one of those phone callers, yelling cheerful well-wishes and participating, as far as possible over the miles that separate us, in the passionate excitement of another landmark day in his life. On his 90th birthday I would like my father to know that watching him move forward into the created contentment of his life in retirement has taught me never to indulge dread, and that I treasure a certain memory of the expression he wore the day he came home to retire because it reminds me of how much we've grown, he and I, over the years.

I know that in our separate cities we will both get red in the face

and moist at the eyes, and that my mother and guests on his side
and a few close friends on my side will have to be on hand to keep
us from getting overemotional. But things will be entirely different
from the day my father came home from the bank where he'd
worked for 45 years. The girl for whom doubt was too much to bear
at age 11 will raise a toast to her father, arrived with such grace and
good health upon the age of 90. Savoring the richness of Irish
Cream, she will thank him for his usefulness to her as a man wise
for his years, and celebrate the privilege of "getting on with things"
in such fine company.

AND MY MOTHER SWAM
IN THE SEA

Elizabeth Apone

W E HAVE RETURNED to the sea. For yet another year's vacation, we come to the Jersey shore the week after Labor Day for peaceful harbors free of summer travelers. My mother has long ago resigned herself to an annual vacation in the same locality, her dreams of a European trip or a Western excursion put back on her mind's shelf. My father is a true homing pigeon, zeroing in on the familiar curve of the Jersey coastline.

"I saw Europe from a foxhole when I was 19. Why go back?" he asks, referring to W.W. II, "The Big One" as Archie Bunker would put it.

My folks have driven in from Pittsburgh, while my fiance, Jeff, and I arrive from Northern Jersey where I now reside. As we pull in the driveway, the house we rent annually looks a little dingier than it used to. From the car window my parents look a little frailer, slightly smaller than I remember. I am gripped by the chill of change.

Recalling a time when my parents seemed ageless, I realize the months that yawn between our visits makes change more pronounced. A slower gait, a grayer head go unnoticed in day-to-day living, but on occasional visits, change stands out like a scarlet letter.

But their smiles and embraces quickly wash away the gulf of time, and as I am held in their grasping arms I become a child again, the "little one" as my grandmother used to say. They look so familiar, swathed in comfortable running outfits, impossibly unhip velour tops, practical shoes. Returning to them is a luxurious break from the day-in, day-out rigors of adulthood. To be taken care of, fussed over, worried about is like being wrapped in a warm, sturdy quilt. It is startling to realize that when they pass on, I will lose this ephemeral island of childhood.

My father, as usual, had stationed himself in the window to be the first one to herald my arrival, his eyes scanning the road through heavy rimmed glasses. "I get first hugs," he hollered, an old ritual. My mother came behind him, just as quickly, laughing, her face a lovely blend of petite features and enormous eyes.

I recall weekends when I would wait until the click of the mailbox lid indicated the arrival of the day's letters. Despite a quick start, I could never quite get there before Dad, and instead of finding mail I would see him gleefully running away, letters under the arm like the football held by the Heisman statue.

I wonder if he can beat me to the mailbox now.

Like the prodigal son, we find food waiting for us, not quite as elaborate as the fatted calf, but sufficient. Jeff eats greedily, fearful of starvation at the hands of my parents. Having cooked for three people under 5 feet, 4 inches for so many years, my mother is puzzled at the prospect of feeding a 6-footer with the appetite of a grizzly. During many of his visits, Jeff would leave my house on the pretense of filling the gas tank, only to raid McDonald's drive-through.

We head to the beach, each of us assuming our preferred vacation pose: my mother and I walking slowly in one direction, my father jaunting briskly the other way, Jeff lying semi-comatose on his back in the sunshine.

Talking leisurely with my mother is a pleasure like no other. Unlike most people I converse with, she is a superior listener who also asks thoughtful, appropriate questions. Inevitably, at work and at parties, she is cornered by long-winded boors who take advantage of her special gift. Speaking to her I am, for once, sure that someone is engaged in my conversation and, more importantly, interested in my thoughts, my dreams. No one ever listens with as much interest as your mother.

She seems happy, looks tan and strong. Always athletic, her frame remains trim. Despite the glow of health, she has problems that accompany age, high blood pressure, occasional dizzy spells. My father, she says, has fewer health problems, yet he visits the doctor perpetually. A slight hypochondriac, he can always find a mole in need of removal, an annoying ingrown toenail. We chuckle over the bag of remedies, potions, pills, and creams he has once again lugged to Jersey.

If my father is anything, he is prepared. He likes to plan ahead for unforeseen problems, complications, ever the diligent Boy Scout. On my last visit to Pittsburgh, I went for the final fitting of my wedding dress and my father asked to see me in it. I told him it would be bad luck. "Something could happen to me between now and then," he countered. "I'm no spring chicken. I want to see you today." I was furious with him for allowing the specter of death to enter my mind.

But I got over it when I showed him the dress and saw his proud, teary expression. It had been a good decision, sharing today with him. Standing there, I realized that life yields few moments of pure, unadulterated happiness. More often our joy is tinged with sorrow, laughter coming through tears.

On the beach are two red floppy dogs. The smaller one ventures over to us; the larger dog stares in our direction from his obedient post beside the master. As we praise and pet the first animal, who proudly displays half a clamshell between his teeth, the other whines to join our group. Freed at last, he bounds up to us, wet nose covered in clinging sand, and almost knocks my mother down with an enthusiastic thwack of his bushy tail against her knees. Somewhat alarmed, I steady her.

My father joins us now; we spotted him long before, pigeon-toed walk and all, heading in our direction. My mother is putting on her white bathing cap, carefully tucking the exposed curls neatly underneath.

"Ah, Esther Williams, I presume," my father says.

We watch her swim, my father and I, from the safety of our beach chairs. Her arms cut a line through the water like scissors through navy silk. She is the voyager among us who fears no rough currents, no chilly water, her face free of worry lines. Those on shore do the worrying for her. A nervous child grown into a cautious adult, I feel the sharp metal edge of my chair and decide that, should a shark attack her, this will be my weapon. Poking the beast's black oval eyes, swatting its tender snout, I'll free her and drag her to safety.

I am her hero, and if I could save her, save him, from any danger in the sea, any looming terror in the night, I would. Unconsciously, like the silent turn of a page, like a faint whisper at dawn, I have become the protector of my parents. Somewhere along the line, at a point I can't place, I entered the prime of my life while they moved unnoticed into their twilight years.

I am thankful to see them now, retired, content and self-sufficient, yet I prepare my heart for the future. My closet empty of the childhood monsters they once banished, I stand gallantly, sword in hand, ready to rage at the possible bogeymen of their tomorrows: senility, sickness, the loss of one by the other, and yes, even a final, inevitable disappearing act by them both. "The Child is Father of the Man," I read in a college poetry course, yet only now does this passage seem understandable and oddly personal.

Patiently I wait on shore for my mother, knowing this is one sea that, for now, she will return from.

A LONG INTERMITTENT WAKE

Burnie Bauer

"I CAN'T RAISE MY MIND. Please help me!" pleaded Helene, my wife of 46 years, as I helped her get dressed the other morning.

It's been a little over three years since we were told she had Alzheimer's disease, although looking back we should have seen it as much as a year earlier. But we thought not remembering phone calls and forgetting the names of close friends was just part of aging. It was only after she fell and hit her head on the basement floor that X-rays led to the diagnosis of Alzheimer's. Since that day, someone has always been with her.

Fortunately, seven of our nine children live in the area and take turns having her at their houses for part of the day so I can go to the office. And our 15 grandchildren are happy to have Grandma about; they take her by the hand in church and lead her around in the stores and show her much consideration.

Every two weeks for two and a half years, we drove into Chicago so Helene could receive treatment at Rush-Presbyterian-St. Luke's Hospital, where she was one of 10 patients participating in the Dartmouth Alzheimer Research Program. The doctors administered a chemical whose deficiency in the brain, researchers feel, causes the loss of memory and awareness that characterizes Alzheimer's. Recently, however, the program was suspended, dashing our hopes. We've now embarked on a multiple vitamin course suggested by my experience while working at Lobund when I was a student.

Generally on those Chicago trips we would arrange to have lunch with our daughter Mary, who lives in Chicago, and get home by evening. Once we got stuck in a snowstorm and had to stay over-night in a roadside home.

Thank God for our large family—now I know why He sent them—and for the nearby nursing homes that will take Helene for a day if it's necessary.

Daily I watch for signs of a comeback, and often I'm rewarded . . . only to see her slip backward in some other area. For instance, she refuses to write her name, but one day she promptly wrote her first and second names, Helene Genevieve, then balked at writing her last name. "I can't do that," she pleaded, and another balloon burst. After not recognizing our second son, Matt, by name for sev-eral months, she suddenly did; but a few days later she asked our oldest son, Pat, who he was. Increasingly of late she asks me where her husband is.

Life with an Alzheimer loved one is like a long, intermittent wake. The body is there but the mind and personality are gone, returning only occasionally and reopening wounds. Helene is like a stranger who knows nothing of our friends, ideas or the events we have shared. Brief lucid moments surprise you, and when she asks, "Is something wrong with me?" the tears choke you.

It is particularly hard when she starts to quote some poetry or a line from a play she was in, and then forgets the last word. One can't help recalling her sharp, supple mind and the poetry and drama con-tests she won in college. But the sadness is tempered by the knowl-edge that she suffers no pain and seems to sense the love she is draw-ing out from family and friends and even strangers when we go out.

Friends from the past 40 years—especially friends from the Chris-tian Family Movement and from Notre Dame—are most supportive and understanding. They stop and talk to both of us when we ven-ture out to eat or to church. Helene seems to enjoy it; she tries to respond, even though she often can't complete sentences. We have often been invited to stay in friends' homes on trips and made to feel like family.

Alzheimer's has been described as the long goodbye. I've already said goodbye to Helene as my wife, but I still have her as a child, not unlike the way my seven daughters were when they were learn-ing to walk and talk—except progress is now in reverse.

I try to hang on to our memories as I take her with me on shopping or small business calls, talking to her as we drive along of the good times we've had together. It's a monologue, but occasionally when I mention the name of a friend or a place she will react with a brief smile and murmur some phrase, generally incomprehensible.

Often I end my frustration by saying the Hail Mary or Our Father; I ask her, with occasional success, to repeat the first few words. That's also the last thing I say to her at night, when she grasps my hand in a drowning person's grip and drifts off to sleep.

Some night it will be forever.

ROOM FOR ONE MORE

Barrie Maguire

WE HAD LOVE to spare, we told ourselves. Plenty of extra love to give the little girl with the black curly hair and the flashing eyes.

Amy was already 8 months old when we met her for the first time at that Wilmington adoption agency. Every time I held her she yelled her head off, but I didn't care. "Oh, yes we want her," we sang to the large, serious woman who was offering Amy to us. Just one week later, we brought her home to meet her four excited brothers and sisters.

Almost from the beginning, Amy's new life in our house was less than ideal. Maybe because she'd arrived almost without warning, maybe because she was adopted, maybe because we didn't have enough love for *five* children after all.

Sadly, after a few months it began to dawn on me that I was feeling fundamentally different about Amy than I was about my other children, my natural children. If Amy's 2-year-old brother woke crying in the night, I would leap from my bed to console him, to reassure him that his daddy loved him, that he was safe. When Amy cried in the night I would wait a bit to see if she was going to stop before I reluctantly dragged myself from bed. It was the same with dropped bottles, thrown baby food, wet diapers. I didn't have the empathy towards her that came automatically with the others. Amy just didn't feel like one of *my* kids.

It was almost as if—and I fought to keep the thought at bay—it was as if I didn't love her.

Distressed, I kept my awful secret to myself.

The night after Amy's first birthday, I lay in bed remembering her delighted face at the party table, her utterly futile attempts to blow out the candle, her fat little fist oozing chocolate icing; if those sweet images hadn't turned me around, nothing would. I reached the dreadful conclusion that Amy would never feel like one of mine, that I would never truly love her. But, oh God, she must *never* know!

I would have to pretend.

I would have to pretend I was happy to see her, pretend I loved being with her, pretend I loved her. The next morning, I lifted her out of her crib and told her how very much her daddy loved her. The words rang hollow in my ears, but I put everything I had into it, hoping, praying I could fool her. From then on I scooped her into my arms at every opportunity, grinning my biggest fake grin, pushing negative thoughts from my mind. "I love you, Amy," I'd say, poking my nose into her tummy or beaming down at her in her crib, "I love you, I love you, *love* you!"

Just as it is impossible to pinpoint the exact moment when the dark of night surrenders to the morning, I don't know precisely when love found Amy and me. But one evening at bedtime, a week or so into my charade, I was kneeling on the floor by her crib, Amy's baby-laughter bouncing off the bedroom walls, when suddenly, stunningly I realized the pretending was gone. The artificial had been made real. Now I was the father of five.

Within a few weeks of the day I fell in love with Amy, Ted was born a thousand miles away. It was another 13 years before he and I first laid suspicious eyes on each other: Ted standing silently on carpeted stairs, his hand on the banister . . . me silhouetted in the doorway . . . his mother turning, a hopeful smile on her face, to introduce her only child to the man she would eventually marry.

Immediately after our wedding, we whisked Ted off, ready or not, to a new home and a new life in faraway Pennsylvania.

Although he stayed in his room a lot, Ted and I developed a good relationship during his high school years. In a way, I was pretending again—conveying a degree of intimacy that really wasn't there—the way stepparents and stepchildren do. It was much easier this time; I didn't have to make room in my heart for Ted, the way I'd had to for Amy. Ted already had parents who loved him. Ted was my *step-*

child, he didn't need my love the way my five kids did. He just needed me to like him. And I did. I helped him where I could, encouraged his dream of becoming a filmmaker. We treated each other with respect, friendship and, at times, affection.

One year after Ted graduated from film school, we all gathered in a sunny, flower-bedecked loft for his wedding. The room was packed with aunts and cousins and parents and grandparents and, of course, Ted's stepbrothers and stepsisters, my five kids.

As Ted and his bride stood facing each other, I could see over her shoulder directly into his amazingly grownup face. His bride had already begun her vows when her voice faltered, then stopped altogether. None of us breathed. A look of alarm flashed across Ted's face and his cheeks began to redden. Then he looked down at her and gave her a tiny smile of encouragement, and a tear appeared in the corner of his eye. His bride regained her composure and began her recitation again, but I didn't hear her. For me, the room, the traffic outside the window, the whole world had grown silent. For me, there was just his face. Ted's face, and that gutsy, grown-up, husbandly tear slowly sliding down his cheek.

Afterward, I put my arms around him and pulled him close as his strong arms tightened around me. What I whispered into his ear surprised both of us. "I love you," I told him for the very first time. "I never knew how much until today."

Sheepishly we released each other, and I turned away to find my tall, beautiful, precious Amy standing behind me. I hugged her and gave her the news: Now I was the father of six.

With both my adopted daughter and my stepson, love took awhile to show itself. I now believe that love was always there, hiding in the dark like the sun hides at night. But when love finally showed its face, the sunrise was spectacular.

A PATCH OF WOODS
ALONG THE LAKE

Kerry Temple

I DON'T KNOW why you go to that place," my friend said. "There's nothing there."

"You're wrong," I told him. "Everything is."

It's a matter of perspective, I suppose, that enables one to see what is and isn't there. The stars shine in the daytime too; the sun's radiance just upstages them. Even city lights dull them at night, but it doesn't mean they're not all up there, like lanterns beaming in the cosmos.

My friend and his family had just returned from Disney World, Epcot Center and Busch Gardens, with a swing back to the Midwest through the nation's capital. He talked about Space Mountain, the Smithsonian and the dancing dolphins at Marineland. So I understood his reservations about my low-budget vacation retreat into the woods with my two sons. What's there, he asked, to entertain or educate adolescent boys ready to spring into the world? After all, we weren't going to the Tetons, Yosemite or the Grand Canyon. Just a patch of woods along Lake Superior.

So in a sense he was right when he said there's nothing there—except for rocks and trees, the crystal beauty of clean, cold water, mud and grass and sand and the solitary nest of a lordly bald eagle. There are no museums, no amusement parks, no golden arches or showers or television sets to turn on at night. That's precisely why we go: to see the stars far, far away from the glare of the city lights. They are so much brighter.

I remember a night and a towering summer sky and a cool, damp wind blanketing us. We had driven that day far out a dirt road to the forested shore of Lake Superior, where we pitched a tent and made ourselves at home. At dusk we began walking along the beach, the cold, dark water slapping against sand and stone. We walked until night fell, until the stars came out, until we stopped and stared. Then we listened to water and wind and beheld the cosmic wizardry.

No one talked—not even when shooting stars flamed across the sky. Not even as time passed and the constellations slid down the galactic dome. Then a toad appeared, a dark, leggy blob hopping along the moonlit beach. Another. And a third.

The trio was soon corralled by two barefoot cowboys, caressed and belly-stroked, played with and confined in a hole dug especially for the occasion but from which they easily escaped, only to be re-captured. Set loose. Observed. Seized and, for purely experimental purposes, flung into the frigid depths of the largest of the five Great Lakes.

In time each toad re-emerged from the tidal foam to be tried again and again—until a whip of a snake slithered into view and distracted the merry scientists from their toad study. The boys set upon the snake, which also showed an impressive ability to boomer-ang ashore—until one final hurl from which it never returned. After a sullen vigil knee-deep in the toe-numbing waters, we agreed the snake must have outflanked us in order to take a less Sisyphian passage to land.

I don't know what time it was when we finally tumbled into our tent and zipped our bags against the chill, but I remember thinking about things—about what makes the water cold, and how long it takes for rocks to be ground into sand, and how many stars are out there, spiriting their light across the mysterious cauldron of life we call the sky. And I weighed something my son had asked: "If the universe is expanding, what is it expanding *into?*" And I thought about God. And the rightness of toads. And the solace of empty places.

And I realized how, when all the stuff that's been close around you gets pushed far away, what has been distant draws very near—until you can look upon nothing and see everything.

* * *

There are four rocks in the glove compartment of my car. I brought them home with us and sometimes they rattle around in there, like talismans reminding me of places where we played. One is as big and red as a human heart. It feels good in my hand. I remember when I saw it—bold red amid the earth-tone stones lodged under four feet of water at the edge of Lake Superior. It gleamed. When I bent to snag it, my face splashed into the cold, clear lake as my hand plunged deeper than I had anticipated. Rarely does water run so clear so deep.

We were on an island. No one else was around, and we had wandered the woods all day. It was hot and close and buggy, and as fatigue enveloped us we saw a bear.

It was a big, black bear high atop a bare, dead tree. We were tired and hot from walking all day when Ross said, "There's a bear." We could see its pink tongue licking, needling at the tree, then it stopped and we looked at each other for a minute or two. The bear seemed surprised to see us, as if it had been caught with its nose in a honey jar. It shimmied down a few feet—its cleat-like claws scrattling over the brittle bark—then stopped and looked at us again. We were all fixed like that for a moment: alien creatures watching apprehensively across some great divide, with no language to span the chasm. Then the bear dropped to the ground, looked once over its shoulder and disappeared into the dense green foliage. We ran the opposite way.

We were still a little high when we made it to the water's edge. The sun was low and we could see a couple of smaller islands across the water to the west. We stood on the cusp of a gentle inlet flanked by tawny cliffs and riddled with boulders and nice climbing rocks scattered along the shore. Despite the water's frigid grasp, I could not resist the urge to swim. So we stripped down to our underwear and plunged into the lake.

We played there a long time, climbing on the rocky shelves, exploring beach and cliff and secluded grotto until the yellow sun eased into the lake. There was no place else we needed to go, no one waiting for us. We could stay out all night if we wished. Our camp was set up in an orchard of birch trees on a tongue of land some ways down the shore. It would be there whenever we arrived. Our excursions had an air of boundlessness about them, an immunity from any limits of time or space.

I watched my barebacked sons in their idle wanderings, watched them devise games out of driftwood and imagination, watched them dodge deer flies and chase sea gulls and lose themselves in this lavish playground of earthwork and whimsy. I like to watch these boys turned loose upon the land. They seem at home, joyously engaged in a sporting life that possesses the heart. "I am glad I shall never be young without wild country to be young in," Aldo Leopold wrote. "Of what avail are 40 freedoms without a blank spot on the map?"

* * *

It was a meaningless and futile activity, and I'm not sure why we started it—except that I wanted to dig my fingers into the earth.

I had been sitting and watching long enough. It is good to observe, waiting for the quiet pieces of landscape to come to you, but sometimes a restlessness sets in when you've been looking too long. And sometimes you can't know a place by what you see.

The boys had been out all morning, climbing mountains of sand, bowling rocks downhill, skipping stones over the lake. Sunlight glinted off their bare shoulders as they, stickmen in the distance, tiptoed in the lake.

I sat by a clear, spring-fed stream that crashed out of the woods and crossed a strip of sand and stone before flowing into the lake. I was enchanted by the raucous whitewater, the liquid brilliance, the way the weaving waters surged and spun and rolled around rocks and whitewashed slabs of wood. Sunlight glistened off its surface, pockmarked with ripples and eddies. Sunlight splashed off the multicolored cobblestones embedded in the bottom. Sunlight made rainbows in the bubbles.

I was entranced by the currents, the wave patterns of rapids and falls, the spiraling showcase of whirlpools that drowned sticks and leaves, only to spit them out later and shove them out to sea. And I thought about the persistence of water. The fluidity of living. The interminability of flow. The liquid confluence of sunlight and stone. The Zen of H_2O.

The stream, emerging from the woods, splayed into three rivulets as it cascaded toward the lake. When the boys came back, I flopped a log across one of the tributaries to serve as a bridge. But with a big splash it landed halfway down in the water and became more of a dam. I decided to finish the job. The boys and I set to work.

We recruited the largest rocks first, packing them snugly between the stream bed and log dam. The water was largely undeterred; in fact, its pace seemed to quicken as it broke into a thousand silver fingers, finding the holes, opening new routes, perforating our dam. We worked quickly to plug the leaks, jamming rocks into any cavities we could see. The water level rose.

Encouraged, we redoubled our efforts. We stationed one stone-layer at the damsite while two gatherers waded upstream, seizing softball-sized rocks and tossing them back to the builder. Occasionally, having learned that surface area counts, we would enlist hunks of driftwood and wedge them into the stone wall. But the water found our gaps, and when Casey tried sealing the crevices with sand he learned he couldn't count on that shiftless material.

Eventually, dripping sweat, I stood to survey our progress and admire the irrepressible ingenuity of water. It was going over the top. It was eroding the banks at each side. It was burrowing underneath. There was no holding it back. What it couldn't dislodge or penetrate, it simply outmaneuvered.

So we moved upstream and tried again at a site more conducive to dam-building. And we applied what we had learned about materials and placement and structure. Two dams would be better than one. When that failed to work, well, we turned to the other tributaries and adjusted their configurations—removing impediments, rerouting the current—so they'd handle more of the river's volume. "We are changing the course of the universe," I said triumphantly as I dug out new channels by hand.

By now the boys were just watching. Hungry, they no longer shared my obsession. But I was having a blast, as happy as a toddler in a sandbox, oblivious to anything beyond the fringes of my imaginary little world—at least until the boys jumped me and we tumbled into the water and rolled around wrestling and rough-housing in a tickling-ticklish heap of arms and legs and laughter. They have grown too large for me to handle two-on-one, so I was the one who cried uncle. I do not like to be tickled; I didn't mind the sand in my face. And I didn't mind that the river was still carrying on as if I were a minor disruption in the natural order of things.

We dismantled the dam and rescattered the rocks. I stashed one in my pocket to keep—as a reminder of the day I spent all day doing nothing—then we walked away to let nature run its course.

* * *

This was the day of rain. We woke to the sound of it drumming on the tent, to the drip of it into the tent, and to a heavy gray sheath subduing the earth. I poked my head out and guessed that it would rain all day. The day proved me right.

The rain—steady, incessant, depressing—presented two choices. The leaky tent left us with one. So we pulled on slickers and ponchos, fired up the stove and had breakfast under water. Then we went for a walk. A wade.

The plan was to scout out a bald eagle's nest, following some loosely diagrammed directions provided by a fisherman. We eventually found the nest after several hours of meandering, but by then the quest was secondary—it was enough to be traipsing through the wet, wet woods, as soggy as river otters on a spree. We were happy. We were drenched. Our shoes had the texture of sponges.

We would have been miserable if we'd stopped, so we kept moving, following a trail and an old twin-rut logging road, skirting a pair of inland lakes, heading toward Lake Superior. We had been walking north for a while and were just beginning to drag when we heard it—the sound of breakers on rock. We raced ahead. Here is what we found.

The big lake was no longer a turquoise and aquamarine lullaby but a raging beast of charcoal swells and frothing whitecaps. We stood on a cliff, our toes clinging to sandstone and shale, and gazed down perhaps 1,000 feet into the surging, abysmal vat of angry water. Our bodies were buffeted by a cold wind that drove the dark clouds low across the sky. Huge fists of water hammered the rocky shore, sending crystal sprays high in the air. I moved the boys away from the cliff's edge and we stood in awe of the power resounding in nature's temper.

We were hypnotized by the constant smack and suck of the waves, by the speed of the low-flying clouds, and by the fragility of the human form in the midst of such violent, indifferent forces. I shuddered to imagine one of the boys adrift in these turbulent waters, their kindling bones pitched into the ancient, inscrutable walls, then dragged into the depths.

We spied a slender crescent of beach, found a passage down to it and flung rocks into the bellies of the crashing waves. Then we saw—offshore, bobbing along the surface, spinning like a candy-colored top—a beach-ball. It rode the undulating crests as it made its fitful way to the beach, where we snagged it out of the water: a toy spewed from the mouth of the cosmic fury.

So we played. We ran and chased each other in games of hotbox and dodge-ball—always mindful of the lake's grim threat and the danger of getting too cold. Then, from some combination of sunset and storm cloud, the world grew dark and the heavens opened up. The rains came harder, drilling the air and drenching us. Thunder cracked and rumbled across the water. Lightning bolts lit up the sky, crackled, flared all around us, snapping at the earth in a torrent of blinding flash-points. We took cover in a hollow of rock, bundling together to watch the show.

We waited out the storm. The sun eventually returned to the western horizon and illuminated the glassy landscape, just before sinking into the lake. The air was cleaned out, cool and still. We tromped back to the tent in the deepening twilight, put on warm, dry clothes and ate. Then we watched the straggler clouds pass like ghosts across the stars, and we nestled into our tent for a good night's sleep. And I put away another rock, this one stolen from a day when we said yes to a world that was moody and mean, for this night when it was so good to have one another.

* * *

The fourth and final rock came from paradise.

There was a beach where we played home-run derby with a tennis ball and driftwood bat. There was a river where we raced sticks, and some steep foothills where we tracked wildlife. At one end of the beach were rocky cliffs beautifully sculpted by wind and water and the touch of some invisible artist. Lively breakers exploded at the foot of these walls, the water shattering into sun-catching jewels.

With courage you could jump into the water from the cliffs. The freefall was scary and exhilarating. The water was deep green, almost pure emerald-green, and when you landed, the water hugged you in a frigid embrace, absorbing you into the liquid greenness. Swimming underwater with my eyes open, I felt I could glide into that greenness forever.

It was late afternoon when the stick races were over and the batting title had been settled. I told the boys it was time to head back to the tent for our last night in the woods. We started out, walking ankle deep in the lapping water. We were the only ones there and it felt like paradise. The sun was an orange ball hanging out over the water near the cliffs, which by now were silhouettes. Orange slivers danced upon the water in a trail leading to the sun.

"Can we go back?" the boys suddenly asked. "Can we jump off the rocks one more time?" I looked out over the water and thought of my shivery body and the chilled air and the hunger in my stomach and what it felt like to be 12 and what it would feel like to be back in my office in two days. I said yes.

The boys hustled back down the beach but I, somehow drawn to the sun and its luminous path, walked into the lake. The water was cold enough to contract my muscles and steal my breath, and I swam toward the cliffs in an urgent breaststroke, occasionally dipping my face into the water. And when finally I arrived at the jumping rocks, the tides nudged me into the cliffs like a bear nuzzling its young.

The boys arrived and we all jumped—over and over again, until we were trembling white prunes of goose-bumps and chattering teeth. Until dark descended and the world became a restful place. I took a stone from there. It is green, with a green vein all the way around it, as if it were two parts somehow fused together.

* * *

I have told the boys that the world is a poem whose meanings are there to be deciphered by those who will see. I have told them that there are different ways of seeing. I have tried to leave it at that.

It is hard sometimes to resist the urge to impose my meanings on things, to explain, for example, the importance of water, the significance of sand, the lessons of rock. I do not always refrain from such instruction, but I try. Look closely, I will tell them: Everything you need to know to get along in the world is right there. Read the poem. The meaning of life is all around you. The lessons are there in the woods. But in the long run it is probably better, rather than telling them *what* they should see, to help them learn *how*.

So I keep the rocks as keepsakes, reminders of a time and a place and a family on the loose, playing tag among the wild things, looking for the Artist's signature on an unfathomable universe, humbled in the knowledge that these stones may be as close to the eternal as we'll ever come. And I listen to the stories they have to tell, to the songs that may be sung but once in a lifetime.

A HOUSE DIVIDED

Helen Heineman

W̲E̲ ̲B̲O̲A̲R̲D̲E̲D̲ ̲O̲U̲R̲ train on a July afternoon, heading westward one last time toward my husband John's old Indiana home. His mother had sold the house and was about to move in with her youngest daughter. At a get-together a year before, all the members of the family had made their requests for furniture, china and other memorabilia that could not fit into Momo's new living arrangements. Now we were en route to help with the cleaning-out chores and, via rented truck, to take home our share of the "heirlooms."

Some years earlier when my own family home was emptied and sold, I was a young mother of four who left the chores to my siblings. As a result, I had not gone through my family's possessions one last time and had not made any requests for tokens of remembrance. Now I resolved to be fully a part of my husband's farewell to his family home.

On Amtrak's Lake Shore Limited, we chugged along the Berkshires and across the Massachusetts countryside. I fell asleep quickly in my tiny bunk, to wake at 5:30 a.m. in Buffalo as a sign flashed rapidly by my window: "Love God with your whole heart." We traveled along the shores of Lake Erie, then through Cleveland and on to Chicago. From there we drove the last leg of the trip with my husband's brother Bob and his family.

In Connersville, Indiana, our destination, we pulled up in sweltering heat to the large, 10-room, white house on Central Avenue. Entering the heavy, leaded glass door, we found Momo waiting for us in the parlor. Brother Bob and his wife had thoughtfully brought along a window air conditioner, and during our week's work this room became our headquarters.

This final stage of separating from the family home began with an evening of conversation. There was a sad seriousness about the remembered stories, a knowledge that this group would have no more such discussions sitting on the ornate parlor furniture, the old pump organ in the corner, the family pictures on the wall above the fireplace, the marble-topped tables and domed lamps shedding light on memories of life during two World Wars.

The next morning we began our work with the upstairs closets, hauling box after box down the stairs, along the steamy hallway, through the glass doors and into the parlor where Momo sat on the couch, waiting to decide the fate of tea cups and saucers, wedding crystal from 50 years ago, and painted vases from excursions to spots long forgotten. The question was always, could she bring the item with her or should it be given to one of the family? By late afternoon she had grown tired, reduced to nodding yes or no and waving objects away with a futile gesture, as if she could no longer take personal responsibility for so much unruly life.

Among our finds were three boxes containing her mother's wedding dress, wedding shoes, and what we'd now call a peignoir, a linen shift worked with an elaborate lace collar and cuffs. The outfit had bloomers, and we all laughed trying to imagine a wedding night in those boyish trousers.

Many of the boxes contained items belonging to Aunt Mary Hassett, who had pinned notes to each explaining where it came from, who had made it, and the date when it was received or given. Many bore warnings: "Never throw this away." Sometimes, she discreetly kept to herself the name of the maker of a shawl or a throw or a scarf, noting mysteriously, "If I named the person, there might be difficulties." As I went through the handkerchiefs, scarves, doilies, fans, beads, gloves and hats, Aunt Mary's words so haunted my efforts that in the end I kept everything, no matter how useless or deteriorated.

One day, overwhelmed by the sheer bulk of our finds, we drove up to Centerville to sell some unwanted things at an antiques mall.

Wandering the aisles, we were surrounded by more of what we'd left behind: milk-glass, Fostoria crystal, jugs, Hoosier kitchens, old sheet music, hats and hat pins, busts of Richard Wagner. These held no attraction for us, of course, unconnected as they were to memories of people from our own past. So we sold our rejects . . . dresses that fit no one, brass candlesticks and a large metal jug that had appeared in the house after a Red Cross drive. Then we drove home to clear more space in our own repository of the past.

The next day the two brothers tackled the barn, a large, dilapidated structure. In its heyday it had been a horse barn, and later it served as a place to store old bedframes and cars that didn't work. During the worst days of the Great Depression, it became a temporary haven for the family of an ex-nanny to some of the children. They constructed a makeshift kitchen in the back, and shared the bathroom facilities of the big house.

Now it was a place for junk and a home for raccoons and mice. No one wanted to clean it out. Bob and John rented a dumpster, defied the 98-degree heat, and all through the morning we could hear the sound of wood and metal being pitched from upstairs windows into the dumpster: old chairs, all the lights and pulls of a marionette theater, 60-year-old window screens, and hoards of toys smashed beyond reclaiming.

From its debris, the barn yielded one treasure. Like most buried treasures, it produced conflicting claimants. Brother Bob's 10-year-old son David had helped with the barn cleanout, lured by what he might find there. His labors ended with a shout of joy when he opened a small box and pulled out a hoard of baseball cards from the 1940s and '50s—Mickey Mantle, Ted Williams, Willie Mays. But the cards belonged to Brother Charles, who still wanted them, though he let David select a few for himself.

Our week was drawing to a close. We boxed up whole runs of newspapers and collections of books and drove to Cincinnati to see if anyone at the historical society there had any interest. They didn't.

Then it was time to pick up our rental truck and drive back to Boston with the pieces we had chosen: The large cherry corner cupboard that had stood in a dark corner of the dining room; another, more modern curio cabinet for one of our sons and his wife; a rocker; an ornate walnut table and its hurricane lamp; the rocking horse that great-grandfather had ridden as a child in the 1880s.

Our packing and loading completed, we climbed the stairs to bed. The weather was still grindingly hot—the fifth straight day of temperatures over 95 degrees—and during the night I lay restless, unable to sleep for the heat. I watched the open window, its gauzy curtains drawn back in the hope of a stray breeze.

Did I feel something brush my cheek? Perhaps instead of mere air it was the spirit of the man who had purchased the house for his family so many years ago, lingering to pay his respects to a new owner—who would not be a stranger but one of the family's grandsons, his flesh and blood after all. The idea persisted that he was watching and waiting, with the patience of spirits or angels sent on impossible missions.

In the early morning we headed out, waving goodbye to Momo, who stood in the driveway smiling tentatively. The moment brought back another parting, 15 years earlier, when we had loaded our station wagon with our four young sons. We all waved goodbye to Dad, who had risen early and was in an upstairs window of the house as I first knew it, in the fullness of its life.

People standing and waving goodbye: How many times, I thought, until the last time? But Mother was going on to a new life with her youngest daughter. Now it was the house that was bidding farewell, not its occupants.

As our yellow Rent-a-Truck rumbled and rattled through Indiana, Ohio and Pennsylvania, I pondered the week's experience: the dismantling, redistribution and sale of a home after the seven children born and raised there had grown up and left, one parent had died, and the other could no longer go it alone.

The grandson who bought it had told us he was planning to bring the house "up to date"—to tear up the old carpeting and refinish the hardwood floors, probably spreading an Oriental rug or two across their polished surfaces, to put a billiard table in the parlor and fill the cherry bookcases with athletic trophies. While the monumental stained glass window separating the bookcases must remain, others in the house were removed to form decorative focal points in the more modern homes of family members. Momo had taken one for herself in the hope of recreating her old home amid new walls. The kitchen cupboards were completely bare: The new occupant was single and would eat most of his meals out.

I found myself wondering if the house as it had been would remain alive somewhere—in remote corners, on back porches, or in the high doors which do not quite fit into their frames—and if its spirit would eventually impinge upon its new owner, who is also the new owner of a Jaguar convertible. On the face of things, such influence seemed to me not a good bet.

CONTRIBUTORS

Burnie Bauer, a 1938 graduate of Notre Dame, is a South Bend businessman. His wife, Helene, died on March 9, 1988, while sleeping in his arms.

Regina Blakely is a part-time poet and full-time trainer with an investment company in Phoenix.

Rebecca Banasiak Code graduated from Notre Dame in 1976 and is now an assistant professor of neurobiology at Texas Woman's University in Denton, Texas. Her husband, Jim, is a dentist and commander in the U.S. Public Health Service in Kings Point, New York. Jim and Becky have lived together a total of 13 years during their 20-year marriage, although Jim is set to retire from military service in 1998.

Walt Collins, a 1951 graduate of Notre Dame, was editor of *Notre Dame Magazine* for 12 years before retiring in 1995.

Brian Doyle graduated from Notre Dame in 1978 and is the editor of *Portland Magazine* at the University of Portland in Oregon. A poet and essayist, he and his father, Jim Doyle, are the authors of a collection of essays, *Two Voices*.

Ann Egerton lives in Baltimore where she writes feature stories, literary criticism, and commentary.

John Garvey, a 1967 Notre Dame graduate, is a *Commonweal* columnist and an Orthodox priest and pastor of St. Nicholas Church in Queens, New York.

Sonia Gernes is a poet, novelist, and professor of English at the University of Notre Dame.

Georgie Anne Geyer is a writer, foreign correspondent, and syndicated columnist based in Washington, D.C.

J. Martin Green, a 1963 graduate of Notre Dame, is an attorney in Beaumont, Texas.

Robert F. Griffin, C.S.C., is a 1949 Notre Dame graduate, longtime University chaplain, and former weekly columnist (for *Our Sunday Visitor* and *The Observer*) whose work has been collected into several books.

Helen Heineman, the author of four literary biographies and numerous

245

articles, is the provost and academic vice president of Framingham State College in Framingham, Massachusetts.

Barrie Maguire graduated from Notre Dame in 1960. He is now a writer, artist, and cartoonist living in Narberth, Pennsylvania.

Joe McKenna was born in Derry, Ireland, and earned a master's degree at Notre Dame in 1988. He is now the director of a community foundation in Berkshire, England.

Elaine Cripe McKeough, a former alumni editor of *Notre Dame Magazine*, is now retired and living in Dowagiac, Michigan.

Kent Meyers is a writer who teaches at Black Hills State University in Spearfish, South Dakota.

Philip Milner, who earned his doctorate from Notre Dame in 1972, is a professor of English at St. Francis Xavier University in Antigonish, Nova Scotia. He is the author of *The Yankee Professor's Guide to Life in Nova Scotia*.

Thomas M. Mulroy, a 1973 Notre Dame graduate, is an attorney in Pittsburgh.

Patricia O'Brien, who lives in Washington, D.C., has written numerous newspaper and magazine articles as well as three novels (*Good Intentions, The Ladies' Lunch,* and *The Candidate's Wife*) and two nonfiction books (*The Woman Alone* and *Staying Together: Marriages That Work*).

Sheryl Miller Overlan is a freelance writer who lives in Boston.

Brooke Pacy is a writer and teacher in Baltimore.

Mark Phillips is a writer who lives in Cuba, New York.

Beth Apone Salamon, who graduated from Notre Dame in 1990, is a writer and public relations officer at Saint Barnabas Medical Center, Livingston, New Jersey.

Scott Russell Sanders, a professor of English at Indiana University in Bloomington, has published numerous articles as well as 15 books, including eight works of fiction. His books of personal nonfiction include *The Paradise of Bombs, Secrets of the Universe,* and *Writing from the Center*. "A Perfect Place" subsequently appeared in *Staying Put* (copyright 1993 by Scott Russell Sanders). It is reprinted by permission of Beacon Press, Boston.

Carol Schaal, who earned a master's degree from Notre Dame in 1991, is *Notre Dame Magazine*'s managing editor.

Breyman Schmelzle, a 1969 Notre Dame graduate, is the outdoor editor of the *Tucson Citizen*. His daughter, Jill, is in high school in Tucson and has won nine Arizona Special Olympics medals, including five gold.

Kerry Temple, who graduated from Notre Dame in 1974, joined the staff of *Notre Dame Magazine* in 1981 and is now its editor.

Virginia Tranel writes essays, poetry, and fiction from her home in Bill-
ings, Montana.
Barb Turpin is a Notre Dame faculty member and an administrator in
the University's graduate school.
Tom Werge is a professor of English at Notre Dame.
Mary Ruth Yoe is editor of *The University of Chicago Magazine.*